HIGH TIME

HIGH TIME

The Legalization and Regulation of Cannabis in Canada

Edited by

Andrew Potter and Daniel Weinstock

Published for the McGill Institute
for Health and Social Policy by
McGill-Queen's University Press
Montreal & Kingston • London • Chicago

ISBN 978-0-7735-5636-2 (cloth)
ISBN 978-0-7735-5641-6 (paper)
ISBN 978-0-7735-5723-9 (ePDF)
ISBN 978-0-7735-5724-6 (ePUB)

Legal deposit second quarter 2019
Bibliothèque nationale du Québec

Printed in Canada on acid-free paper that is 100% ancient forest free
(100% post-consumer recycled), processed chlorine free

We acknowledge the support of the Canada Council for the Arts, which last year
invested $153 million to bring the arts to Canadians throughout the country.

Nous remercions le Conseil des arts du Canada de son soutien. L'an dernier,
le Conseil a investi 153 millions de dollars pour mettre de l'art dans la vie des
Canadiennes et des Canadiens de tout le pays.

Library and Archives Canada Cataloguing in Publication

High time : the legalization and regulation of cannabis in Canada /
edited by Andrew Potter and Daniel Weinstock.

Issued in print and electronic formats.
ISBN 978-0-7735-5636-2 (cloth). – ISBN 978-0-7735-5641-6 (paper). –
ISBN 978-0-7735-5723-9 (ePDF). – ISBN 978-0-7735-5724-6 (ePUB)

1. Cannabis – Government policy – Canada. 2. Marijuana – Government policy –
Canada. 3. Drug legalization – Canada. I. Potter, Andrew, editor II. Weinstock,
Daniel, 1963–, editor

HV5822.C3H54 2019   362.29'5   C2018-905751-3
                                             C2018-905752-1

This book was typeset in 10.5/13 Sabon.

Contents

HIGH TIME

Introduction

ANDREW POTTER AND DANIEL WEINSTOCK

Of all the promises made by the Liberals during the 2015 electoral campaign, marijuana legalization seemed, at first glance, to be the easiest to achieve. Whereas electoral reform, which ended up being abandoned early on by the Trudeau-led government, raised a host of issues both technical and constitutional, ending a prohibitionist regime with respect to marijuana that had clearly failed to meet its objectives over the years seemed comparatively easy. All you needed to do to legalize marijuana, it seemed, was, well, to *legalize marijuana*. That is, you just had to eliminate the criminal prohibitions against it that existed.

This is a case where first appearances would have been enormously misleading. The legalization of marijuana in Canada turns out to be a hugely complex and risky venture, one that raises serious concerns, and that will continue to elicit controversy, across a wide range of policy domains that cut across federal, provincial, and municipal jurisdictions.

The first source of complexity stems from the fact that Canada is striking out into the unknown. No other country has legalized marijuana in quite the same way that Canada has. Uruguay's regime, for example, is much more restrictive than Canada's will be. For example, marijuana producers in that country must apply for licenses, and the drug is at present still sold only through pharmacies. At the other end of the spectrum, the tolerationist regime currently in place in the Netherlands makes no effort to control supply.

Canada's legal regime will vary from jurisdiction to jurisdiction. In some cases, marijuana that has been supplied by licensed producers will be sold through provincially run cannabis stores; in others, it will be sold through more private retail outlets. But regardless of the specific sales regime, legal cannabis will be available to all adult Canadians from coast to coast, while at the same time the regime will strive to keep it out of the hands of under-aged Canadians. The Canadian government is not so much lifting criminal prohibitions on the existing, thriving, illegal marijuana economy as it is setting up a parallel, legal marketplace for the drug, which, it hopes, will ultimately drive the illegal market out of existence.

The policy quandaries raised by this seemingly simple move are legion. For one thing, given the limited range of policy levers that are actually at the disposal of the federal government in Canada, much of the work in setting up the nuts and bolts of the new marijuana market will fall to the provinces. The potential for federal-provincial squabbling is great, as evidenced by another recent move by the federal government to suspend criminal prohibitions on controversial practices whose regulation actually falls to the provinces – namely, the case of medically assisted dying. All the evidence of history suggests that the provinces and the federal government will not naturally and spontaneously align on a whole host of issues over which they will ultimately have to agree, ranging from taxation to the permissibility of small-scale home cultivation of cannabis.

The possible sticking points range from the local and technical to the highest levels of international law. Closest to home is the question of where marijuana users will be allowed to consume the drug. Under the prohibitionist regime, the answer is, of course, "nowhere," even though, as a matter of fact, the rather lax enforcement of laws against use and against simple possession have made it the case that the real answer, at least in some parts of Canada, seemed to be "everywhere." Yet even before legalization took effect, some municipalities (such as the Montreal suburb of Hampstead) passed motions or bylaws banning smoking in public, while city councilors in Gimli, Manitoba, voted to ban the retail sale of cannabis.

Another issue that legalization raises has to do with public safety. Again, prohibition allows law enforcement to put its head firmly in the sand as far as systematic, non-arbitrary detection of marijuana in drivers is concerned. You don't have to come up with ways to detect levels of THC in the blood of drivers that might actually impair their ability to drive when the substance is entirely illegal. Under legalization, marijuana will become like alcohol – a substance about which law enforcement will have to be able to make fairly fine-grained distinctions and determinations at the roadside. But unlike the situation for alcohol, the technology for making these sorts of determinations for cannabis in a way that is accurate and reliable enough for law enforcement is still in the development stage and largely untested. At the very least, we can expect to see a large number of court cases challenging the validity of the various tests law enforcement will deploy.

International implications are also legion. How will the problem of marijuana consumption by Canadians be dealt with at the US border? How does the fact that Canada is a signatory to various international legal instruments square with the fact that it has now made the most widely used drug legal? How will the Canadian banking system respond to the risks of being associated with an industry that most of the rest of the world continues to prohibit?

Finally, what mix of policy measures is most likely to drive illegal producers and suppliers out of the Canadian market, without generating further perverse consequences? Pricing marijuana low, and creating other inducements to bring users into the legal marketplace, may give rise to a situation where organized crime no longer thinks it worthwhile to supply the marijuana market. But will this simply mean that it will double down on other, more dangerous drugs? Does the logic of the "harm-reduction" approach that the federal government has implemented not, at the end of the day, require lifting criminal prohibitions against all drugs as a condition of depleting the oxygen within which organized crime operates?

As it became clear that the unresolved policy questions around the legalization of marijuana in Canada would multiply and ramify throughout the Canadian institutional network, we saw an opportunity to bring together a number of experts from diverse fields to hash them out. Along with experts on the law, the economics, the politics, and the epidemiology of marijuana, we heard from politicians who had been central to the legalization process in Parliament, and with business people who will be instrumental to the creation of a multi-billion-dollar marijuana economy in Canada. Our ambition was not necessarily to resolve the myriad policy issues that legalization raises, but to begin to identify them, to flag potential problems with present policy proposals, and more generally to open up a space for ongoing interdisciplinary dialogue that might inform the evolution of policy in Canada going forward.

Accordingly, the *Institute for Health and Social Policy* and the *McGill Institute for the Study of Canada* held a major international conference on the policy challenges surrounding marijuana legalization in Canada on 28 and 29 May 2018. The conference attracted close to 200 participants from academia, industry, government, and civil society.

To the extent that one theme emerged from these two days of presentations and discussion, it is that Canada is in a sense taking a stab in the dark. There is no reliable evidence from other jurisdictions that it can draw on to orient its policies. Accordingly, policy in this area will perforce be fallibilistic. We have to try some things that seem plausible on the face of it, but stand ready to modify policy as evidence comes in as to its effectiveness in reaching its objectives. Yet flexibility at the level of policy is notoriously difficult to achieve. Any set of policies creates sets of stakeholders who do well under them, and who are thus disinclined to adapt when different policies are felt to be needed. And there is well-known inertia at the level of governments that make them loath to try new things when evidence suggests that the old ways aren't working.

Given the stakes associated with legalization, in terms of public health, of public finances, of public safety, and the like, it is important nonetheless that Canada get this right, or at the very least, that it not get it too awfully wrong. The papers collected here look at the present palette of policies that will be enacted by different levels of government, and attempt to determine where changes might have to be made. It will be important, however, that researchers devote intensive study to the impacts of the laws that will go into effect after 17 October 2018, in order to provide decision-makers with evidence through which to guide the evolution of policy in what will most likely be a highly volatile and fluid policy domain.

Montreal, September 2018

PART ONE

Politics

In Praise of Political Opportunism, or, How to Change a Policy in Only Fifty Years

ANDREW POTTER

I

In 1964, a NASA engineer named Gary Flandro was given the job of studying the various possibilities for exploring the gas giants of the outer solar system. Flandro soon figured out that in the late 70s, the solar system would be aligned in a way what would allow a spacecraft to visit all of the outer planets using gravity assists, slingshotting its way past Jupiter, Saturn, Uranus, and finally Neptune. NASA quickly started making a plan for what they dubbed the "Grand Tour," which would take less time and cost a lot less money than it would to send individual probes to each planet. There was a certain amount of urgency to the project, since this alignment happens only every 175 years.

They almost missed their chance. Thanks to a combination of political infighting, costs concerns, and bureaucratic stonewalling, the tour was cancelled in 1971. But creative rebranding of the project led to the Voyager program, which was supposed to explore just Jupiter and Saturn. However, thanks to some sneaky planning work by the NASA scientists, Voyager 2, which launched in 1977, kept on going and managed to complete the Grand Tour in 1989 with a flyby of Neptune.

This is a good metaphor for how serious policy reform gets done in Canada. For any major change to happen, the planets of the policy universe need to be aligned just so. For reform to the criminal law, this means that the relevant policy work has to be in place, and public opinion, stakeholder interests, and the courts all need to be onside. And as the case of marijuana legislation shows, we can go decades between favourable conditions. But it is not enough for the planets to align. As the case of the NASA engineers suggests, we also need politicians willing to take advantage of the opportunity the cosmos presents.

When people talk of "political opportunism," they don't usually mean it in a good way. Opportunism is something distasteful, unsporting, even unethical. It is when a politician jumps on a brief shift in public opinion or on the temporary weakness of the opposition to gain an unfair advantage. Opportunism, when it comes to political behaviour, is typically denigrated as the height of cynicism.[1] But if politics is the art of the possible, then cynicism is the politician's muse. As such, opportunism should be rightly considered a legitimate element of the creative leader's palette. In a fractious federation like Canada, opportunism can and should be considered a political virtue.

II

One of the more curious features of the criminalization of marijuana in Canada is that no one really knows how it happened. The most widely accepted view is that the policy has its origins in the anti-immigrant and, in particular, anti-Chinese, campaign against opium use that culminated in the Opium Act of 1908 (for this, see Owusu-Bempah et al, "Unequal Justice," in chapter 8 of this volume). The criminalization of marijuana in 1923 is typically read as a widening of that campaign due in large part to the work of Emily Murphy, who is best known for her part in the long struggle to see Canadian women legally recognized as persons. But Murphy was also an outspoken eugenicist and anti-immigrant activist. In a series of essays she wrote for *Maclean's* magazine in the early 1920s, she claimed that a syndicate of immigrant groups including Blacks, Chinese, and Mexicans she called "the Ring" was conspiring to get white Canadians addicted to drugs so as to enable the takeover of the country. These essays were eventually published in the best-selling book *The Black Candle*, which included a new chapter on the growing threat from marijuana, of which she warned: "There are three ways out from the regency of this addiction: 1st-Insanity. 2nd-Death. 3rd-Abandonment... a direful trinity and one with which the public should be cognizant."[2]

The hysteria Murphy raised over reefer madness is widely blamed for having led Parliament to criminalize cannabis in 1923. But the truth is that very little is known about how, or why, cannabis was added to the schedule of prohibited drugs. There is no record of any deliberations in the House of Commons or the Senate, and no indication that any member of either legislative chamber was much influenced by Murphy's writings. The historian Catherine Carstairs says that if anything, Murphy was widely considered to be somewhat of a crank on this issue, and suggests that the link between Murphy's writings and criminalization is most likely spurious.[3]

Regardless, the upshot was that Canada became one of the first countries in the world to criminalize marijuana, doing so a full fourteen years before the United States. But for decades, no one really gave it much thought, and until 1960 or so the prohibition on marijuana was widely seen as a matter of a solution wandering around in search of a problem. Between 1923 and 1945, there were a total of 25 arrests in Canada on marijuana-related charges. Over the next thirteen years, there were only an additional 45 charges. Annual arrest rates didn't hit double digits until 1958, and when Canada signed the *UN Single Convention on Narcotic Drugs* in 1961, which committed the country to outlawing the production and supply of marijuana, annual arrests for marijuana use were under two dozen.[4] By just about any measure you can name – criminal justice, social order, public opinion – by the early 1960s marijuana use, and its criminalization, were simply not an issue in Canada.

That started to change by the middle of the decade. Between 1966 and 1972, cannabis-related arrests (overwhelmingly for possession) roughly doubled every year, a pattern that continued well into the 1970s. Canada suddenly had a marijuana problem, but it wasn't just about the sheer number of arrests. The arrival of the sixties counter-culture and its sex, drugs, and rock 'n' roll ethos meant that lots of white, middle-class youth found themselves facing criminal records for doing what pretty much everyone who was anyone seemed to be doing – getting a little high with a little help from their friends. Public opinion started to shift as people began to wonder if maybe the problem wasn't with marijuana use but with the law itself. And so, after almost fifty years of relatively inconsequential prohibition, Canada turned its attention to reforming its cannabis laws.

III

When it comes to reforming something like the criminalization of cannabis, the actual space of policy options is fairly limited. One possibility, of course, is the status quo. Just because a policy isn't perfect or has negative effects doesn't mean there is a better policy on offer; so you can always opt to do nothing. As a second option, you might choose to double down on the law enforcement side. You can increase the penalties for possession, sale, and trafficking; pour more resources into policing, drug enforcement and interdiction, and so on; and engage in anti-drug public awareness campaigns.

A third option is decriminalization. Usually paired with a harm-reduction policy agenda, decriminalization can involve everything from treating drug offences as akin to bylaw infractions or dropping penalties altogether, to diverting users or abusers away from criminal justice and into the health care system, while tolerating or tacitly encouraging recreational use in certain defined areas.

Finally, you can end prohibition altogether and opt for legalization. Again, legalization comes with a fair amount of latitude in how it is implemented and regulated. Different models include whether to treat cannabis in the same way we treat a vice like tobacco, or, alternatively, like alcohol. There are also competing retail models, as well as a host of decisions to be made surrounding production, advertising and marketing, legal age of purchase, and so on. But essentially, policy makers are looking at four options: the status quo, increased criminalization, decriminalization, or outright legalization.

As minister of justice in the Pearson government, Pierre Trudeau took responsibility for a radical rethink of the relationship between the state and public morality. In 1967, he introduced a far-reaching omnibus bill that included the decriminalization of homosexuality and the legalization of contraception and abortion, and later moved to liberalize the law concerning divorce. After he became prime minister in 1968, Trudeau would continue to push this laissez-faire attitude towards the activities of consenting adults. The question of whether recreational drug use, and the lifestyle and politics that tended to accompany it, should be a matter of public concern was top of mind for many Canadians at this time, and in 1969 the Trudeau government launched the Commission of Inquiry into the Non-Medical Use of Drugs, better known as the Le Dain Commission after its Chair, Gerald Le Dain.

The commission's mandate was to investigate the role of the state in prohibiting and regulating the use and distribution of drugs for "nonmedical" purposes, though it expanded its mandate to include a discussion of social values more generally. What followed was four years of public policy work, a period that saw the commissioners review hundreds of submissions from all relevant stakeholders including police services, health care professionals, and provincial and municipal authorities. They floated a number of trial balloons in the form of interim reports, and the commissioners released their final findings in May of 1972. But they were not able to reach a consensus on the question of what to do about marijuana, so the commission ended up with three separate recommendations. The majority found the existing regime to be "grossly excessive," and recommended a suite of policy reforms broadly aimed at decriminalizing possession of drugs and reducing the penalties for trafficking. One commissioner, Marie-Andrée Bertrand, went further in advocating outright legalization and proposed treating marijuana in more or less the same way we treat alcohol.[5]

What is useful to note here is that virtually all of the hard intellectual work on marijuana policy was done fifty years ago. Aside from the obvious caveats regarding the state of research on the physical and psychological effects of cannabis consumption and addiction more generally, the Le Dain commission was an exhaustive exploration of the available policy-decision space – a space that has not changed in size or shape since then. Another notable outcome was the political response: following a time-honoured pattern in Canadian policy making, the Trudeau government thanked the commissioners for their work and proceeded to do nothing.

There were good reasons for the government to park the idea of reforming the nation's drug laws. In the federal election in the fall of 1972, the Liberals barely hung on to power, reduced to a two-seat minority government just ahead of the Progressive Conservatives. There were lots of other things to occupy the federal government's attention, including the upcoming Montreal Olympics, rising oil prices, skyrocketing inflation, and growing unrest in Quebec. But the Le Dain report marked the beginning of what has been well described as a repeating cycle of "promise, hesitation, and retreat."[6] The government would express some interest in reforming the nation's drug laws, a plan would be put forward that would suggest shifting the focus of our approach to marijuana regulation from the criminal justice system to a public health regime, and nothing would ever come of it.

Still, Trudeau continued to pay lip service to the notion that, in an ideal world, getting high wouldn't be a criminal offence. In 1977, Trudeau – now enjoying the renewed support of a majority in the House of Commons – reiterated his support for some degree of relaxation of prohibition. The Liberal throne speech that year called for an end to jailing people for individual possession; as Trudeau told a group of students at the University of Toronto: "If you have a joint and you're smoking it for your private pleasure, you shouldn't be hassled."[7]

IV

Yet drug-related arrests – the majority for cannabis possession – continued to climb, reaching a decade-long high of over 58,000 in 1977, and peaking with over 65,000 arrests in 1981, a period that also saw the highest levels in Canadian history of drug arrests per 100,000 people.

By this point, international developments, most significantly in the United States, had made any further progress towards reform in Canada virtually impossible. Beginning with Nancy Reagan's anti-drug "Just Say No" campaign in the early eighties, opposition to marijuana use got wrapped up in the broader campaign that was sparked by hysteria over the growing problem of cocaine use, in particular crack cocaine. In one notorious episode in 1986, just two days after Ronald Reagan made a public speech declaring a "war on drugs," Conservative Prime Minister Brian Mulroney went off-message during a prepared speech to announce that "drug abuse has become an epidemic that undermines our economic as well as our social fabric."[8]

Mulroney never really elaborated on this remark, and it seemed to catch the members of his government as well as senior bureaucrats off guard. But it did lead to the investment in 1987 of $250 million towards a national drug strategy, which was actually framed in the hopeful language of harm reduction. This hope was reflected in new legislation that was introduced first by the Conservatives in 1992 and re-introduced by the Liberals under Jean Chrétien in 1993. The key development was to create a new cannabis offence that would allow possession under 30 grams of marijuana or one gram of hashish to be dealt with by summary proceedings. When the new law came into effect in 1996, the government hailed it as a form of de facto decriminalization, despite the obvious consideration that it was still embedded in the criminal law, still allowed for incarceration, and still left offenders with a criminal record.[9]

This was happening at a time when enforcement and public opinion were going in opposite directions. A Health Canada survey conducted in 1995 showed strong public support for some form of decriminalization, with 69 per cent of Canadians in favour of either a non-criminal fine or no legal restraints on cannabis possession at all. Meanwhile, after declining significantly from the late eighties and through the first half of the nineties, drug arrests started to climb once again, reaching record levels in the second half of the decade. And as usual, simple possession of cannabis made up of over half of the arrests. What really forced the issue was a new tactic brought to bear by activists looking to challenge the basic criminal justice foundations of Canada's cannabis control regime: political activism and court challenges premised on the right to access marijuana for personal medical purposes.

V

Canada has a long-standing organized activist community dedicated to reforming the country's drug laws. The Canadian branch of the US-based National Organization for the Reform of Marijuana Laws (better known as NORML) was founded in 1978, and has been pushing for outright legalization ever since, while a network of head-shop owners and compassion clubs has quietly worked to provide cannabis and cannabis-related paraphernalia to recreational and medical users. In 1997, Marc-Boris St-Maurice (best known at that point as the bassist for the Montreal punk band Grimskunk) founded the Bloc Pot, a Quebec political party devoted to the legalization of cannabis. St-Maurice and his allies took their campaign national for the 2000 federal election, in which they ran seventy-three candidates across the country.

But at both the provincial and federal levels, Canada's political system remains highly resistant to single-issue parties or narrowly targeted political interests (just ask Elizabeth May), and neither the Bloc Pot nor the Marijuana Party of Canada were able to elect any members. However, even as the activists found themselves shut out of the political process, the courts system became highly amenable to rights-based activism, largely focused on the right to access marijuana for personal medical purposes. Most claimants brought actions based on section 7 of the Charter of Rights and Freedoms, claiming violations of their right to life, liberty, and security.

In the most important of these cases – especially *R v. Parker* and *R v. Krieger*, both in 2000 – the courts ruled that the nature of the punishment (Parker) and lack of access (Krieger) violated the claimant's Charter rights. And so the courts demanded changes to the law, which implicated not just medical users but recreational users as well. The government tried to ring fence the court rulings in 2002 by instituting a medical marijuana access regime run by Health Canada, but the courts weren't having it. In a series of subsequent decisions, judges continued to throw out possession charges and insist on changes to the existing criminal law. In this way, medical marijuana turned out to be a legal Trojan horse that put into question the entire cannabis regulatory regime.

Slowly but surely, the planets were starting to move into position: the courts were pressing for legislative reform, while public opinion had settled quite comfortably into a solid two-thirds in favour of some form of relaxation of the prohibitionist regime, with somewhat more in favour of decriminalization than outright legalization. And so, with pressure to do something building from both the courts and the public, Parliament tasked two committees with studying once again the problem of illicit drugs in Canada, and in 2002 both the House of Commons Special Committee on Non-Medical Use of Drugs and the Senate Special Committee on Illegal Drug Use released reports. The House report recommended some form of decriminalization, while the Senate report (usually called the Nolin Report after the committee's chair, Pierre Claude Nolin) advocated outright legalization.

The Nolin report in particular was hugely influential. In framing its recommendations, the committee noted that while public opinion on cannabis, especially with respect to medical marijuana, had liberalized substantially over the preceding decade, and that while there was a general tendency to believe that it was not a dangerous drug, this was tempered by significant concern over organized crime and the relevant threats to youth and children.[10] After noting that when it came to reducing the supply and consumption of marijuana the current regime was a "complete failure," the Nolin report recommended a harm-reduction approach based on the regulation of the production, distribution, and consumption of cannabis – that is, legalization.

Forced into acting, in early 2003 the Liberals under Jean Chrétien introduced a decriminalization bill. Possession under 15 grams of marijuana would have been subject to a fine, while cultivation of up to seven plants would have been a summary offence. The bill looked almost sure to pass, and *The Economist* magazine famously ran a cover story entitled "Canada's New Spirit," featuring an illustration of a moose in sunglasses. After thirty-five years of desultory work on the file, Canada was well on its way to enacting the most significant change in its cannabis laws since 1923.

But as is so often the case, politics intervened. Parliament took its time with the bill, in large part due to pressure from the American Drug Enforcement Agency, which was threatening to increase searches of Canadians at the border. But what ultimately killed it was the proroguing of Parliament that fall to accommodate Paul Martin's increasingly high-pressure leadership ambitions. In 2004, a year after he essentially deposed Chrétien and took over as prime minister, Martin reintroduced the bill, but it too died when he called an election a month later. After he won re-election with a minority government, Martin yet again reintroduced a decriminalization bill, but it sat in committee untouched for a year. Then his government fell on a vote of non-confidence, and when Stephen Harper took power in 2006, he promptly announced that marijuana-law reform was not on his agenda. In fact, just the opposite: Harper turned away from even the milder harm-reduction measures the Liberals had introduced, choosing instead to double down on the criminalization of recreational drugs. The Conservatives under Harper introduced a new national anti-drug strategy based on increased criminal penalties, promising to set mandatory minimum sentences for drug traffickers and those running marijuana grow operations.

The window for reform had closed, and it remained shut for the duration of Harper's near-decade in office.

VI

Yet even as Stephen Harper was pushing for increased criminalization as the solution to Canada's drug problems, the courts continued to find problems with the Controlled Drug and Substances Act and its relationship to the medical marijuana access regulations. In a pair of cases in 2007, the Ontario Court of Justice ruled that the prohibition of possession of cannabis was unconstitutional, since the exemption for medical cannabis relied on the government agreeing to supply it as a matter of policy.[11] A few years later, both the the the BC Superior Court and the Supreme Court of Canada fired cannonballs through the rigging of the medical marijuana regime, making the status quo increasingly untenable.[12]

But the key development came on the political side, with Justin Trudeau's 2013 victory in the race to succeed Michael Ignatieff as leader of the Liberal Party of Canada. Shortly after taking over the leadership, Trudeau gave a remarkable speech at a rally in Kelowna, BC, where he plumped for the outright legalization of marijuana. "I'm actually in favour of legalizing it; tax and regulate it," he told the crowd. In language that could have been taken straight from the Nolin report, Trudeau went on: "It's one of the only ways to keep it out of the hands of our kids, because the current war on drugs, the current model, is not working. We have to use evidence and science to make sure that we're moving forward on that."[13]

In reaction, Trudeau was widely accused of engaging in political "opportunism," notwithstanding the fact that he also admitted to having smoked marijuana at a party not three years before, while sitting as a member of parliament. Conservatives jumped on this with glee, accusing him of sitting as a lawmaker who thought it was fine to break the law.[14] That is why many observers were surprised when legalization of marijuana was included in the party's campaign platform for the 2015 general election. But again using language mirroring the main themes of the Nolin report, the Liberal platform included a plan to legalize marijuana on the grounds that the prohibitionist system helped support organized crime and gave many Canadians criminal records for minor offenses, and put young people at risk while failing to keep anyone from actually using the drug. And so, the Liberals promised, "To ensure that we keep marijuana out of the hands of children, and the profits out of the hands of criminals, we will legalize, regulate, and restrict access to marijuana."[15]

Not everything in an election platform gets implemented, of course, especially when it comes to promises made by a party that was in third place in the polls when the platform was being written, and had every reason to think it might not have to actually deliver on any of the promises. And even after they won a majority government (surprising perhaps even themselves), the Liberals were not shy about stalling on promises that were going to be tricky or problematic. This included the pledges to get Canada back into peacekeeping, to enact the recommendations of the Truth and Reconciliation Commission, and – most notoriously – the complete reversal on the promise to make the 2015 election the last one held under the "first past the post" electoral system.

Still, there were reasons to think that cannabis legalization wouldn't be so easily abandoned. To begin with, shortly after taking power, Trudeau appointed a panel, known as the Task Force on Cannabis Legalization and Regulation, to explore the various policy options for legalization. The panel was chaired by Anne McLellan, the former Liberal cabinet member who held both the health and justice portfolios. The rest of the panel was made of highly respected representatives of the major stakeholder groups, including health research, law, policing, and social work. But perhaps more importantly, the legalization file was being steered by some of the most skilled ministers in Trudeau's cabinet, including Health Minister Jane Philpott, but especially Justice Minister Jody Wilson-Raybould and her parliamentary secretary, former Toronto chief of police Bill Blair.

Nothing of any significance happens in the Canadian political system, however, without the explicit and forceful backing of the prime minister. As the example of the failed swing at electoral reform demonstrates, if the prime minister is not willing to put his political capital on the line in support of a major policy initiative, then it simply won't happen. As matters evolved, there was never any daylight between Trudeau, his ministers, and the senior bureaucrats over legalization, despite considerable grumbling from some provinces (especially Quebec), and requests from various groups, including indigenous organizations, to delay it all for at least a year. And so it came to pass that on 17 October 2018, ninety-five years after it was first criminalized, cannabis became legal in Canada.

VII

There are many outstanding questions surrounding issues such as the elimination of the black market, how we will handle drugged driving, whether we can manage to keep cannabis out of the hands of youth, and what impact this will have on Canada's standing in the international community. Many of the rest of the papers in this book are devoted to exploring these concerns. But as large as the stakes may be for the Liberals, they are even bigger for Canadians, who stand to benefit from legalization being done right, but have a lot to lose if it goes badly. Legalization is the beginning of the process, not the end, and we should all hope that this government, or its successors, will have the political courage to alter course if any harms from the new policy demonstrably outweigh the benefits. But for now, the Liberal government can take credit for managing to do what no government has been able to do in almost half-a-century of trying.

There are two big lessons here. The first is that serious policy reform in Canada can take a very long time, even after the hard intellectual spadework has been done. It took decades after the Le Dain commission for a government to find not only the will but also the political sea room to grasp the opportunity as it arose.

The second lesson is that, in policy reform as in space exploration, it isn't enough for the planets to be in friendly alignment; you need people able to take advantage of the movements of the cosmos. This is what got Voyager 2 to Neptune, and it was what ultimately led to the legalization of cannabis in Canada. If this is political opportunism, then Canada could use a lot more of it.

NOTES

1   For a discussion of the normative dimensions of cynical politics, see Andrew Potter, "The Naive and the Cynical," http://authenticityhoax. squarespace.com/blog/2012/12/18/politics-the-naive-and-cynical.html

2   Emily Murphy, *The Black Candle* (Toronto: Coles Publishing Co., 1973), 337.

3   Daniel Schwarz, "Marijuana Was Criminalized in 1923, but Why?"CBC News, 3 May 2014, https://www.cbc.ca/news/health/marijuana-was-criminalized-in-1923-but-why-1.2630436

4   Source: http://cannabislink.ca/legal/

5   Marcel Martel, *Not This Time: Canadians, Public Policy, and the Marijuana Question* (Toronto: University of Toronto Press, 2006), 150.

6   P.S. Giffen, S. Endicott, and S. Lambert. *Panic and Indifference: The Politics of Canada's Drug Laws* (Ottawa: Canadian Centre on Substance Abuse, 1991).

7   Richard Starnes, "The Joint Proposal," *Ottawa Citizen*, 25 January 1997.

8   P.G. Erickson, "Recent Trends in Canadian Drug Policy: The Decline and Resurgence of Prohibitionism," *Daedalus* 121 (3): 239–67.

9   Benedikt Fischer, Kari Ala-Leppilampi, Eric Singe, and Amanda Robins, "Cannabis Law Reform in Canada: Is 'The Saga of Promise, Hesitation, and Retreat' Coming to an End?" *Canadian Journal of Criminology and Criminal Justice* 45 (3) (2003): 265–98.

10   Pierre Claude Nolin and Colin Kenny, *Cannabis: Our Position for a Canadian Public Policy*, Summary Report of the Senate Special Committee on Illegal Drugs. Ottawa - Ontario : Senate. September 2002.

11   *R. v. Long 2007* and *R. v Bodnar/Hall/Spasic*, Ontario Court of Justice.

12   *Allard et al v Regina* (2016) and *R. v Smith* (2015)

13   Andrea Janus, "Trudeau Makes Headlines for Calls to Legalize Marijuana," CTV News, 25 July 2013, https://www.ctvnews.ca/politics/ trudeau-makes-headlines-for-calls-to-legalize-marijuana-1.1383738.

14   See for example Thomas Walkom, "Justin Trudeau's Clever Marijuana Gambit," *Toronto Star*, 23 August 2013.

15   *Real Change: A New Plan for a Strong Middle Class*, The Liberal Party of Canada (2015), https://www.liberal.ca/wp-content/uploads/2015/10/New-plan-for-a-strong-middle-class.pdf.

2

Legalized Cannabis in Canada: Federalism, Policy, and Politics

MALCOLM G. BIRD

By the fall of 2018, if all goes according to plan, Canada will be the first country in the Organization for Economic Co-operation and Development (OECD) to have fully legalized recreational cannabis. Justin Trudeau's Liberal government has fulfilled a central pillar of its 2015 electoral campaign, and in doing so, moved the party towards a left-of-centre stance appealing to many young, urban Canadians. For the federal government, legalizing cannabis required new legislation, as well as amendments to the *Controlled Drug and Substance Act* and the *Criminal Code*, among other regulatory, legislative, and policy changes. A majority in the House of Commons will ensure that the legislation will pass and, aside from a few amendments from the (semi-)independent Senate (most of which were rejected), Bill C-45 will pass and become the law of the land. Minister Bill Blair, a former Toronto police chief, spearheaded the government's efforts on this file and in late April attended a conference on cannabis legalization, where he emphatically reminded attendees (which included the author) that "public health" concerns were fundamental to the government's plan, and that in no way were they setting out to "promote the use of cannabis" among the citizenry. While many details had yet to be fully worked out, he recognized that legalization was a complicated matter and that it was best to view the entire endeavour as more of a "process" than a fixed "event." So far, so good. Legal cannabis is coming to Canada.

Implementing legalized cannabis will raise numerous policy, political, public health, and moral issues. But this is of little concern to the federal government, since these problems will be managed by

Canada's ten *provincial* and three *territorial* governments, along with their civic appendages. It is these governments that are charged with implementing this new policy and, in doing so, will be left to deal with an entirely new set of challenges related to managing a new legal narcotic drug. It is not that cannabis and its illegal status did not pose problems (particularly the criminalization of its distribution system), but, in raw political terms, its illegal status meant that its use in society could be safely ignored by the provincial state – the "let sleeping dogs lie" adage applied to the policy world. The federal government's stance on cannabis, then, foisted a new issue onto the laps of the provinces and was taken with no real consultation. Legalized cannabis, given the failure of promised electoral reform, will be a key component of the 2019 Liberal re-election strategy as the party seeks to capture much of the "progressive" vote from their New Democratic Party (NDP) rivals. All the political and electoral rewards will accrue to the Liberal federal government, while all the associated problems with implementation will be borne by the provinces. This must be an example of Justin Trudeau's new "co-operative" federalism at work.

I: IS ILLEGAL CANNABIS A PROBLEM?

Cannabis's increasingly ubiquitous presence, particularly within many sub-communities, is often a rationale cited for legalizing it. "Everyone is doing it anyway, so why not legalize it?" is a commonly used rationale that is frequently accompanied by illustrating the damage alcohol and tobacco use cause society. A recent substantial research paper confirms this view: in 2014, total substance use cost Canada a whopping $38.4 billion, which was divided amongst alcohol ($14.6 billion), tobacco ($12 billion) and cannabis ($2.8 billion), among other substances.[1] However, damage caused by two legal intoxicants is not necessarily a strong justification for introducing a third, given the additional costs and problems cannabis legalization will bring about – although such views do illustrate well the hypocrisy and contradictions of legalized substance use policy! Further, while criminalizing and incarcerating individual users and distributors is not a desirable outcome, decriminalization of cannabis (either de facto or de jure) would be one way to address this matter without embarking on full-fledged legalization. Readers, and Canadians more generally, need to think hard about whether cannabis's current illegality constitutes a real "problem" that requires the attention of the political sphere. In practical and political terms, does the median voter, or the suburban soccer mom or gray-haired senior citizen, really care about cannabis's illegal status? How does this issue rank in relation to healthcare, education, and, most important of all, the state of the economy in the mind of your average voter? Does prohibited cannabis keep Canadians awake at night, as one might worry about their job or the health and security of their family? For your average voter, legalized cannabis is a low priority.

Cannabis legalization is diverting energy from more pressing matters. Governments, much like individuals, companies, or any other organization, have limited time, energy, and resources to dedicate to resolving the problems that they face; as a result, they must prioritize their efforts. Readers must appreciate that most of a government's time and resources are spent responding to the problems that emerge from all of society (including the economy) that are not able to be managed by firms, families, individuals, or other organizations – this is why we require the state in the first place! Natural disasters, plant closings, political scandals, environmental calamities, economic turmoil – among many other acute, pressing issues that perpetually emerge – all require effective political management from the state. This, of course, is in addition its role allocating scarce resources amongst a never-ending cascade of demands from every conceivable interest group that is demanding ever-more-publicly provided goods and services – and always doing so backed up by clever arguments, ample data, and solid rationales. Compounding this dynamic is the highly centralized decision-making character of Canada's Westminster Parliamentary system, whereby political power is focused in the offices of the first ministers and the members of their Cabinets.

As a result, the actions of Canadian governments are deeply constrained. Particularly when it comes to proactive policies; i.e., not merely responding to societal problems, and going about implementing policies that might meet their partisan, ideological, or electoral goals (such constraints also explain why their actions are guided by intense pragmatism as well). So, the legalization of cannabis is only a "problem" for Canada's provincial governments because their federal counterpart foisted it onto their agendas, and few would have opted to make it their own matter, given the complexities involved and the fact that the federal government's control of the *Criminal*

Code would have mooted such efforts, even if they were desirable. In political terms, then, cannabis legalization confers significant "opportunity costs" on provincial governments, since it will require resources that otherwise would go towards alternative issues they must manage. For Manitoba, a province that struggles with 11,000 children in state care; major urban decay in its capital, Winnipeg; and an annual deficit of over $800 million, amongst other problems, our provincial government has more than enough challenges in dire need of effective responses. The hierarchical character of our federal system places the provinces in a subservient position to their federal counterpart, which, in the case of cannabis legalization, will necessitate the allocation of considerable resources.

II: FEDERALISM IN CANADA: DIVIDING UP THE POWER

Cannabis legalization is a viable policy largely due to the relationship between Canada's federal and provincial governments. This constitutional dynamic explains why the provinces will bear the burden for legalization, and how this plays out in the case of legal cannabis tells us a lot about the current state of our federation. Canada is unique among many countries, since its sub-national units (i.e., the provinces) play the dominant role in many key policy arenas in relation to their federal counterpart.[2] In fact, all the critical public goods and services that citizens rely upon are provided by the provincial state. Healthcare and education (at all levels) are the two key arenas solely in the provincial domain, but other areas such as transportation, social and child welfare, employment rules, and much of the regulatory frameworks shaping daily and working life, among many others, fall within the purview of the provinces. Municipalities also provide many vital services to citizens and will play a central role in the legalized cannabis regime, but they remain, to an overwhelming degree, as appendages of their provincial patrons. The most critical function of the federal government is to collect taxes (and redistribute revenues to the provinces). Overall, despite taxation, along with overseeing the Canadian Broadcasting Corporation (CBC) and Canada Post, there are remarkably few things the federal government controls that have a tangible effect on peoples' day-to-day lives. Defense, foreign affairs, and trade are important policy sectors, but they are also rather ephemeral and a have limited immediate impact on people's daily lives. Sectors such as criminal justice and immigration, for instance, are "hybrids" in the sense that they are shaped by federal legislation and actions, but much of the implementation of these polices falls within the domain of the provincial state and their civic counterparts.

The work of implementing legal cannabis falls within the provincial domain. It is both the complexity of implementing this new regulatory regime, in and of itself, and the significant political risks that are associated with implementation, that make this issue so daunting. The lack of experience, not surprisingly, means that the province must proceed very slowly and cautiously, despite the firm and short deadlines imposed by the federal government, and accept that mistakes will be made and will often be publicized by media outlets, causing additional grief for provincial governments. Several provinces, including Quebec and Nova Scotia, are using provincial liquor boards to distribute cannabis because they have the experience and the infrastructure to handle substances with narcotic properties, but the provinces are also likely using them because they provide an additional layer of political insulation if (or more likely, when) errors are made and an individual or an organization needs to be held to account. Firing or a timely resignation of a corporate leader oftentimes suffices in such a situation.

In terms of distribution, a host of crucial issues must be addressed. Where will cannabis be sold? Where specifically will retail locations be permitted to operate? How will the wholesale and retail markets be structured? What hours will they operate? If using a private sector retail model, as Manitoba will be doing, who will get the (lucrative) right to sell cannabis? (Remembering, of course, that the allocation of these licenses needs to be an open and transparent process.) What types of products will be offered? Which firms will supply cannabis? How will it be packaged? What will be its potency? How much will it cost? How will governments eliminate illicit products and the illegal market? How will enforcement agencies differentiate legally acquired cannabis from its illicit counterpart? These, of course, are among a long list of other critical logistical problems. Each one of these matters requires considerable thought and research and holds the potential to create both policy challenges and political embarrassment for a sitting government.

Following distribution of cannabis, other complexities emerge. Where and when can one consume it? Who will enforce these new rules, and how will they do so? How, exactly, are governments going to keep youths from acquiring and using cannabis? What will be the extent and tone of the public education campaigns? Once this new narcotic is introduced, many public agencies, firms, and other organizations will need to develop and implement policies towards its use. Among provincial agencies such as workers' compensation boards to social housing providers to educational institutions, adapting to this new regime will further complicate their normal operations. A cornucopia of regulations, from human resources to insurance to human rights, will have to adapt to this new, intoxicating, and legal narcotic, and must integrate its use into routine human resources processes. But perhaps the largest set of problems lies with cannabis use and vehicle operation. While cannabis use interferes with the capacity to operate a motor vehicle, there is not yet an accurate and immediate – let alone judicially and legally tested – means to determine how "high" an individual is and to what degree this will affect their capacity to operate a motor vehicle safely. Developing and implementing these policies throughout the provincial sector, not surprisingly, will require significant efforts and financial and human resources.

III: THE "NEW" CANNABIS REGIME?
INFLUENCING BEHAVIOURS

How states regulate indulgences has a causative effect on their consumption. In the medium and longer terms, provincial governments will have to determine the "optimal" cannabis consumption levels. Think for a moment how people's attitudes and the corresponding rules, regulations, and social norms (the regulatory regime, to use a formal term) have changed with regards to alcohol, tobacco smoking, and gambling in Canada over the last fifty years. In the mid-1960s, gambling, for the most part, was illegal, smoking tobacco was ubiquitous (even permitted in hospitals!), and alcohol was heavily restricted (expensive and difficult to acquire, among other restrictions). Since then, attitudes towards and levels of consumption of these indulgences have changed dramatically. In the case of tobacco, governments have recognized the public health hazards and costs associated with smoking, and in response they have levied taxes on tobacco products and, more generally, made purchasing and consuming it more difficult and inconvenient. Such efforts complemented public health and other educational campaigns to "de-normalize" and stigmatize tobacco use. Other efforts include strict indoor and even outdoor user restrictions, graphic images and warning labels on packaging, and a ban on all advertising and promotion, among many other constraints. As a result, societal attitudes have shifted dramatically towards tobacco consumption, so much so that smokers are equivalent to modern-day lepers. These endeavours have yielded tangible results, and in 2013 just under 15 per cent of Canadian adults were regular users in contrast to the mid-1960s, when half of the adult population were daily smokers.[3]

In stark contrast, expanded legalized gambling has led to an increase in wagering. Today, punters have numerous venues to indulge in, from video lottery terminals to lottery tickets to casinos, and the many online betting options available, and oftentimes these gambling opportunities are actively promoted by provincial gaming authorities. Largely because of this more liberal regime, gambling expenditures have grown considerably: per capita spending has soared in real terms from $128 in 1992 to $528 in 2008.[4] Similarly, strong correlations between how alcohol is sold, and at what price, has a positive influence on how it is used. Tim Stockwell and his research associates demonstrate how polices making alcohol easier to acquire (higher retail store densities, for instance) increased alcohol-attributable hospital admissions, while more expensive drinks were strongly correlated with fewer emergency room hospital visits.[5]

These same institutional dynamics, it is reasonable to assume, will apply to cannabis. Remember too that in the case of cannabis, much like tobacco, alcohol, and gambling, a relatively small proportion of users are the heaviest consumers; in the case of cannabis, 20 per cent of users consume 80 per cent of the product.[6] To a large extent, provincial governments will be tasked with regulating (and moderating) the consumption of a heavy-using sub-group. They will have to determine which factors most influence consumption and then take steps to (re) shape how consumers and citizens view and use cannabis and its associated products. This will require dedicated sections of health policy departments to collect data and, to the best of their ability, determine the "costs" of cannabis use in terms of social, health, and economic factors, and then to balance those costs with the "benefits" of using it. Adding further complexity to these decisions will be a well-organized and financed cannabis growing and distribution lobbying sector that will now be active attempting to influence government behaviour. As well, given the regulatory powers of the federal government in this sector, it may (or may not) have congruent interests as their provincial counterparts in terms of the character of the new regulatory regime.

IV: REVENUES? TAXING INDULGENCES

In theory, cannabis legalization will raise revenues for provincial governments. Since cannabis was previously illegal and therefore untaxed, this represents new monies for provincial coffers. What is unclear is how large in absolute terms these revenues will be (considering there is a functioning illicit market providing cannabis for between $6 and $10 per gram), and whether there will be a net gain once the total costs of legal cannabis are accounted for. The federal government, in contrast, most likely will see a net gain in revenue, but that is largely because it is less burdened by implementation costs, and it is actively embarking on a cost-recovery program to recoup the costs associated with regulation. It is true that the current (illegal) cannabis regime imposes significant costs on society in social, health, and criminal justice matters, to name a few, and earns no revenues for governments, but in political terms, this was a moot point because the provincial government could reasonably ignore such matters – largely because it could do very little to change the situation. In this sense, legalization has brought these costs, like all the additional regulatory challenges, to the forefront of problems faced by the provincial state.

There are several key general points regarding revenues derived from indulgences.[7] First, these revenues are concentrated, and the costs are diffused. Revenues are concentrated since they are derived from tax levies and/or profits earned by provincially owned and operated liquor and gaming firms, and as such, they are relatively easy to identify and quantify. The costs of such indulgences, however, are far more difficult to measure, since they are diffused across various groups and institutions and over a long period of time. Second, the intensity of the state's regulatory regime is strongly correlated with where and to whom these costs accrue. Contrasting the tobacco and gambling regulatory regimes will illustrate these two points. Tobacco has been vilified as a public health hazard partly because it is relatively easy to link its use to specific diseases (lung cancer, emphysema, etc.), and the costs of managing those illnesses is borne by provincial health insurance plans. Many provinces, in fact, have successfully sued tobacco firms to recover some of these healthcare costs. In contrast, as legalized gambling has expanded, more people are indulging and, not surprisingly, there has been a stark increase in individuals with gambling addictions. However, what is critical is that the costs associated with problematic gambling (racking up personal debt, associated mental and physical health issues, and stress on intimate relations, to name a few) are incurred by the individuals themselves and their families, and not the provincial government directly. Perversely, in fact, provincial governments and their gambling appendages earn significant revenues from problem gamblers.[8]

Finally, and perhaps most importantly, the total societal costs are far greater than the revenues these indulgences earn for governments. It is the form those revenues take that give the illusion that these indulgences earn positive revenues. A recent and very extensive study provides well-researched estimates of the total costs associated with substance use in Canada in 2014, accounting for losses due to healthcare expenditures, reduced productivity, criminal justice, and other direct costs. Total costs to Canadian society due to alcohol use were $14.6 billion, while alcohol excise revenues that year were $10.5 billion; similar numbers for tobacco estimated $12.0 billion in costs and $7.8 billion in related revenues to governments.[9] The total costs associated with cannabis use in 2014 were estimated at $2.8 billion, and so future revenue projections will have to take this base cost into account. If legalization of cannabis brings about higher consumption (due to increased ease of purchase, higher social tolerance for use, etc.), this will motivate provincial governments to develop models that will determine total societal costs, and to account for where and to whom those costs accrue. Yet another policy and political challenge for provincial governments to fund and manage in the future.

V: MORAL DILEMMA: NORMALIZING CANNABIS?

Canadian governments will need to adopt a coherent message regarding cannabis use. Bill Blair at our April conference stated emphatically that the federal government will not "promote the use of cannabis," which is a reasonable statement in the abstract. But what, then, will be the official state-sanctioned narrative in public educational campaigns regarding cannabis and its use? Strenuous efforts have sought to "de-normalize" and stigmatize tobacco in Canada, and these endeavours have yielded significant results in changing how Canadians view and use tobacco products. Is the federal government willing to use a similar narrative for cannabis? The federal government, it is worth noting, has been lauded for its strong stance against tobacco. Such a strategy is coordinated by Health Canada through its Tobacco Control Directorate, which implements Canada's much-lauded Tobacco Control Programme, whose overarching goal is to create, implement, and coordinate policy to eliminate tobacco use in Canadian society. Will a similar bureau be created to regulate cannabis? If so, what "tone" will the government's messaging take? A strong anti-cannabis messaging to discourage use, akin to the tobacco regime; or a more moderate, non-judgmental dynamic that highlights the negative sides of use but leaves the ultimate decision in the hands of the consumer? Remember, too, that legalization will make acquiring cannabis easier for most of the population (no concerns regarding arrest, easy-to-find retail locations, among other changes), and while the research is still nascent, the Parliamentary Budget Officer, while recognizing the complexity of factors that shape consumer behaviour, concludes that it is likely consumption will rise following legalization.[10] Already we have seen the intentions (and actions) of the federal and provincial governments come into conflict when the House of Commons rejected amendments to Bill C-45 that sought to reserve the provinces' right to restrict home cultivation, as Quebec and Manitoba intend to do. It is likely that conflicts will continue as governments seek the optimal "tone" regarding the state's sanctioning of cannabis use.

More generally, what message does legalization in and of itself send to the general population regarding narcotics use? Legalization is, in many respects, a very public endorsement – or, at the very least, the removal of a formal sanctioning regime – of a substance that has the potential for significant harm. And when one considers the poor record of the state mitigating and moderating the harms caused by other legal narcotics such as tobacco, alcohol, and opioids, one can't help but wonder if this is really such a good idea.[11] With legalization, we as a society in general, and the numerous cannabis companies that will eagerly set about to promote their products specifically, are sending a message that using cannabis is okay and it could, and should, be integrated into one's lifestyle. Is that really a healthy message to pass along to our citizens, especially our youngest ones?

CONCLUSIONS: MOVING FORWARD ON CANNABIS

Two main observations inform this chapter's negative views on cannabis legalization. First, that provincial governments have much more pressing problems to manage, and that, in political terms, cannabis's illegal condition is not a real, tangible policy problem congruent to, say, the challenges facing our healthcare and education systems. And second, that this matter was foisted onto the provinces, largely against their will, and is a viable policy only due to the unique dynamics of our federal system, whereby the central government will earn all the political credit for this shift, and the provinces will be left to implement the policy and cope with all its associated problems. Canada's status quo policy regime regarding cannabis, while not an ideal condition, was – again, in political terms – working fine. But these quibbles are moot, since we are moving forward with legalization, and will need to think about how it might work in practice and the effects it will have on federal/provincial relations. Following are some concluding thoughts regarding implementation that might help to mitigate the fallout.

The federal government ought to extend the timeline past 17 October 2018. This would provide the provinces with more time to plan and implement their retailing and regulatory regimes. Such a significant policy shift as cannabis legalization should not be subject to partisan and electoral calculations (with the federal election coming up in late 2019), and more time would allow for a more thorough and complete implementation process. Next, such a significant shift should occur as part of a step-by-step process, with decriminalization occurring first, either in an official or an unofficial capacity. This would allow for the governments' legalization response to be informed by the experience with decriminalization. Relaxing the timeframe could also permit more meaningful consultations amongst and between the federal government and its provincial counterparts. As would a formal initiative to revisit cannabis legalization and the legislative and policy changes in a set timeframe (say three to five years), to assess its effects and outcomes, with a commitment to make further legislative and policy changes, if so required. The federal government should also permit the provinces to implement cannabis regimes that fit with their provincial cultures, political climates, and the like. This would mean permitting a variety of retailing and regulatory regimes, including the right to not participate in establishing a retailing system at all, instead relying on mail-order or internet-based transactions – much like how municipalities in some provinces have the right to prohibit cannabis and, historically, alcohol sales. Permitting Canadians to grow cannabis at home, for example, as the current legislation allows, significantly infringes on the provinces' capacities to manage this new drug. Canadian governments in general and provincial governments specifically, need to think long and hard before further expanding the cannabis market to edibles and a host of alternative means of cannabis ingestion, from tinctures to drinkable products and various spray-type consumption means. Such products will make consumption easier and control more difficult and, most critically, are aimed at increasing the market appeal of this new narcotic, particularly to attract older consumers and women.

Finally, it is worth noting that legalization will mean more state control of our daily lives. Cannabis legalization is often touted by advocates as a liberation-motivated policy – giving individuals the legal choice to indulge (or not) by consuming cannabis – but legalization, in fact, will have the opposite effect. Rather, it will be the provincial state that will determine how and when individuals indulge, and will bring further scrutiny regarding their actions once they have used (driving restrictions being the most significant), but all aspects of cannabis use will now be subject to state control. Consumption, for instance, will most likely be restricted to private residences. This will not be an ever-present "4:20" celebration, where people can smoke freely when and where they wish, but rather, cannabis consumption will become yet another behaviour controlled and enforced by the state. For those of us who fret about liberties and the imposition of a single, hegemonic set of values onto the citizenry, this is another example of the ever-expanding role of the state into all aspects of our daily lives.

NOTES

1   Canadian Substance Use Costs and Harms Scientific Working Group, *Canadian Substance Use Costs and Harms (2007–2014)* (Ottawa: Canadian Centre on Substance Use and Addiction, 2018), 8, https://uwaterloo.ca/tobacco-use-canada/sites/ca.tobacco-use-canada/files/uploads/files/tobaccouseincanada_2015_accessible_final-s.pdf.

2   Michael Atkinson et al., *Governance and Public Policy in Canada: A View from the Provinces* (Toronto: University of Toronto Press, 2013).

3   Jessica Reid et al., *Tobacco Use in Canada: Patterns and Trends, 2015 edition* (Waterloo: University of Waterloo Propel Centre for Population Health Impact, 2015) 14–15, https://uwaterloo.ca/

tobacco-use-canada/sites/ca.tobacco-use-canada/files/uploads/files/
tobaccouseincanada_2015_accessible_final-s.pdf.

4   Garry Smith, "The Nature and Scope of Gambling in Canada," *Addiction*
    109, no. 5 (May 2014): 706–10, https://doi.org/10.1111/add.12210.

5   Tim Stockwell et al., "Minimum Alcohol Prices and Outlet Densities in
    British Columbia, Canada: Estimated Impacts on Alcohol-Attributable
    Hospital Admissions," *American Journal of Public Health* 103, no. 11
    (November 2013): 2014–20, https://doi.org/ 10.2105/AJPH.2013.301289.

6   John Hudak, "On 4/20, Top Minds Discuss Critical Issues in the
    Marijuana Policy Debate," *Brookings Institute*, 20 April 2016, https://
    www.brookings.edu/blog/fixgov/2016/04/20/on-420-top-minds-discuss-
    critical-issues-in-the-marijuana-policy-debate/.

7   Malcolm Bird and Christopher Stoney, "Government Approaches to the
    Regulation of 'Sin'," in *How Ottawa Spends 2006–2007: In From the
    Cold: The Tory Rise and the Liberal Demise*, ed. Bruce Doern (Montreal
    and Kingston: McGill-Queen's University Press, 2006).

8   Robert J. Williams, Yale D. Belanger, and Jennifer N. Arthur, *Gambling in
    Alberta: History, Current Status, and Socioeconomic Impacts* (Lethbridge:
    University of Lethbridge, 2011), 7, https://prism.ucalgary.ca/bitstream/
    handle/1880/48495/SEIGA%20FINAL%20REPORT-Apr2.pdf?sequence=
    3&isAllowed=y.

9   Canadian Substance Use Costs and Harms Scientific Working Group,
    Canadian Substance Use Costs and Harms (2007–2014), 8; "Tax
    Revenues from Tobacco Sales," Physicians for Smoke-Free Canada, last
    modified November 2017, http://www.smoke-free.ca/factsheets/pdf/
    totaltax.pdf; "Table 10-10-0012-01 Net income of liquor authorities and
    government revenue from sale of alcoholic beverages (x 1,000)," Statistics
    Canada, last modified 28 August 2018, https://www150.statcan.gc.ca/t1/
    tbl1/en/tv.action?pid=1010001201.

10 Michael DeVillaer, *Cannabis Law Reform in Canada: Pretense and Perils*
    (Hamilton: McMaster University Peter Boris Centre for Addictions
    Research, 2017), 34, https://fhs.mcmaster.ca/pbcar/documents/
    Pretense%20&%20Perils%20FINAL.PDF.

11 DeVillaer, *Cannabis Law Reform in Canada: Pretense and Perils*, 41–56.

3

Cannabis Legalization and Colonial Legacies

JARED J. WESLEY

In the era of reconciliation, cannabis legalization is one of the first hard tests of federal and provincial governments' commitments to inclusive national policymaking. Through their collective endorsement of the Truth and Reconciliation Commission's (TRC) Calls to Action, and the principles of the United Nations Declaration on the Rights of Indigenous Peoples (UNDRIP), upon which they were based, governments pledged to pursue meaningful, government-to-government engagement with Indigenous people and communities in matters that affected them. How well have these commitments withstood the early challenges of legalizing cannabis? Held up to their own standards and promises, federal and provincial governments have not performed well to date.

In their initial three-year drive to end the ban on recreational marijuana, federal and provincial governments established broad objectives to enhance public safety and public health for all Canadians. Issues of social justice and reconciliation were explicitly sidelined in their first wave of policy frameworks, as governments focused their resources on standing up a nationwide regulatory system to replace prohibition. From a policy standpoint, it is both conceivable and desirable that federal and provincial governments will meet their commitments to engage meaningfully with Indigenous governments to address the adverse effects the "war on drugs" had on their communities, once legalization takes effect in October 2018. Yet questions remain as to why and with what consequences they chose to pursue a settler colonial approach to policy development in the first three years of the process.

This chapter explains governments' prioritization of regulation over remediation as the by-product of expediency and settler colonialism. Faced with tight, self-imposed time constraints, the federal government ignored its commitments to respect the inherent right to Indigenous self-government and pushed back questions of social justice and reconciliation in favour of a broader focus on public safety and public health. Under tight timelines, provincial governments defaulted to existing policy frameworks, namely those dealing with alcohol and tobacco, when approaching the regulation of cannabis in their jurisdictions. In doing so, federal and provincial governments closed off much debate as to the applicability and effectiveness of the existing policy regimes to cannabis, while also limiting the scope of engagement with those having the most at stake in legalization: Indigenous people and communities. These choices will impact the ability of all governments to achieve the public health and public safety outcomes they have established for legalization, as redressing generations of harm done through incarceration, substance use, and stigmatization remains integral to the success of the new regime. These choices also call into question the strength of federal and provincial governments' commitment to reconciliation and collaborative government-to-government relationships with Indigenous people when self-imposed time constraints and competing interests are at play.

I: JURISDICTIONAL ISSUES

In countries as large and diverse as Canada, creating an effective nationwide policy framework for something like cannabis regulation is a daunting collective action problem. These challenges are compounded by the need to reconcile Crown authority with inherent rights of Indigenous people to self-government. Placing tight timelines on the policy development process makes it even more difficult, forcing governments to prioritize in terms of the issues they want to address and the partners they wish to engage.

Canadian policy makers often view such challenges through the lens of federalism, which is designed to solve conflict through a combination of self- and shared-rule. While sometimes efficient from a collective action perspective, federalism "organizes out" political communities like Indigenous people, who are improperly seen as lacking jurisdiction to govern themselves. In this sense, the default to federalism is also a symptom of persistent settler colonialism in

Canada: the enforcement or belief in the supremacy of European settler institutions over those of Indigenous people and communities. This includes treating Indigenous governments as subordinate to federal and provincial authorities.

In line with this federalist approach, early federal-provincial-territorial (FPT) consensus divided jurisdiction over cannabis into three main categories. First, the federal government was seen as having sole authority to determine policy in areas including criminality, production (commercial cultivation, processing, package labelling), and the medical cannabis system. Second, provincial governments held jurisdiction over distribution, consumer retail, and workplace or public consumption. Third, federal and provincial governments shared (or, in the case of home cultivation, disputed) jurisdictional responsibilities over elements like personal production, taxation, public safety, and public health.

The role of Indigenous people and communities is seldom addressed in these jurisdictional discussions. Viewed exclusively through the lens of Sections 91 and 92 of the *Constitution Act, 1867*, jurisdictional authority over all aspects of the legalized cannabis regime falls exclusively to the federal or provincial governments, respectively. This settler colonial practice transforms Indigenous leaders from partners into subordinated stakeholders (often in the same breath as interest groups or municipal councils), thus contradicting the inherent right to self-government found in the Constitution (Section 35), affirmed by the courts, and acknowledged by a host of federal and provincial policies.

II: COMMITMENTS TO RECONCILIATION

Among them are FPT governments' commitments to uphold the UN Declaration on the Rights of Indigenous Peoples and the TRC's Calls to Action, both of which contain assurances that no decisions about Indigenous people will be made without their input and consent.[1] For instance, Calls to Action 18, 19, and 36 committed the federal government to measure and address health outcomes, including substance abuse and dependency, in collaboration with Indigenous people.

As Allan Clarke notes, the federal government's acknowledgement of Indigenous authority is also embedded in its own policies, including the *Renewed Framework to Address Substance Use Issues among First Nations People in Canada* and its *Principles Respecting*

the Government of Canada's Relationship with Indigenous Peoples.[2]
A key principle of the former is

> Recognition of the individual, shared, and collective levels of
> responsibility to promote health and well-being among First
> Nations people. This begins with individuals managing their own
> health and extends to families, communities, service providers,
> and governments who all have a shared responsibility to ensure
> services, supports, and systems are effective and accessible, both
> now and for future generations.

The 2018 federal *Principles* document confirms ten federal commitments toward building a better relationship with Indigenous peoples.
These include recognition that:

> Indigenous self-government and laws are critical to Canada's
> future, and that Indigenous perspectives and rights must be
> incorporated in all aspects of this relationship. In doing so, we
> will continue the process of decolonization and hasten the end of
> its legacy wherever it remains in our laws and policies [...]

The *Principles* also acknowledges the importance of "involving
Indigenous peoples in the effective decision-making and governance
of our shared home [...] [and ensuring] space for the operation
of Indigenous jurisdictions and laws." Under Principle 8, the federal government pledged to build "a fairer fiscal relationship with
Indigenous nations," which could include "new tax arrangements,"
new transfer arrangements, and other mechanisms. As detailed
below, if the development and content of its first cannabis policy
framework is any indication, the federal government has much
work to do to live up to these commitments in the next phase of
legalization.

While they have their own internal policies and practices, provinces and territories, as a collective, do not have a comparable set
of principles to guide their engagement with Indigenous people
and communities on issues like cannabis legalization. This said,
premiers have met with National Indigenous Organization (NIO)
leaders on an annual basis since 2004. In 2009, they established a
joint Aboriginal Affairs Working Group consisting of NIO leaders
and ministers responsible for Indigenous relations, which morphed

into the Federal-Provincial-Territorial (FPT) Indigenous Forum in 2015. These venues have proven effective in highlighting, if not addressing, key priorities, including Aboriginal children in care and missing and murdered Indigenous women.[3] According to public records, cannabis legalization has not been discussed in great detail at any of these multilateral tables; yet this could be by consensus of Indigenous organizations, which have the ability to negotiate and set the agendas at these meetings, in collaboration with their FPT colleagues. Instead, federal, provincial, and territorial governments have held high-level discussions at the ministerial level (health, justice, finance), and have created over a dozen official-level task teams to share information and address subjects of common concern. Indigenous organizations have been noticeably absent from these FPT forums and discussions, meaning that the overall objectives, strategies, and operational choices are being developed without the partnership of Indigenous people.

III: FEDERAL/PROVINCIAL OBJECTIVES

The federal government has been the driving force behind cannabis legalization in Canada, with provincial governments playing a supporting role. The pledge to decriminalize cannabis was a key plank in the Liberal Party of Canada's 2015 campaign platform and, after commitments to electoral reform and ambitious plans to combat climate change stalled months into their mandate, the Liberal government made expedient fulfillment of this pledge a priority. According to the 2015 Liberal platform:

> We will legalize, regulate, and restrict access to marijuana.
> Canada's current system of marijuana prohibition does not work.
> It does not prevent young people from using marijuana and
> too many Canadians end up with criminal records for possess-
> ing small amounts of the drug. Arresting and prosecuting these
> offenses is expensive for our criminal justice system. It traps too
> many Canadians in the criminal justice system for minor, non-
> violent offenses. At the same time, the proceeds from the illegal
> drug trade support organized crime and greater threats to public
> safety, like human trafficking and hard drugs. To ensure that we
> keep marijuana out of the hands of children, and the profits out
> of the hands of criminals, we will legalize, regulate, and restrict

access to marijuana. We will remove marijuana consumption and incidental possession from the Criminal Code, and create new, stronger laws to punish more severely those who provide it to minors, those who operate a motor vehicle while under its influence, and those who sell it outside of the new regulatory framework. We will create a federal/provincial/territorial task force, and with input from experts in public health, substance abuse, and law enforcement, will design a new system of strict marijuana sales and distribution, with appropriate federal and provincial excise taxes applied.[4]

Missing from this pledge were promises of meaningful engagement with Indigenous people and communities, and the importance of addressing the negative consequences of the prohibition regime. The promised task force notably excluded Indigenous communities and leaders (in the end, it also excluded provincial and territorial governments, with the federal government launching its own task force without their co-leadership). Moreover, mentions of social justice, in general, and redress for Indigenous and racialized communities most impacted by the "war on drugs," in particular, were noticeably absent from the campaign pledge.[5] In their place, the federal government prioritized the broader, dual objectives of improving public health and enhancing public safety. These goals were to be accomplished by focusing on youth and eliminating the black market, respectively. Discussed below, achieving gains in either of these policy areas will require more focus on Indigenous communities than is planned at the time of writing.

As it was, the federal Task Force's *Framework for the Legalization and Regulation of Cannabis* made little mention of specific measures to address the unique situation of Indigenous people and communities.[6] This was not for lack of input. The report acknowledged that, through roundtables, meetings, and online submissions involving Indigenous experts, organizations, governments, and Elders, the Task Force had gained "valuable perspectives and a better understanding of the interests and concerns of First Nations, Inuit, and Metis communities."[7] Indeed, the volume of input from Indigenous organizations was relatively high, with 17 per cent of all online submissions provided by Indigenous governments or groups.

Yet, recommendations specific to Indigenous people and communities remained limited to calls for more engagement, primarily on economic issues. For example, the Task Force recommended that the federal government "should prioritize engagement of Indigenous governments and representative organizations, as we heard from Indigenous leaders about their interest in their communities' participation in the cannabis market." This was based on the fact that the Task Force had heard from Indigenous leaders and organizations about "economic opportunities which may contribute to creation of new jobs in their communities. A particular interest of Indigenous representatives is the opportunity for Indigenous governments or individuals to acquire cannabis production and distribution licenses." Discussion over the necessity of Indigenous governments to obtain permission from the federal government to grow and distribute cannabis on their lands remained unexplored in the report.

The Task Force also encouraged the federal government to consider revenue-sharing models that included Indigenous communities, but stopped short of acknowledging the authority of Indigenous people to engage directly in taxation. Instead, Indigenous governments were treated as recipients of federal tax revenues, grouped together with municipal councils in that regard. According to the Report,

> The federal government, in co-ordination with its provincial and territorial counterparts, should conduct the necessary economic analyses to determine a tax level that achieves the balance between public health objectives and reducing the illicit market. *Municipalities and Indigenous national organizations and representatives should be included in discussions regarding the equitable allocation of revenues* [emphasis added].

Beyond these economic and fiscal concerns, there were only two mentions of Indigenous people in the federal Task Force report. One involved a call for the federal government to "engage with Indigenous communities and Elders to develop targeted and culturally appropriate communications," which is based on a request made by an Elder "to develop culturally appropriate messaging on the risks of cannabis use for Indigenous youth." The second mention suggested "[p]rograms should be tailored to meet the needs of different communities. For instance, Indigenous representatives told us that programs should be tailored to the unique circumstances of Indigenous communities." No specific recommendations were offered in terms of the process of developing those programs, nor their suggested content.

For their part, provincial governments tacitly endorsed the Task Force report, albeit with concerns over sufficient time and resources to implement the new regime. These caveats pertained to their own abilities to stand up regulatory systems and retail markets, and raise sufficient revenue to offset anticipated costs related to law enforcement and health care. None voiced significant concerns over the exclusion of Indigenous people from the legalization process, nor requested an investment of funds, or attention into matters like social redistribution or pardons.

Provincial and territorial premiers struck their own Provincial-Territorial (PT) Working Group on Cannabis Legalization in July 2017. Led by their respective health and justice ministers, the Working Group was tasked with producing a report identifying "common considerations and best practices to cannabis legalization and regulation, guided by the objectives of reducing harm, protecting public safety, and reducing illicit activity" – the same overarching objectives on which the federal Task Force mandate had been based.[8] Likewise, in its report, the PT Working Group made limited mention of Indigenous people and communities. When reference was made, they were considered alongside municipalities as subordinate bodies facing fiscal challenges similar to those confronted by provincial and territorial governments. This is embodied in the categorization of Indigenous communities under a section titled "Municipal Cost Pressures."

At times, the Working Group appeared to speak on behalf of Indigenous communities, without having engaged them in the drafting of the report. In reference to the breadth and depth of policy changes required to implement legalization, for instance, the PT Working Group noted, "All of these activities are complex, and have significant resource implications for provinces and territories, as well as municipalities and Indigenous communities (including those that have entered into self-government agreements)."

Despite these common challenges, when discussing the authority of Indigenous communities to govern their own affairs as it pertained to the regulation of cannabis, the PT Working Group was clear that the ultimate authority rested with the Crown:

Several provinces and territories also recognize that there will be Indigenous communities, particularly those in remote and northern regions, which may be looking to enact community restrictions on cannabis, similar to present approaches to alcohol. While recognizing that care needs to be taken as to not frustrate the federal intent, many provinces and territories are working with Indigenous communities and governments to discuss the *mechanisms through which Indigenous communities will have the opportunity to make their own decisions on how they deal with social issues related to drug and alcohol abuse* [emphasis added]. Discussions are also being held in several jurisdictions as to how self-governing First Nations will be enabled to establish their own laws and approaches to cannabis legalization.

The PT Working Group also acknowledged the cost pressures confronted by Indigenous communities as a result of legalization, but grouped them together with municipalities and limited their constitutional authority to an administrative role. "Provinces and territories recognize that municipalities and Indigenous communities or governments will also be responsible for implementing components of the regulated distribution and retail system including providing oversight for zoning of retail operations (in a private model), public education, and community consultation."

Only once did the PT Working Group mention the importance of developing culturally sensitive, targeted programs and services related to Indigenous people and communities, noting "it will be critical to develop well researched and targeted campaigns for Indigenous and newcomer populations to prevent a widening of the gap in health status. The general failure of tobacco cessation campaigns among Indigenous populations in particular has demonstrated how critical it is to be culturally relevant and respectful."

Like their federal counterparts, some provinces held separate engagement events for First Nations outside the Council of the Federation process, but their input was rolled into larger stakeholder reports. Important exceptions occurred in the three territories, where unique relationships and processes exist. In the South, however, there was little to no widespread discussion about Indigenous self-governance over cannabis regulation on-reserve, special support for Indigenous entrepreneurs seeking to enter the industry, or taxation powers or revenue-sharing for cannabis sales.

In short, the federal and provincial focus was placed firmly on maintaining their own jurisdiction over public safety and public health, with little mention of the authority of Indigenous governments or the importance of social justice.

IV: IMPACTS OF POLICY REPLICATION
AND SETTLER COLONIALISM

In rolling out Canada's new legalized cannabis regime, federal and provincial governments largely replicated their own existing approaches to alcohol and tobacco regulation. This was particularly true of consumption – with regulations largely mirroring tobacco regulations – and possession, distribution, and retail largely mirroring alcohol rules. There were exceptions to these patterns. (Manitoba opted to impose a minimum age of 19 for cannabis consumption, for example, a year higher than the minimum alcohol.) But such cases are notable because they are the exception. Overwhelmingly, provincial governments chose to incorporate cannabis into to their existing regulatory frameworks for tobacco and alcohol, which were already separate and distinct from jurisdiction to jurisdiction.

A patchwork of cannabis laws and regulations has arisen as a result, creating challenges for the orderly implementation of the federal government's objectives to promote public safety and public health across the country. "Going it alone" put provincial governments at odds with those law enforcement, medical, and industry professionals who sought greater policy alignment across the country. It also raised concerns over equating cannabis use with alcohol consumption, on one hand, or tobacco smoking, on the other, with health experts noting important differences among the three substances.

At the same time, by employing the same processes and pursuing the same policy paths that mistreated traditionally marginalized communities in the first place, and failing to consider innovative policy options that would empower them, federal and provincial governments also missed a valuable opportunity to pursue reconciliation with Indigenous communities. Regulatory regimes for alcohol and tobacco were developed decades ago, based on a settler colonial interpretation of the Canadian constitution. Space constraints do not permit a full examination of the harmful effects of the introduction of alcohol and commercial tobacco into Indigenous communities by settlers. To this day, however, alcohol and tobacco remain highly regulated by federal and provincial authorities, which in many cases determine the type, volume, and price of the products

sold and consumed in Indigenous communities. Decades of negoti-
ations have resulted in some Indigenous people being exempt from
federal and provincial tobacco taxes, but full regulation remains elu-
sive for Indigenous communities. By replicating these frameworks
for cannabis, PT governments are perpetuating this settler colonial
approach in terms of substance and process.

Consider taxation. Indigenous communities have the ability to
raise revenue through the regulation of cannabis on their territory.
For First Nations, the federal government has acknowledged this
capacity through the *First Nations Fiscal Management Act* and, as
part of Budget 2018, even made mention of "the important role that
tax revenues play in supporting self-sufficiency and self-determina-
tion for Indigenous governments, [and] the Government of Canada
is committed to continuing to negotiate direct taxation arrangements with Indigenous governments." Such arrangements have yet
to be negotiated in the cannabis field, and are unlikely to begin until
after the first two years of legalization. That is when the federal-
provincial revenue-sharing agreement expires, allowing the federal
government to consider vacating tax room for Indigenous governments. Until that time, should governments wish to keep the price
of legal cannabis competitive with that in the illegal market, there is
little tax room available for Indigenous governments.

In terms of process, Indigenous people have not been involved
directly in much of the policymaking process surrounding cannabis legalization. As discussed, policy replication has recreated
consultative systems that reduce Indigenous leaders to the role of
quasi-municipal officials, business entrepreneurs, and stakeholders.
According to Clarke,

> As [2018] Senate hearings have shown, First Nations, Inuit and
> Métis leaders have presented compelling testimony that they
> were left out of the engagement and deliberation on the legisla-
> tion, both on the important and related public health issues and
> on how the laws governing cannabis will be administered in the
> future. This assertion seems to have been validated by the [fed-
> eral] Minister of Health when, in response to a question from
> Senator Scott Tannas, she was unable to state even one change
> the government had made to its draft legislation as a result of
> engagement with Indigenous peoples.[9]

The realization that they had been cut out of revenue discussions prompted the Assembly of First Nations to formally request that the federal government delay the implementation of legalization by a full year, so that potential public health, safety, and revenue implications for Indigenous people and communities could be more fully assessed.[10] The Senate Standing Committee on Aboriginal Peoples echoed this call, but it went unheeded.

In terms of substance, the exclusion of Indigenous people and communities from a meaningful role in policy development is particularly problematic, given that Indigenous people have a greater stake than most in the outcomes associated with cannabis legalization. Distinct from the settler population, Indigenous people have had unique experiences with various facets of the previous cannabis regime.[11] The "war on drugs" approach has had a disproportionate impact on Indigenous people through increased incarceration rates and sentences,[12] and the negative public health effects of substance dependence are higher among Indigenous compared to non-Indigenous people in Canada.[13]

Racialized communities have also faced disparate effects under the old regime [see Owusu-Bempah's chapter in this volume]. And their concerns are not being addressed in the first round of FPT policy frameworks, either. As Owusu-Bempah wrote elsewhere,

> Lessons from [the United States] are instructive here as some American jurisdictions that have legalized cannabis are working to incorporate reparations and equity measures into law, policy and practice. There are three main areas that should be addressed: 1) pardoning the convicted; 2) social reinvestment of tax revenue from legal sales and; 3) incorporation of those affected by prohibition into the licit cannabis industry.[14]

None of these issues have been on the agenda during the first three years of legalization policy development. The federal government has delayed discussions about criminal record suspensions until after legalization, which will in all likelihood push the debate into or beyond the 2019 federal election campaign. Similarly, there have been no FPT discussions about social reinvestment of new government revenues into the communities most impacted by prohibition to address ongoing substance dependence and related issues. Instead, governments plan to invest more broadly in public health, public safety, and research. And the federal government and most provinces, outside BC, have decided to exclude those with previous cannabis convictions from participating in the newly legal industry as distributors and/or retailers. Overall, inaction by FPT governments in these areas is likely to have substantive effects on Indigenous people and their communities without their input.

CONCLUSION

This chapter assessed federal and provincial governments according to their own standards and commitments when it comes to "doing policymaking differently" in the era of reconciliation. Promises to engage meaningfully with, and respect, the inherent right to self-government of Indigenous people will confront a host of conflicting interests that challenge governments to maintain their resolve. In the case of cannabis legalization, competing concerns included the perceived need to end prohibition within a single election cycle, and to prioritize the overall health and safety of the Canadian public over the unique needs and challenges of those people and communities most heavily impacted by the war on drugs. Beyond a doubt, a primary responsibility of governments is to prioritize the issues they will address and the partners they will engage. Commitments to reconciliation, like the TRC's Calls to Action, were designed to guide governments in making these determinations. To date, they have not affected federal and provincial approaches to cannabis legalization, which have involved replicating settler colonial frameworks for the regulation of alcohol and tobacco.

This is particularly disappointing from a policy perspective, given that Indigenous people and their communities have more at stake in legalization than their settler counterparts. Indigenous people have been disproportionately affected by the prohibition of cannabis, yet neither federal nor provincial governments have engaged them meaningfully in discussions over key policy areas like reprieves, revenues, and rehabilitation. These results run counter to the federal government's stated intent, and PTs' shared objective, to create a strong regulatory regime in support of public health and public safety for all Canadians.

In short, by replicating existing policies through conventional processes, FPT governments have also excluded Indigenous people and racialized communities from meaningful involvement in a policy-making process whose greatest impact will be on them.

The author thanks Willissa Reist for research assistance.

NOTES

1   Kiera Ladner, "An Indigenous Constitutional Paradox: Both Monumental
    Achievement and Monumental Defeat," in *Patriation and Its
    Consequences: Constitution Making in Canada*, ed. Lois Harder and Steve
    Patten (Vancouver: UBC Press, 2015).

2   Allan Clarke, "Feds Must Allow First Nations to Tax, Regulate
    Cannabis," *Policy Options*, (22 May 2018), http://policyoptions.irpp.org/
    magazines/may-2018/feds-must-allow-first-nations-tax-regulate-cannabis/;
    Health Canada, *Honouring Our Strengths: A Renewed Framework to
    Address Substance Use Issues among First Nations People in Canada*
    (Ottawa: Health Canada, 2011), http://publications.gc.ca/collections/
    collection_2011/sc-hc/H14-63-2011-eng.pdf; Justice Canada, *Principles
    Respecting the Government of Canada's Relationship with Indigenous
    Peoples* (Ottawa: Department of Justice Canada, 2018), http://www.
    justice.gc.ca/eng/csj-sjc/principles.pdf.

3   Jared Wesley, "National Indigenous Groups and the Premiers' Meeting,"
    Policy Options, 16 August 2017, http://policyoptions.irpp.org/magazines/
    august-2017/national-indigenous-groups-and-the-premiers-meeting/.

4   Liberal Party of Canada, *Real Change: A New Plan for a Strong Middle
    Class* (Ottawa: Liberal Party of Canada, 2015), https://www.liberal.ca/
    wp-content/uploads/2015/10/New-plan-for-a-strong-middle-class.pdf.

5   See Owusu-Bempah chapter in this volume.

6   Task Force on Cannabis Legalization and Regulation, *A Framework for
    the Legalization and Regulation of Cannabis in Canada: The Final Report
    of the Task Force on Cannabis Legalization and Regulation* (Ottawa:
    Health Canada, 2016), https://www.canada.ca/content/dam/hc-sc/
    healthy-canadians/migration/task-force-marijuana-groupe-etude/
    framework-cadre/alt/framework-cadre-eng.pdf.

7   Task Force on Cannabis Legalization and Regulation, *A Framework for
    the Legalization and Regulation of Cannabis in Canada: The Final Report
    of the Task Force on Cannabis Legalization and Regulation*, 13.

8   Provincial-Territorial Working Group on Cannabis Legalization and
      Regulation, *Report on Cannabis Legalization and Regulation* (Ottawa:
      Council of the Federation Secretariat, 2017), http://www.canadaspremiers.
      ca/wp-content/uploads/2017/12/COF_Report_on_Cannabis_Legalization_
      and_Regulation-Final.pdf.

9   Clarke, "Feds Must Allow First Nations to Tax, Regulate Cannabis."

10   Jorge Barrera, "Assembly of First Nations Wants Provinces, Territories to
      Butt out of First Nations Pot Sales," CBC *News*, 2 May 2018, https://www.
      cbc.ca/news/indigenous/assembly-first-nations-provinces-
      marijuana-sales-1.4645525.

11   Shelley G. Marshall, "Canadian Drug Policy and the Reproduction of
      Indigenous Inequities," *The International Indigenous Policy Journal* 6,
      no. 1 (2015).

12   Catherine Carstairs, *Jailed for Possession: Illegal Drug Use, Regulation,
      and Power in Canada, 1920–1961* (Toronto: University of Toronto Press,
      2006); Steven Hayle, Scot Wortley, and Julian Tanner, "Race, Street Life,
      and Policing: Implications for Racial Profiling," *Canadian Journal of
      Criminology and Criminal Justice* 58, no. 3 (July 2016), https://doi.
      org/10.3138/cjccj.2014.E32.

13   Tara Elton-Marshall, Scott T. Leatherdale, and Robin Burkhalter,
      "Tobacco, Alcohol and Illicit Drug Use among Aboriginal Youth Living
      Off-Reserve: Results from the Youth Smoking Survey," *Canadian Medical
      Association Journal* 183, no. 8 (May 2011), https://doi.org/10.1503/
      cmaj.101913.

14   Akwasi Owusu-Bempah, "Let's Repair the Harms of Canada's War on
      Drugs," *Toronto Star*, 10 July 2017, https://www.thestar.com/opinion/
      commentary/2017/07/10/lets-repair-the-harms-of-canadas-war-on-
      drugs.html.

4

Cannabis and Conflict of Interest: Is It Wrong for Public Officials to Profit from the Legalization of Cannabis?

CHRIS MACDONALD

Is it ethically problematic for public officials to profit from the legalization of cannabis? In Canada, concerns have been raised about numerous instances in which public officials of various kinds have profited – either during or following public service – from their involvement in the cannabis industry. This chapter examines this issue through the lens of conflict of interest. Does profiting privately in this way imply improper behaviour in a situation characterized by conflict of interest, or something close to that?

I: BACKGROUND

Against the backdrop of legalization, ethical questions have arisen about the actions of a number of public officials – elected and otherwise – who have roles or who have moved to take on roles in various parts of the for-profit cannabis industry. This includes, for example, not just one but both leaders of the country's federal Task Force on Cannabis Legalization and Regulation. The task force was chaired by former federal Minister of Public Safety Anne McLellan,[1] and its vice chair was McGill University professor Dr Mark Ware. McLellan, for her part, has been a senior advisor at Bennett Jones LLP – a prominent advisor to the Canadian cannabis industry – since 2006. And Professor Ware announced in May of 2018 that he was taking a leave from McGill to become Chief Medical Officer at Canopy Growth Corp. Canopy is an established provider of medical marijuana and had announced plans to supply the recreational marijuana market too, in the wake of legalization. Other ethical questions that arose were less closely tied to legalization, but seem part of the larger story: for example, Julian Fantino, the former Ontario Provincial Police Commissioner and former Minister of Veterans Affairs, announced in the fall of 2017 that he would be opening a medical marijuana company. Fantino, once a vocal critic of legalization, was at pains to stress that his company – Aleafia Total Health Network – was involved only in medical, and not recreational, marijuana. But critics saw at least a tension between his former administrative opposition and his new-found entrepreneurial zeal.

But the point of this chapter is not to render judgment about the propriety of any particular individual's behaviour. Rather, the hope is to sketch the relevant terrain in sufficient detail to allow others to reach their own conclusions with regard to cases that they take to be of concern. The use of the word "propriety" here is conscious and intentional. While the matter at hand is one of ethics, ethical discourse is too often focused on determining whether a particular behaviour is entirely "ethical" (i.e., ethically good or at least neutral) or entirely "unethical" (i.e., categorically ethically bad). That is, ethics is too often treated as binary: either a behaviour is ethical, and hence entirely unobjectionable; or unethical, and hence intolerable. The method of analysis used in this chapter encourages a rather subtler approach, one that is typical of professional discussions of ethics, if not typical of public discussions of ethics. Under this approach, there are indeed some behaviours that are categorically ethical – entirely unobjectionable. And there are indeed some behaviours that are categorically unethical – entirely wrong. But there are also other behaviours that are somewhere in between: behaviours that rightly raise eyebrows, that are in some sense morally regrettable even if not fully unethical. Behaviours that might be referred to as unseemly. While we will in this chapter occasionally refer simply to whether a particular activity is "unethical," the reader ought to think of this as a kind of shorthand, and bear in mind the range of more subtle possibilities.

It is also crucial here to distinguish the question of whether a given activity is ethical (or seemly) from the question of whether it is legal. The activities discussed in this chapter are within (or at the very least akin to) the range of activities covered by a number of legal and regulatory documents relevant to the behaviour of Canadian government officials, including at least the *Conflict of*

Interest Act and the *Conflict of Interest Code for Members of the House of Commons* (both of which are administered by the Office of the Conflict of Interest and Ethics Commissioner). And while reference will be made to such documents, and inferences drawn from what those documents have to say, legal analysis *per se* is beyond the scope of this chapter.

The relationship between ethics and the law is of course a subtle one, about which philosophers and legal scholars have written an enormous amount. Ethics and the law have much in common. Both seek to civilize our interactions with other members of society and are intended to guide individual and collective behaviour as a mechanism for doing so. And ethical and legal *reasoning* are alike in many ways as well: both involve reasoning about the propriety of some past action or proposed course of action, with reference to the relevant facts (who did what?), behavioural norms (trust, integrity, and so on), and principles of reasoning (such as the requirement to treat like cases alike). Yet ethics and the law have different sources and overlapping but different content. Not all that is legal is ethical – for example, cheating on one's spouse, or breaking an important promise to a friend. And not all that is illegal is unethical – for example, many acts of civil disobedience. Thus, legal standards provide at best an imperfect guide to ethical analysis, and the present chapter will not simply apply the relevant legislation and professional codes to the question of cannabis.

A further connection between ethics and law makes it relevant, however, to cite legal restrictions in the course of ethical analysis. Laws, when they are good laws, are motivated by ethical reasons: good laws seek to protect persons and communities from harm and from violations of their rights. The fact that a particular behaviour is illegal, or that it has even been thought plausibly to violate the law, is often a strong but imperfect indicator that the behaviour is ethically questionable too. Laws, especially those that pertain to the operations of complex institutions, often embody years of experience and the considered opinions of experts. Canada's *Conflict of Interest Act* is no different in this regard. When a given behaviour has been made illegal in any reasonably well-governed society, we ought to take that into consideration as part of our ethical assessment of that activity. Hence this chapter makes occasional reference to conflict-of-interest laws and regulations. But this will always be part of an ethical analysis, not a legal one.

II: WHAT IS CONFLICT OF INTEREST?

What is conflict of interest? Definitions vary, but there is considerable agreement among scholars as to most of the key elements. Scholars tend to agree, for example, that conflict of interest as such is a category of situations that occur primarily in professional or institutional settings. They also agree that conflict of interest involves professionals or officials either providing advice or using judgment on behalf of someone else. Scholars also tend to agree that conflict of interest occurs in situations requiring trust, such as for example when a judge is trusted by the public to render judgment impartially, when a physician is trusted by a patient to offer professional advice motivated only by the patient's best interest, or when a government minister is trusted by citizens to render policy in pursuit of the public good. Finally, scholars also agree that conflict of interest occurs in situations in which the professional or official involved has some personal interest – often but not always a financial one – that might tend to bias the official or professional's advice or judgment.

How should we define conflict of interest? Canada's *Conflict of Interest Act* serves as a decent starting point. Section 4 of the Act says the following:

> For the purposes of this Act, a public office holder is in a conflict of interest when he or she exercises an official power, duty or function that provides an opportunity to further his or her private interests or those of his or her relatives or friends or to improperly further another person's private interests.

This definition is flawed in one noteworthy way, namely in its reference to *exercising* official power. That is, under this definition, a conflict of interest doesn't exist unless and until the official actually takes action in an improper way. This fails to correspond to the views of the leading scholars in this area, according to whom conflict of interest is a kind of situation, not a kind of action. According to this latter view, a conflict of interest exists as soon as an official finds him- or herself in a certain kind of situation, namely one in which he or she has the opportunity to act in a way that opens up the possibility of bias. Such an official is already – blamelessly – in a conflict of interest.

A more suitable definition would be as follows: a conflict of interest obtains in…

...a situation in which a person has a private or personal interest sufficient to appear to influence the objective exercise of his or her official duties as, say, a public official, an employee, or a professional.[2]

According to this definition, *all* that is required for the existence of a conflict of interest is the existence of a certain kind of professional duty, one that is (loosely speaking) in tension with some personal interest that stands to affect judgment. The essential link here is the need for the professional or official to exercise judgment. This is diagnostically crucial. A conflict of interest does not exist simply because some professional or official has a personal interest in some matter of, for example, public policy. In order for a conflict of interest, strictly defined, to exist, the individual must be in a position to make a decision or offer advice on the matter. If there is no opportunity to exercise judgment, there is no conflict of interest – though there may be the appearance of one.[3]

It is worth spelling out why conflict of interest is considered a problem. Two reasons are generally recognized. First, and perhaps most obviously, conflict of interest is considered a problem because we worry in such situations that if the professional or official in question goes ahead and renders judgment or offers advice, in spite of the existence of an un-remediated conflict, her decision may be one that fails to serve those she is sworn to serve. A judge, for instance, adjudicating a case involving a relative, might impose a sentence that is not a just one. Or a government minister might end up instituting a policy that serves the interests of friends, or lines her own pockets, rather than best serving the public interest.

Perhaps more important, however, is that where conflict of interest occurs, and where it is dealt with improperly, there is the possibility that confidence in the decision-maker, and indeed the institution in which decision-making is embedded, will be shaken. Seen from this perspective, the problem with the conflicted judge is not just that she may make a bad decision, but that citizens will lose faith in the justice system as a whole. The problem with the conflicted public official is not merely that bad policy may result, but that voters will lose faith in public policy-making more generally. This is in fact the moral crux of conflict of interest. In modern society, individuals rely in an enormous number of ways on the decision-making of professionals, policy-makers, and experts. Such reliance is necessarily grounded in trust, and "this trust is imperiled if people *even suspect* that experts or office-holders, who are inherently difficult to monitor, might be in a position to improperly profit from their privileged status."[4]

In spelling out these worries, it is crucial to point out that, properly understood, conflict of interest is not an accusation. Conflict of interest itself is not, for example, a form of corruption. Indeed, conflicts of interest can arise entirely innocently, as when a small-town judge finds that a close relative has been charged with a crime and brought before her. The judge here has done nothing wrong. But she is clearly in a conflict of interest: her job is to render judgment in all cases impartially, and yet in the present case she would clearly have an "other" interest – namely a presumptive interest in not seeing her relative go to jail – and that interest could very plausibly interfere with her judgment. In this situation, the judge is not to be *accused* of conflict, but simply needs it pointed out if she hasn't noticed it already. If she *handles* the situation badly – for instance, if she goes ahead and presides over the case – then she is of course rightly to be criticized for that.

What should the individual do, then, when she finds herself in a conflict of interest? First, note that the fact that conflict of interest is not an accusation goes hand in hand with the realization that the integrity of the individual is no solution. When a true conflict exists, it is insufficient for others to encourage her to take care, or for the individual to point to her own integrity. The claim (or even the fact) that a given professional or official "would never" allow personal interests to shape decision-making is entirely beside the point:

> Even cases in which the professional is morally and psychologically committed to serving her client's interests to the best of her abilities, and even when she could not conceive of being tempted or influenced by some personal interest that is in conflict with her client's, we still may say that she is in *a conflict of interest situation* and that *because* she is in such a situation she *has* a conflict of interest....[5] [emphasis original]

The individual who finds herself in a conflict of interest is in a situation in which her personal interests may – entirely subconsciously – sway decision-making in ways she cannot possibly predict. Against such subconscious forces, the integrity of the individual, and an honest intent to "do my best," is simply impotent. And even if the individual had a high degree of certainty in her ability to be impartial, that doesn't mean that observers would be so certain, and it doesn't mean that trust in the institution would not still be eroded.

Most experts on conflict of interest (and most institutional conflict-of-interest policies) recommend three key steps to dealing appropriately with conflicts of interest: avoid them when you can, disclose conflicts to relevant individuals, and remove yourself from decision-making where at all possible. Each of these prescriptions, however, poses certain difficulties. Avoidance, for example, in some cases is simply impossible: as noted above, sometimes professionals find themselves thrust into situations characterized by conflict of interest, through no doing of their own.

Disclosure, too, poses difficulties. When notified of a conflict of interest on the part of a professional or an official, are we to discount that individual's judgment entirely? We might think that, once notified of the possibility of bias, we can at least "keep our eyes open" for it. But in most cases, we rely on professionals and officials precisely because we lack the sort of technical knowledge that would allow us to monitor them effectively. I go to a doctor because I don't have the knowledge that would be required to monitor my doctor's decision-making for signs of bias. When a professional or an official declares a conflict, what, even in principle, should we do with such a disclosure? The answer is unclear. And Daylian Cain and co-authors have provided experimental evidence casting doubt on the effectiveness of disclosure as a remedy. According to them, there is good reason to think both that clients are unlikely to know what to do with professional disclosures of conflict of interest (in order to adjust their own decision-making), and further, that professionals who disclose a conflict of interest may actually give more biased advice than those who fail to disclose one.[6]

Finally, removing oneself from decision-making (known technically as "recusal") is sometimes impossible. In some institutional settings, for example, the limited number of individuals with the relevant expertise may make it impossible or impractical for a given individual to decline to make a particular decision; special knowledge may make a given individual an essential part of the process. If you are the only accountant at a small company, your judgment may well be essential in hiring further accountants, even if one of the applicants is a close friend of yours. And in some cases, recusal may not even be effective in achieving its nominal goals. Imagine, for instance, the situation of a corporate board member who declares a conflict on some matter and steps out of the room while a vote is taken. The *other* members of the board may quite possibly find their own decision-making biased by the very interest revealed by an individual whom they regard as a valued colleague, and perhaps even a friend. On the other hand, it might be that while the practical value of disclosure is unclear, interested parties still have a right to know that an individual in whom they are placing their trust is in a conflict of interest. A good argument can be made here. After all, a great many norms that apply in institutional settings are ones grounded in principle, rather than strictly speaking in the pursuit of better outcomes.

III: TWO KINDS OF CASES

With regard to Canadian government officials profiting from the legalized cannabis industry, two very different types of situations must be differentiated. One is the situation faced by some government officials during their time in office. The other concerns the ethics of post-government employment. That is, it pertains to the question of the propriety of *former* government officials profiting from the cannabis industry after having left a government position that involved some meaningful role in matters pertaining to that industry.

The first question – concerning the behaviour of government officials while in office – is relatively straightforward. These cases are dealt with directly by the *Conflict of Interest Act*. Under the Act, public officials[7] are obligated, for example, to arrange their own affairs "in a manner that will prevent the public office holder from being in a conflict of interest," and to abstain from decision-making regarding matters in which they have a private interest. These are the most general requirements of the Act. A subset of public officials (including, for example, cabinet ministers and the Chief Electoral Officer, all of whom are designated as "reporting public officials" under the Act) are required to submit to the office of the Conflict of Interest and Ethics Commissioner a confidential, written description of assets and activities that might tend to result in conflicts of interest if relevant decisions were to arise in the course of the official's duties, and to update the Commissioner if their situation changes.

Setting aside quibbles about the definition of "conflict of interest" offered in the Act (see above), the Act does provide decent basic guidance to public officials seeking to satisfy the main requirements of ethical behaviour in the face of conflict. It exhorts officials to avoid conflicts (namely by arranging their financial affairs appropriately upon taking up public office), disclose conflicts (in writing, to the Commissioner, who then posts them on her office's website), and to recuse themselves from decisions regarding which they have a conflict.

Let us next examine a couple of hypothetical examples. First, imagine a cabinet minister – say, the Minister of Public Safety and Emergency Preparedness[8] – is offered an opportunity to invest in a commercial venture growing recreational cannabis. Needless to say, profiting from cannabis would put the minister in a fairly serious conflict of interest. The minister would be responsible for setting policies that affect that industry, and would be engaged in high-level discussions about the federal government's entire policy direction with regard to it. Given our general impression that the cannabis industry will be increasingly profitable, this situation embodies one in which the minister would pretty clearly have an "interest sufficient to appear to influence" her judgment with regards to setting policy. At the very least, such an investment would have to be disclosed, as a matter of basic integrity and as required by the Act. What about recusal? Arguably, the Minister of Public Safety and Emergency Preparedness would play such a central role in policy-setting with regard to cannabis that recusal would be wildly impractical. And, further, even if a way were found to keep the minister "out of the loop," there would be every possibility that her senior advisors and officials within the ministry, along with cabinet colleagues, would find themselves biased by their feelings of allegiance to the minister. In such a situation, the minister would be obliged simply to decline the opportunity. This would have been the case had Anne McLellan, for example, been asked to join Bennet Jones while she was still Minister of Public Safety.

Next, let us consider the case of a non-governmental expert in cannabis biology, agriculture, or commerce, asked to take on an official role that involves making policy recommendations to government with regard to the legalization of cannabis. Such an expert would, in all likelihood, have gained the relevant expertise through professional activities of a money-making kind: it is unlikely that a mere hobbyist would gain sufficient profile to attract the (positive) attention of government and to be asked to render service. Mark Ware would be in this category – a scientist with ties to industry.[9]

If still engaged in those money-making activities, any such expert would likely (perhaps unless retired) have the kind of interest in the outcome of the relevant policy debates that would be sufficient to appear to influence judgment. Of course, as mentioned above, this might be hard to avoid. Disinterested experts may be hard to find. And asking experts to "arrange their affairs" so as to avoid conflict – that is, to divest themselves of their financial interests – might well be so burdensome as to pose a serious barrier to recruitment. The result might be a situation in which the government is faced with recruiting someone with an obvious, unresolvable conflict of interest, and then doing what could be done to *manage* the conflict.

One plausible mechanism for doing so might be to minimize the impact of the conflicted expert's possible bias by using multiple experts, perhaps as part of a panel that consists of a range of individuals with sufficiently varying perspectives. Indeed, that may have been the government's strategy in recruiting members to the task force in addition to Dr Ware and Ms McLellan. Both of them declared conflicts of interest, and none of the other members of the task force did.[10] Other members of the task force included a criminology professor, a municipal politician, a senior police officer, and a senior health administrator, among others. This is not to say that such diversity makes the problem go away. Some observers would surely still be worried that Dr Ware and Ms McLellan would bring their biases (or the biases critics assume they have) to the table, and as chairs exert undue influence over their task force colleagues. But for the reasons adduced above, diversity might be the best way of *managing* a conflict that cannot reasonably be avoided.

The second question that must be explored is what is known in the literature as "post-government employment." This is the question of the propriety of government officials *leaving* government and *then* taking up employment in an industry over which they once had influence. This is more or less the situation that applies to Dr Ware in his taking a leave from McGill to become Chief Medical Officer at Canopy Growth Corp. The question of the propriety of instances of such behaviour is considerably more difficult to assess than the ethics of straightforward conflicts of interest that occur while holding public office.

The difficulty in discussing post-government employment arises first, perhaps, because worries about post-government employment are typically so different from worries about traditional conflicts of interest. After all, in traditional conflicts of interest, the worry is that a private interest will warp an official's decision-making. But, where the individual in question has left office, there is no longer any public decision-making role to be jeopardized. Andrew Stark points out that although this sort of "private gain from public office comes within the colloquial embrace of conflict-of-interest problems, it in fact involves no conflict of interest."[11] This is very far, however, from saying that there is no ethical *problem* when officials gain privately from having held public office.

Post-government employment in fact raises a number of significant worries. The first worry is that former public officials will be all too effective in the private sector, in particular as lobbyists, using their status and connections to advance the cause of their new, private-sector employers. This is surely the reason for the Act's total prohibition on lobbying activities related to cabinet ministers' former portfolios in the year following their departure from office,[12] and the Act's lifetime ban on ministers lobbying their former cabinet colleagues.[13] This means that Ms McLellan, for instance, as a former cabinet minister, is forbidden from lobbying her former colleague Ralph Goodale, who was Minister of Finance when she was in cabinet, and who now is Minister of Public Safety and Emergency Preparedness. Julian Fantino, for his part, is currently (legally, at least) free to lobby as he wishes: though a former cabinet minister, he was part of a Conservative government, and so none of his former colleagues are now members of the Liberal cabinet. However, should the Conservatives return to government, and should, for example, Fantino's former colleague Robert Nicholson return to his previous portfolio as Minister of Justice, Fantino would be forbidden under the Act from lobbying Nicholson. The ban on lobbying former cabinet colleagues is, under the Act, a lifetime ban.

A further worry is that any former official of sufficiently high rank will have had special access to privileged information – and in the most extreme cases, classified information. In less serious cases, the worry remains that former officials have information and experience that gives them a unique, and thus perhaps unfair, advantage over others who have not served in the specific public-sector roles they themselves have. The worry about fairness is pervasive. Writing about the history of restrictions on post-government employment in the American context, Kathryn Stone pointed out that worries about unfair advantage underpin many of the limitations on post-government employment. Former government officials have knowledge, insight, and influence that are likely to be unparalleled in the private sector. "Congress," she writes, "continued to worry that the information, influence, and access that these former government employees acquired during their government employment would provide an unfair and improper advantage to the outside interests that hired them."[14]

A final worry (though perhaps not exhaustive of the history list of worries) regarding post-government employment has to do with the doubt that such employment casts upon an individual's motives for having sought public office in the first place. Applied to the present case, the question might be why Dr Ware would take time from his other duties to serve on the Task Force. This is seldom a worry with regard to career civil servants (and legal restrictions on post-government employment typically acknowledge this difference). Presumably no one spends forty years in public service, at a comparatively meager salary, specifically in anticipation of landing a lucrative private-sector contract upon retirement. The worry, rather, applies more specifically to those who enter public life, either as elected or appointed officials, for a briefer period, and find themselves enjoying a "bump" in income upon returning to the private sector. But the worry here is not or should not be the lucre to be gained through having served as a public official. Money, *per se*, is not a bad thing. The worry, rather, has to do with the light it casts back on the individual's time in office. First, there is a worry about motives: was this person perhaps *motivated* to serve in public office specifically by the prospect of later financial gain, rather than by more noble motives? Second, there is a worry about how a person so motivated might have *behaved* while in office. As Stark puts it, "Officials motivated by possibilities for private gain to enter or serve in public office have a conflict of interest (their in-role decisions and actions could be affected by their desire to optimize possibilities for private gain)."[15] The problem, Stark continues, "...lies with the extension of private motivations into the [official] role, not with the extension of the role into private activities."[16] To the extent that those who worry about Dr Ware's career move are justified, the worry must be about whether foreseeing such a move might have influenced his work on the task force, rather than about him "carrying" his task force experience into the private sector.

Because of worries of this sort, the *Conflict of Interest Act* stipulates that, quite generally, "No former public-office holder shall act

in such a manner as to take improper advantage of his or her previous public office." Just what constitutes "improper" advantage is,
for the most part, left unclear. The relevant subsections of the Act
mention things such as use of privileged information, and lobbying
("making representations to") government in the year immediately
following leaving a position.

It is worth pointing out, however, that the Act does not outlaw all
post-government employment. To ban all subsequent private gain
from having held public office is of course impossible. In many cases,
the private gain to be had (and it may be significant) lies simply
in the fact of having held public office, or having held a relevant
one. Having held public office is after all something that goes on
one's resumé, so to speak, and becomes part of one's credentials. It
is a non-trivial form of work experience. To forbid individuals from
benefiting from their government experience would in practice be
to forbid them from future employment altogether, or force them to
work in fields far from their own expertise and in which they would
have few prospects.

CONCLUSION

This chapter has provided a brief sketch of the ethical terrain relevant to the question of government officials – current and former –
profiting from the legalized cannabis industry, and has touched upon
how the relevant considerations might apply to key individuals such
as the chair and vice-chair of the Task Force on Cannabis Legalization and Regulation. There is, in a sense, nothing special about
cannabis in this regard. The extent of interaction between government and industry today makes such questions incredibly common.
Government, faced with regulating an ever-more-complex range of
industries, has an enormous need for information and insight, much
of which must inevitably be recruited from the private sector. Individuals such as McLellan and Ware are inevitably going to be asked
to be part of advisory bodies such as the Task Force. When this happens, they are not to be accused of conflict of interest, but rather, the
conflict is to be acknowledged and managed.

As argued above, the proliferation of situations involving or
approximating conflict of interest is the inevitable result of our
growing dependence on complex institutions and on professional
judgment. This is, on the whole, not necessarily a bad thing. The

institutions and professional relationships that raise these issues also do an enormous amount to make our lives better, and richer, and safer. The key is to do what we can to understand the relevant risks, and to mitigate them where we can. It is worth pointing out that conflict of interest is as poorly understood as it is common. While most people understand that conflict of interest is problematic, and have some vague sense of what it consists in, public discourse on the topic is regrettably crude, and tends not to reflect a sophisticated understanding of the essential elements. Such an understanding is an essential first step toward dealing appropriately with the range of situations – including ones clearly constituting conflicts of interest, ones clearly not constituting such conflicts, and ones somewhere along the edges. A cautious approach, one that begins with careful understanding before moving on to judgment, is particularly appropriate in the context of a controversial and polarizing policy domain such as the legalization of cannabis.

NOTES

1 Ms McLellan has in fact held a variety of cabinet posts at various times, including Minister of Justice, Minister of Health, and Deputy Prime Minister, among others.

2 Chris MacDonald, Michael McDonald, and Wayne Norman, "Charitable Conflicts of Interest," *Journal of Business Ethics* 39, no.1–2 (August 2002): 67–74, https://doi.org/10.1023/A:1016379900781.

3 The term "appearance of conflict of interest" is properly used to designate situations that look, misleadingly, like conflicts of interest, but which in fact lack one or another of the key elements of conflict of interest.

4 Wayne Norman and Chris MacDonald, "Conflict of Interest," in *Oxford Handbook of Business Ethics*, eds. George Brenkert and Tom Beauchamp (Oxford: Oxford University Press, 2009), 464.

5 Norman and MacDonald, "Conflict of Interest," 447.

6 Daylian Cain, George Loewenstein, and Don A. Moore, "Coming Clean but Playing Dirtier: The Shortcomings of Disclosure as a Solution to Conflicts of Interest," in *Conflict of Interest: Challenges and Solutions in Business, Law, Medicine and Public Policy*, eds. Don Moore et al (New York: Cambridge University Press, 2005).

7 It is worth noting that the term "public official" (as defined in the Act) designates a substantial range of individuals, including, for example,

cabinet ministers, parliamentary secretaries, members of ministerial staff, the Parliamentary Budget Officer, and most Governor in Council appointees. It does not include other members of Canada's public service – that is, rank-and-file civil servants. It also does not include, for example, judges and provincial lieutenant governors.

8   At time of writing, the Minister of Public Safety and Emergency Preparedness is the Hon. Ralph Goodale. But the present example is intended to be purely hypothetical, and the author does not intend to imply that Mr Goodale has ever been engaged in the cannabis industry.

9   In addition to being employed by McGill University, Ware was and is executive director of the Canadian Consortium for the Investigation of Cannabinoids (CCIC), a nonprofit funded at least in part by the cannabis industry.

10   "Summary of Expertise, Experience, and Affiliations and Interests," Task Force on Marijuana Legalization and Regulation, Health Canada, last modified 30 June 2016, https://www.canada.ca/en/health-canada/ programs/consultation-toward-legalization-regulation-restriction-access-marijuana/task-force-marijuana-legalization-regulation/summary-expertise-experience-affiliations-interests.html.

11   Andrew Stark, "Beyond Quid pro Quo: What's Wrong with Private Gain from Public Office?," *American Political Science Review* 91, no. 1 (March 1997): 119.

12   *Conflict of Interest Act*, SC 2006, c 9, s 2, s. 35(2).

13   *Conflict of Interest Act*, SC 2006, c 9, s 2, s. 35(3).

14   Kathryn Stone, "The Twilight Zone: Postgovernment Employment Restrictions Affecting Retired and Former Department of Defense Personnel," *Military Law Review* 142 (Fall 1993): 67, 82.

15   Stark, "Beyond," 115.

16   Stark, "Beyond," 115.

PART TWO

Public Health

5

Will Legalization Protect Our Kids?

DANIEL WEINSTOCK

Many considerations undoubtedly conspired to lead the Liberal government of Justin Trudeau to decide to legalize marijuana. Court-ordained legalization for medical purposes has led to a complex and arguably unsustainable situation for courts and for law-enforcement officials. The libertarian argument, according to which a modern society such as Canada should move away from criminalizing victimless crimes, has figured among the pressures that have placed legalization on the legislative agenda of Liberal governments since the early 1970s. Reports of manna-like tax dividends rolling into public coffers in US states that have legalized in the past few years have likely had an effect as well.

But the public justification of legalization that has been put forward by the government from the moment the Liberal party began campaigning on the issue before the last federal election, all the way to the preamble of the Bill that ended up being passed by Parliament in June 2018, has had to do with the impact of a prohibitionist regime on children. Time and time again, Justin Trudeau, both as candidate and as prime minister, has emphasized that our children were being harmed in myriad ways by the prohibitionist regime. Otherwise law-abiding adolescents had to consort with criminals in order to buy marijuana. They risked ending up with criminal records that would follow them throughout their lives. And the lack of any control or regulation on the product that they were purchasing on the illegal market meant that they were putting their health at risk. Illegally purchased marijuana might very well be laced with toxic substances, or contain THC concentrations that vastly increase the mental-health risks associated with marijuana consumption, especially for adolescents, whose brains are still developing.

I want to suggest in this paper that the mix of measures that have been put in place by the federal government and by the provinces risks failing with respect to this central objective. As a society, we risk ending up with a situation in which adults are able to purchase marijuana and other cannabis products that have been rigorously quality-controlled, from seed to store, while adolescents end up suffering the consequences of a prohibitionist regime now targeted at them alone. To jump to my conclusion, there is an argument to be made for the perhaps counter-intuitive idea that, unless we can ensure that we will be able to keep illegal marijuana out of the hands of our kids, we might as well let them have access to the safer marijuana that will be available in the legal market.

MARIJUANA: A (WIDELY AVAILABLE) YOUNG PERSON'S INTOXICANT

When marijuana becomes legal in Canada on 17 October 2018, a multi–billion dollar legal recreational marijuana economy will come into being, literally overnight. As anyone who has walked around any of Canada's major cities with a functioning olfactory apparatus will readily attest, this is *not* to say that there does not already exist a thriving illegal marijuana economy. According to a Statistics Canada study published in 2015, Canadians spent somewhere in the neighborhood of $7 billion dollars on marijuana and other cannabis-derived products. That figure is admittedly only about a quarter of what they spent on alcohol, but it becomes quite impressive when one considers that marijuana is still technically illegal.

Unlike alcohol, it would seem that, at least under the prohibitionist regime, marijuana is a young person's intoxicant. Almost 30 per cent of young adults aged 18 to 24 admit to having used the drug in the past year. But not that far behind are 15-to-17 year olds, 17.5 per cent of whom are reported by the study as having used the drug. Marijuana use tends to taper off as people get older, however. The same study suggests that only somewhere on the order of 1.5 per cent of older Canadians used marijuana in the previous year. That is quite different from consumption patterns for alcohol.

The widespread use of unregulated marijuana among younger segments of the population represents a significant public-health concern. That's because the deleterious health impacts of the drug tend to be most severe among people whose brains are still developing. Brain development occurs until roughly the age of 25. That means that people who consume marijuana in the highest proportions are those who are also most at risk from it. Those older segments of the population of whom it is likely true to say that marijuana is, for them, no more dangerous than alcohol, do not seem to be using marijuana very much at all (though whether consumption goes down as people get older because of the legal status of the drug or because of its distinctive properties is something we will have a better idea about after legalization).

The deleterious impact of marijuana among the young is actually a function of two aspects of the unregulated product that they can presently (quite easily) acquire on the illegal market. The first aspect is the THC potency of the marijuana currently available on the illegal market. THC is the psychoactive ingredient in cannabis, and evidence suggests that the long-term mental-health effects of the substance increase due to potency as measured by THC concentration. There are two ways in which a legally regulated market can offset this aspect of the illegal market. First, it can simply prohibit the sale of marijuana products above a certain concentration of THC. Second, it can provide information as to the THC content of legally available marijuana. (Ex hypothesi, illegal sellers are under no obligation to inform their customers as to the potency of the drugs they are selling, or of the consequences that might ensue from the consumption of marijuana products at different levels of potency.)

The second aspect that leaves consumers in an illegal market at risk is the fact that no reliable regulatory apparatus exists to ensure the purity of the product they are consuming. It is well-documented that illegal producers and dealers are wont to lace the product they sell with toxic substances that increase the effect of the drug upon consumption. The risks attendant upon marijuana consumption in virtue of its unregulated contents distribute more homogeneously across age groups than do the risks that flow from high THC concentration. But a fortiori, the risks that this poses to the general population are also risks for adolescents.

What I've wanted to establish with this thumbnail sketch of the *status quo ante* is that there exists a substantial marijuana economy in Canada prior to legalization. Legalization will not create such an economy *ex nihilo*. Rather, legal marijuana will have to compete in

the marketplace with a well-established illegal market. Will the regulatory apparatus that will be put in place by the federal government
and by the provinces succeed in driving illegal producers and suppliers out of the marketplace? And more to the point of the present
essay, will they succeed in protecting our children from the baleful
health effects of unregulated, illegal marijuana?

WILL THE GOVERNMENT'S REGULATORY APPROACH WORK?

The legal market in marijuana will, to be sure, avail itself of a set of
powerful tools relative to the players presently populating the illegal
marketplace. First, and most obviously, consumers who purchase marijuana through legal suppliers, and who conform themselves to laws
concerning the quantities that they can legally possess at any one time,
will find themselves on the right side of the criminal law, and will therefore not have to fear any legal consequences. Though laws prohibiting
simple possession are spottily enforced at present in Canada, there is
still a risk of sanction. That risk is, moreover, not evenly distributed
across the population, but tends to focus on racialized minorities. The
incentive to move to the legal market will be all the stronger if law-
enforcement officials apply laws against the illegal supply of marijuana
more stringently than they presently do. This is something that share-
holders in the giant companies that will, for the foreseeable future, be
dominating the legal market in Canada, will insist upon.

Second, the conditions under which consumers purchase marijuana will be routinized and rendered just as banal as the purchase
of alcohol. In Quebec, they will purchase their marijuana and other
cannabis products from high-street stores, in which trained consul-
tants will be able to assist them in meeting their needs with arguably
greater precision than is presently the case in the illegal market. In
Ontario, where the private sector will be tasked with distribution,
coffee giant Second Cup is considering transforming a large number
of its coffee outlets into marijuana stores. And Canadians from coast
to coast will of course be able to purchase marijuana online, and
have it delivered to their homes by Canada Post.

Third, consumers will not have to worry about the risk of purchasing product that has been laced with unwanted and dangerous
toxic substances. The legal market will, unlike the situation in a
"tolerationist" regime, such as that which exists in the Netherlands

(where "coffee shops" abound but supply is still unregulated), allow into the marketplace only licensed producers who will be subject to exacting standards of quality control.

Fourth, companies that bring marijuana to market will be able to engage in limited forms of advertising. Though the aim of legalization is not to make the consumption of marijuana more attractive, but rather to minimize the harms associated with it, it seems at present as if the regulations surrounding the commercialization of marijuana will resemble those that alcohol producers and suppliers are constrained by, rather than the far more stringent rules that presently apply to tobacco products.

Finally, the legal market has at least the potential to drive the illegal one out through pricing. Though there is also a strong incentive on the part of the federal and provincial governments to use the legalization of marijuana to levy tax revenues, they can at least in principle undercut the competition as well.

Whether this palette of regulatory tools will suffice to drive the competition out remains to be seen. The fact is that, especially in the wake of the legal grey area that has been created by the legalization of marijuana for medicinal purposes, the purchase of marijuana has *already* become routinized, at least for broad swaths of the population. Many suppliers have long-term, regular customers for whom they have to compete with other suppliers, and who provide them with a strong economic incentive to enact quality controls and a strong customer service ethos. Though technically illegal, the marijuana market in Canada today often functions in many respects like a legal one. It is therefore not a matter of logical necessity that consumers will abandon their present suppliers once the legal market comes on line.

Thus far, I have been considering the likelihood that the policy measures that have been adopted by the federal and provincial governments will succeed in driving out illegal producers and suppliers in the case of adults. As is the case for pretty much every aspect of this complex issue, we won't know how successful these measures will be until we try them. Trial and error will be essential. Given the unprecedented nature of the way in which Canada is going about legalization, we can't really look at other jurisdictions to see what has happened there. There are just too many differences among extant regimes of legalization and decriminalization.

But it must be acknowledged that the set of measures that will be at the disposal of governments to improve on the present criminal

regime are quite powerful, and may very well succeed. The point
I want to make here, however, is that the regime that will be in
place in the case of adolescents will be quite different. Whereas the
governments are adopting a harm-reduction approach to marijuana
in the case of adults, they are for the most part still attempting to
implement, and indeed to reinforce, a prohibitionist regime in the
case of minors.

Harm-reduction policy measures are premised on the observation
that, with respect to a given behaviour, prohibition is either undesirable, impossible, or so onerous as to be practically impossible. Take
the case of sex work. Many argue that, as reasonable people can
disagree about whether the sale of sexual services is, in and of itself,
morally defensible, prohibitionist policies are unattractively perfec-
tionist. Others argue that whatever one thinks about sex services
from a moral point of view, the enforcement of a prohibitionist policy is likely to fail, whatever the resources poured into the attempt
by law enforcement. Whatever route one takes to the observation
that prohibition won't work, the conclusion that, rather than trying
to prohibit, one should instead regulate the practice so as to minimize the harms associated with it, suggests itself quite readily.

Harm reduction is very much at work in Canadian policy in the
case of legalization for adults. But the intention for minors is not
to reduce the harms associated with consumption, but rather to
prohibit consumption. There are a number of measures that will
be implemented that have as their goal to keep marijuana out of
the hands of adolescents altogether. First, a variety of educational
measures will be put in place to alert adolescents to the harms of
marijuana use on the developing brain. Second, there will be a strict
prohibition on advertising targeted at adolescents. And third, there
will be more stringent enforcement of criminal laws prohibiting
anyone from providing marijuana to minors. The law that has been
enacted by the Liberal government allows for sentences of up to
fourteen years of imprisonment for anyone found to be in violation
of the law. While presumably the intent behind this draconian sentencing policy is to prevent the sale of marijuana to minors, the language of the law also creates legal jeopardy for anyone who provides
marijuana to children, by whatever means.

The question is whether this ensemble of policies will succeed in
achieving the prohibitionist intent that the new regime intends for
minors. There are many reasons to think that it will not. First, what

the policies will have to succeed in doing is not to prevent a new product newly introduced into the market from making its way into the hands of minors, but rather to stop the flow of a product that is currently being used by close to 20 per cent of adolescents aged 15 to 18. That is, to say the least, a tall order, one that at the very minimum will require a mobilization of law-enforcement resources far greater than that which is presently being deployed to enforce the (ineffective) across-the-board prohibition the present policy is supposed to replace.

Second, and perhaps most obviously, the fact that marijuana is presently illegal has not prevented public authorities from engaging in educational campaigns aimed at getting young Canadians to become more aware of the dangers of marijuana use. What reasons do we have to think that campaigns carried out in a new legal context, one in which marijuana is now readily available to adults, in the case of Quebec in state-run stores, will be more effective than they presently are? Legalization for adults will at least to some degree "normalize" marijuana use, and while legalization should not be equated with encouragement or approval, it is nonetheless the case that Canadian youth will be receiving messages much more mixed than they are at present. Walking down the streets of Canadian cities will bring them into contact with outlets of the "Société du Cannabis du Québec" or repurposed Second Cups, which, presumably, will trade on the loyalty that has already been developed among Canadian consumers toward their brand to achieve a significant proportion of market share.

Now, to be sure, the normalization of marijuana that will be given rise to under legalization may cut both ways. On the one hand, it might make the messaging that educational campaigns will have to engage in more difficult to calibrate. Rather than pointing to the across-the-board dangers of marijuana consumption, it will have to fine tune the message so as to bring out the specific dangers of marijuana usage *for young consumers*. On the other hand, normalization may in and of itself soften the appeal of marijuana at least for some youth for whom the appeal of the substance lies precisely in its being *ab*normal, frowned upon, and disapproved of. There may be nothing more effective to dampen the enthusiasm of Canadian youth for the drug than to see their parents offer it up with *aperitifs* at their middle-class dinner parties.

Finally, restrictions on advertising are, in the age of social media and internet saturation, difficult to achieve, to say the least. Restricting access of young Canadians to media in which some form of advertising is permitted is far more difficult than it might have been in an earlier age, when prohibitions could be effectively enforced on, say, television programs and magazines that kids were more likely to be exposed to. If marijuana producers and suppliers are permitted to advertise, then their advertisements will reach adolescents.

There are thus reasons to doubt that the arsenal of measures that will be enacted by different levels of government in order to keep marijuana out of the hands of youths will be wholly, or even substantially, effective in achieving the goals of a prohibitionist policy. The fact is we don't know. One of the most challenging dimensions of policy innovation of this kind means that we cannot look to any other jurisdiction to make even educated guesses about what will happen here. Prudence dictates, as I have already mentioned, that we adopt a radically fallibilistic approach with respect to all aspects of marijuana policy, which will have to be reactive to evidence as it comes in. Among the aspects of the policy we must be ready to revisit are those that have to do with the health of Canadian youth. If a prohibitionist strategy based on the policy prongs we have just briefly considered fails, then what?

A HARM-REDUCTION APPROACH FOR ADOLESCENTS?

I've argued thus far that while the move to a harm-reduction policy approach with respect to adult consumers of marijuana makes sense, and may very well immunize adult users from some of the harms associated with an unregulated, illegal market, the parallel deployment of a prohibitionist approach with respect to young Canadians seems, on the face of it, less obviously likely to meet its policy objectives. What if it doesn't work?

The first thing we need to determine is what will count as the threshold of success. What I want to suggest here is that this is an ethical, rather than a straightforwardly factual question. For the sake of argument, let's hypothesize (since we have no data to go on) that increased enforcement, better educational programs, and a ban on advertising aimed at young Canadians will reduce youth consumption by 50 per cent in the 18-to-25 age group. (Let's assume, moreover, what seems to me to be entirely unlikely, namely that increased enforcement will not itself bring in its train a variety of new or exacerbated harms, such as selective enforcement targeting already vulnerable groups).

This would mean that roughly 10 per cent, rather than the roughly 20 per cent who obtain the drug at present, would continue to consume unregulated, and *ex hypothesi* more dangerous marijuana. Would that count as success, or as failure?

Consider an analogy. Prohibitionists and defenders of a harm-reduction regulatory model in the case of sex work have been arguing for years about how best to interpret data coming out of Scandinavian countries that have adopted what has come to be known as the "Nordic model," one that targets demand rather than supply – that is, that criminalizes "johns" rather than sex workers themselves. The debate among partisans of the two approaches has not to do, as far as I can tell, with whether this model has reduced the amount of commercial sex transactions that occurs in the countries that have adopted a prohibitionist approach. Clearly, it has. What is at issue is how to evaluate, morally, the situation of the sex workers that are still operating in a prohibitionist regime. According to critics of the model, though there may be fewer sex workers, they operate in conditions that make them far more vulnerable to violence and disease than would be the case under a harm-reduction model. The question they raise is the following, and it does not admit of an easy answer: is it preferable, morally speaking, to have a greater number of sex workers operating openly in regulated conditions, in which they receive the protection of police and of the health-care system, or to reduce the number, though the reduced number operates in perilous conditions?

My own view is that the latter option is morally unacceptable. Unless we can confidently achieve prohibition, or something very close to it, then we are foreseeably relegating substantial numbers of people to predictable vulnerability and suffering. If it is possible to enact policy that will make it the case that *all* those who take part in an activity, of which some members of society disapprove on moral grounds, do so in safe conditions, then it is morally wrong not to.

Now let's return to the case of marijuana, and of the attempt to prohibit its use among Canada's youth. In my view it would be wrong to knowingly set in train a sequence of events through the implementation of policy that would foreseeably give rise to a significant proportion of the 18-to-25 age group consuming marijuana, in conditions more dangerous than those that we could create through the implementation of a harm-reduction based policy. (Unless, of course, we can reduce consumption through prohibitionist policies to very low numbers indeed, something which, I am hypothesizing, is not likely to occur in Canada under the policies currently being enacted by federal and provincial governments.)

The analogy between the sex work and the drug cases is of course not perfect. In particular, while sex for a fee between consenting adults is in and of itself not harmful, the consumption of marijuana by the young is potentially harmful in and of itself – that is, independent of the specific legal and social conditions in which consumption occurs. Still, it is at least a debatable moral issue whether the morally "least bad" option, in a context in which prohibition is for all intents and purposes impossible, is one in which 10 per cent of Canadian youth are relegated to having to consume unregulated marijuana. Or whether it is one in which the same number of youth who presently consume marijuana do so in safer conditions, both in terms of being immunized from adulterated marijuana, and in terms of their having reliable information over the degree of potency, as measured by THC concentration, of the drug they consume.

What I am suggesting is that, as evidence comes in regarding the success of Canada's policies in "keeping marijuana out of the hands of our kids," we may want to contemplate moving toward a harm-reduction approach for young Canadians as well. This would mean making safe, regulated, marijuana available to them as well as to adults. A harm-reduction approach to marijuana consumption among the young would accept what seems to me to be likely: that prohibition is unlikely to succeed, and that the best that we can do might be to ensure that all those who consume marijuana do so in conditions that are as safe as possible.

MAKING HARM REDUCTION POLITICALLY PALATABLE

I have argued that, as evidence comes in, we should at least be ready to contemplate radically different policy approaches, including that of extending the harm-reduction approach that we will, as of 2018, have deployed with respect to adults, to adolescents. We may in other words want to contemplate the possibility of reducing the age at which regulated marijuana can legally be purchased to, say, 16, rather than where it is presently pegged, namely at 18 or 19 (depending on the province).

I have no illusions as to the political "saleability" of this policy proposal. In this last section, I want to make a set of remarks aimed at softening our resistance to this proposal at least somewhat. (I confess that even I found myself resisting the conclusion even as my arguments led inexorably toward seeing it as at least plausible).

A first remark is that we have been down this road before. That is, we have already gone from considering that some kinds of behaviour should be proscribed for adolescents, to thinking that they will engage in those forms of behaviour regardless of what we do, and that given that fact we had better reduce the harms associated with the behaviour in question. The most obvious example is sex. It is now commonplace for high schools to make condoms available to teens, whereas this would have been inconceivable just a couple of generations ago.

This example suggests a second, more general point. The decisions that we make about how to mark off adulthood and childhood, and more specifically about when it is considered acceptable for individuals to begin engaging in certain kinds of behaviour associated with "adulthood," do not track any deep facts about humans. Ages of eligibility are sometimes fixed (and changed) on the basis of changes in the evidentiary record. They are also often fixed by evidence-resistant conventions. What's more, the general trend in a society such as Canada has been to revise eligibility requirements downwards. "Mature minors" can make a greater range of decisions concerning their medical treatment than they could only a generation ago. The voting age was lowered from 21 to 18 only in 1970. It would now seem ludicrous for anyone to suggest raising it to 21. To the extent that there exists pressure for changes to the voting age, that pressure is downwards.[1]

What's more, there are great variations among countries, which reinforces the view that decisions about when individuals can begin to engage in different kinds of behaviour do not track facts of the matter about when "childhood" ends and "adulthood" begins. With respect to drug policy (broadly understood), the variations are quite great, even among liberal-democratic countries of comparable political culture. The US prohibits anyone under 21 from purchasing alcohol or consuming it in commercial establishments, whereas 16 and 17-year-olds can drink wine and beer if consumed with a meal in the company of adults. The drinking age in Austria is 16.

If we were to decide to make legal, regulated marijuana available to 16 and 17-year-olds, we would not so much be making it available to children as we would (hopefully) be responding to evidence as to how to delimit prohibitionist and harm-reduction policies in a manner that gave rise to the best results.

Even if evidence did suggest that the least bad results would be generated by a policy that made marijuana available to adolescents as of the age of 16, there would be evidence-resistant opposition. Robert MacCoun has shown that moral opposition, and in particular moral outrage, is predictive of whether people will favour prevalence-reduction of harm-reduction policies with respect to different kinds of behaviour.[2] To the extent that people view consumption of marijuana by adolescents as something that they feel strong emotional reactions to, this will lead to endorsement of policies that will aim at prohibition, even where evidence can be presented that suggests that we protect our children better through policies other than prohibitionist ones.

It is entirely possible that the policies that are being put in place in Canada will "keep marijuana out of the hands of our kids." Possible, but it is far more likely that the evidence will soon show that a significant number of young Canadians are still consuming marijuana, but are consigned by policy to the riskier marijuana that is made available to them on the illegal market, rather than being able to avail themselves of the safer product available to their elders. In which case, I for one hope that we will have the policy courage to follow the evidence rather than making our children hostage to emotional reactions that all too quickly reach for prohibitionist tools.

NOTES

1 Kathleen Harris, "Elections Chief Says Lowering Voting Age to 16 Is an Idea 'Worth Considering'," CBC News, 19 March 2018, https://www.cbc.ca/news/politics/chief-electoral-officer-voting-age-16-1.4579051.

2 Robert MacCoun, "Moral Outrage and Opposition to Harm Reduction," Criminal Law and Philosophy 7, no. 1 (January 2013): 83–98.

6

Legalize It (But Don't Advertise It): The Public Health Case for Cannabis Legalization

JEAN-FRANÇOIS CRÉPAULT

> Singers smoke it,
> And players of instrument too
> Legalize it, yeah yeah
> That's the best thing you can do
> Doctors smoke it
> Nurses smoke it
> Judges smoke it
> Even lawyer, too
>
> So you've got to legalize it
>
> And it don't criticize it
> Legalize it, yeah yeah
> And I will advertise it
>
> It's good for the flu
> Good for asthma
> Good for tuberculosis
> Even numara thrombosis
>
> Go to legalize it
>
> Peter Tosh, "Legalize It" (1976)[1]

Marihuana is that drug – a violent narcotic – an unspeakable scourge –
The Real Public Enemy Number One! Its first effect is sudden, violent,
uncontrollable laughter; then come dangerous hallucinations – space
expands – time slows down, almost stands still ... fixed ideas come next,
conjuring up monstrous extravagances – followed by emotional distur-
bances, the total inability to direct thoughts, the loss of all power to resist
physical emotions ... leading finally to acts of shocking violence ... ending
often in incurable insanity.

Reefer Madness (1936)[2]

* * *

Despite claims by its most ardent proponents and opponents, cannabis is neither elixir of life nor devil's weed. Cannabis use comes
with health risks that, while modest compared to other commonly
used psychoactive substances, remain substantial. And to properly
mitigate these risks, cannabis use must be made legal.

While there might appear to be a contradiction here, the public
health sector has long recommended cannabis policy that treats it
like a health issue and not a criminal one. Drug use can cause harm
– but so can drug policy. Cannabis prohibition has done more harm
than good, and decriminalization is a flawed alternative. Society is
best served by legalizing cannabis, strictly regulating it, and managing the risks through the health system.

PUBLIC HEALTH APPROACHES TO DRUGS

The Liberal government has consistently stated its commitment
to "a *public health approach* to legalizing, strictly regulating and
restricting access to cannabis."[3] In both the design of Bill C-45 and
its shepherding through Parliament, the Liberals have referred to
and relied upon the research and arguments of organizations that
have called for cannabis to be legalized with public health principles
as the overriding imperative.[4] This notion, then, has been central to
the legalization debate and process. It has also been used and abused
– both misunderstood and misrepresented.[5]

A public health approach to the control of psychoactive substances
begins from the premise that humans have used these substances
since the dawn of time, for many different reasons, and that not all
use results in harm. Rather, drug use occurs on a continuum from

beneficial/benign to risky/harmful. Thus, a public health approach to drug policy is not primarily concerned with drug use *per se*, but with drug-related *harms*. Here, harm is a multidimensional concept of which health is a central – but not the only – component. A public approach also considers *social* harms: the harms of a drug are a function not only of its chemical properties but of the rules governing its use. A public health approach to drug policy in general – and cannabis in particular – seeks to reduce these harms. Achieving this involves placing a primary focus on population-level (as opposed to individual-level) factors and outcomes, deploying policy measures that "attempt to control the *determinants* of incidence, to lower the mean level of risk factors, [and] to shift the whole distribution of exposure in a favourable direction."[6] In other words, rather than simply prohibiting drug use, interventions are aimed at underlying risk factors.

A BRIEF HISTORY OF CANADIAN CANNABIS POLICY

The legalization of cannabis use for recreational (or, more properly, non-medical) purposes is, in many ways, a novel and radical policy shift. Yet Canada has taken steps toward substantive cannabis policy reform before, only to turn back before implementation.

Before delving into this history, let us acknowledge that the concept of "drugs" is socially constructed.[7] Which psychoactive substances are permitted, and which are proscribed, varies across time and place. Societal norms pertaining to the permissible use of licit substances, and the penalties applied to the use of illicit ones, have also shifted over time. In Western societies, Canada included, the term "drugs" has served as a legal tool to indicate which psychoactive substances are permissible and which are not.[8] Recognizing that definitions of licit versus illicit drugs and permissible versus reprehensible use are historically contingent and culture-bound allows us to view cannabis legalization as part of a longer-term social process.

The possession and use of cannabis were made criminal acts by an act of Parliament in 1923. By all accounts, cannabis was a last-minute inclusion in the 1923 *Opium and Narcotic Drug Act*, and was added without explanation or debate.[9] Cannabis was little-known in Canada at the time; the first recorded cannabis arrests and seizures did not occur until 1937, and even by 1960, there had been just 121 cannabis-related offences across the country.[10] For these reasons the criminalization of cannabis has been described as having "remained a solution without a problem for many years."[11]

Annual cannabis arrests became more common in 1960, doubling almost every year until they exceeded 5,000 by 1970.[12] While drug arrests did occur in Canada throughout the 1940s and 1950s with little public outrage, the demographics of cannabis use (and arrests) in the 1960s were different: for the first time, most people being arrested were white, young, and middle-class. By 1969, "the adverse criminal consequences of criminal cannabis prohibition were increasingly viewed by many as a bigger problem than the drug itself,"[13] and the federal government struck the Le Dain Commission of Inquiry into the Non-Medical Use of Drugs to investigate these issues.

The commission spent three years carrying out research, conducting hearings, and processing submissions from the public, hearing from more than 12,000 Canadians in the process. Its final report made several recommendations to the federal government – among them a repeal of the prohibition against personal possession, cultivation, and use of cannabis. Notably, the commissioners' rationale centred on the notion that criminalizing cannabis did nothing to address the health risks, while also causing significant social harm.

These recommendations were rejected by the government of the day, but the underlying issues continued to simmer. Thirty years after Le Dain, a new commission – the Canadian Senate Special Committee on Illegal Drugs – echoed its findings that "continued criminalization of cannabis remains unjustified based on scientific data on the danger it poses."[14] This commission went one step further than Le Dain, recommending the legalization and regulation of cannabis. This recommendation too was ignored by government, though bills to decriminalize cannabis possession and use were introduced in 2003 and again in 2004 by minority Liberal governments. At the time, drug policy experts wondered whether the tide might finally have turned, but for different reasons, these bills were never voted upon, and the cannabis policy "saga of promise, hesitation and retreat" continued.[15]

Like many other psychoactive substances, cannabis can be used for therapeutic as well as recreational purposes. This distinction is blurry, and even to some extent arbitrary. Though rigorous scientific evidence of its effectiveness is currently lacking for all but a few conditions (notably neuropathic pain, and spasticity),[16] it is commonly used for dozens of ailments and symptoms. It should be mentioned

Table 6.1 Relative risk.

	Alcohol	Tobacco	Cannabis	Amphe-tamines	Heroin	Cocaine/Crack
Lethality*	50	0	0	20	100	22.5
Damage to physical health	80	100	20	30	20	40
Impairment of mental functioning	65	0	30	60	30	80

* Expressed as ratio of lethal dose and standard dose

Table reproduced from CAMH, "Cannabis Policy Framework," 5. Data from Nutt, King, and Phillips, "Drug Harms in the UK: A Multicriteria Decision Analysis."

that the status of cannabis as a controlled substance under international law has greatly hindered research.

Beginning in 1996, a series of court decisions forced the federal government to establish and expand a program governing access to medical cannabis. The most significant regulatory changes occurred in 2014.[17] Although the Conservative government of the day promoted a "tough-on-crime" agenda that included the introduction of mandatory minimum sentences on a number of drugs, including cannabis, it also presided over an unprecedented expansion of legal cannabis consumption. Most significantly, the Conservatives opened production to the private sector – essentially creating, at the stroke of a pen, a cannabis industry. The number of licensed cannabis producers went from just one in 2014 to well over 100 today, and collectively they have been valued at nearly $30 billion.[18] The number of authorized medical cannabis users has risen exponentially. It had gone from under 500 in 2002 to just 37,000 by the end of 2013; following these regulatory reforms, the number of registered users rose to 175,000 in March 2017 and 297,000 in March 2018.[19] It seems fair to question the extent to which this explosion reflects an increasing need for *medical* cannabis, and also to acknowledge the irony of the Harper Conservatives opening these floodgates, creating a system that has aptly been called a "sneaky side door" to legal cannabis.[20]

The year 2014 was also the year the Liberal Party of Canada added cannabis legalization to its platform, as covered elsewhere in this volume. Here, it will suffice to note that it was a public health approach to cannabis legalization that the Liberals embraced and adopted.[21]

ON CANNABIS-RELATED HARMS

Cannabis use can cause significant health harms, both short-term and chronic.[22] It is, however, a less risky psychoactive substance than many; alcohol, tobacco, and opioids, for example, are all more harmful substances (see Table 6.1).[23]

Cannabis-related harms can be grouped into three categories of risk:

- *Pattern of use.* Direct harms from cannabis are more likely when use is very frequent (daily or near-daily) and/or begins at a young age (e.g., early adolescence). In fact, harms are concentrated among the relatively small group of users who use it heavily and have done so since adolescence. Use in childhood or adolescence can impair brain development. Heavy use can impair cognitive function, and while these effects may diminish for adults when use is discontinued, they may be permanent in some adolescents. Heavy use can also lead to cannabis use disorder.

- *Mode of delivery.* Smoking cannabis can cause respiratory issues, including lung cancer. These effects are intensified if tobacco is smoked along with the cannabis.

- *Potency.* Frequent cannabis use is associated with mental illness, though the relationship is not yet well understood. The more potent cannabis is – that is, the higher its THC content – the higher the risk. Some groups, notably adolescents and people with a personal and/or family history of mental illness, are particularly vulnerable to these effects.

In terms of disease burden – a concept used by epidemiologists to quantify the mortality, morbidity, and lost productivity that can be attributed to a particular source – by far the most significant cannabis-related harms are motor vehicle accidents caused by impaired drivers, respiratory disease (including lung cancer), and cannabis use disorder.[24]

An important point follows from this discussion of the risk profile of cannabis. These risks, as well as the others discussed above, are for the most part modifiable, and this has practical implications: cannabis users can reduce their risk exposure by, for example, using less potent products, not driving immediately after use, and ingesting through means other than smoking. (Indeed, "lower-risk cannabis use guidelines" have been developed in order to offer this information to the public in an accessible format.)[25]

As noted by the Le Dain and Senate commissions, the prohibition of cannabis does not dissuade people from using it. In fact, the severity of jurisdictions' drug penalties does not correlate with their level of use.[26] As an example, we can cite the fact that Canadian youth have one of the highest rates of cannabis use in the world, but one of the lowest rates of tobacco use – even though the former is illegal while the latter is legal.[27] Whatever the objectives of cannabis prohibition – and as we have seen, Canada's cannabis laws were not particularly well thought through – it neither prevents nor mitigates the health risks of cannabis use. In fact, it exacerbates them in several ways, and gives rise to social harms as well.

Criminalization pushes cannabis users to a black market in which the provenance, properties, quality, and potency of the product are unknown. Given that risks to mental health seem to rise more or less linearly with THC content, and that emerging research suggests that CBD (the second most common cannabinoid) may help protect against these risks, the lack of reliable information is a significant problem.[28] Further, while the idea that cannabis is a gateway drug has never been proven,[29] the fact of its illegality means that users must purchase it in environments where they may be exposed to other, more harmful drugs and other criminal activity. Criminalization of drug use is also known to drive users away from treatment services.

Under prohibition, cannabis users have been subject to a range of criminal penalties and encounters with the criminal justice system, and these have had a devastating impact on individuals and communities.[30] Compounding this problem is that cannabis possession laws – and drug laws in general – are unequally enforced from place to place and from person to person. For instance, in 2014 it was estimated that police in Saskatoon were four times more likely to lay charges than those in Halifax.[31] Further, racialized individuals have been disproportionately affected by drug laws, having a much higher likelihood of being arrested, tried, and convicted for drug use offences. In Toronto, for example, an investigation found that "Black people with no history of criminal convictions have been three times more likely to be arrested by Toronto police for possession of small amounts of marijuana than white people with similar backgrounds."[32] Thus, hundreds of thousands of Canadians have experienced the social harms associated with cannabis criminalization – harms that are not only severe but also highly arbitrary and, in the case of racialized communities, discriminatory and inequitable.

DECRIMINALIZATION: A HALF MEASURE

We have established that cannabis is not benign, and that certain groups are especially vulnerable to its health risks. It does not necessarily follow, however, that it should be illegal. Robin Room and colleagues put it best:

> In modern societies, a finding of adverse effects does not settle the issue of the legal status of a commodity; if it did, alcohol, automobiles, and stairways, for instance, would all be prohibited, since use of each of these results in substantial casualties.[33]

Of course, there are many points between criminalization and legalization on the drug policy continuum (see Figure 6.1). Why not decriminalize instead of legalizing and regulating?

Many models of decriminalization are possible,[34] but in all cases, cannabis possession and use remain illegal. The main change is that *criminal* penalties for possession and use of small amounts of cannabis would no longer be applicable; instead, depending on the model, they would be replaced by civil penalties (e.g., fines) and/or diversion from the criminal justice system (e.g., drug-treatment court), or other administrative sanctions (e.g., formal warning or caution). Decriminalization of cannabis use is an improvement insofar as it reduces some of the social harms and costs of criminalization, but from a public health perspective it is at best a half measure, for two main reasons:[35]

Criminalization			Decriminalization				Legalization	
Death penalty	Incarceration	Fine (with criminal record)	Diversion	Formal warning system	Civil fine	Personal possession	Retail sales (strict regulation	Retail sales (light/no regulation

Figure 6.1 Drug policy spectrum.
Adapted from Canadian Centre on Substance Use and Addiction, "Cannabis Regulatory Approaches" (Ottawa, 2016), 1, with permission from CCSA.

- It does not address the health risks. As long as cannabis is illegal, government gains no additional control tools; the product itself and the environment in which it is consumed remain unregulated.

- It is unlikely to effectively and equitably reduce the social burden of cannabis prohibition. Given that the opportunity for police discretion remains under decriminalization, it would likely reproduce and perpetuate the arbitrary and discriminatory law enforcement practices described above.

By contrast, legalization provides an opportunity to reduce the harms associated with cannabis use by exerting control over the risk factors associated with those harms.[36]

This approach does not necessarily lend itself to all drugs. The case for legalization and regulation of cannabis is based partly on the fact that it is so widely used, and more importantly, on its risk profile relative to other psychoactive substances. Ultimately, the level of control applied to a substance should be proportionate to the level of risk it poses.[37]

ON THE NEED FOR LEGALIZATION –
AND STRICT REGULATION

Legalization of cannabis is a public health opportunity. It is, however, only a first step:

CANNABIS

ESTABLISH A GOVERNMENT MONOPOLY ON SALES

Control boards provide an effective means of controlling consumption.

CAMH recommends legalization with strict regulation

PROHIBIT MARKETING, ADVERTISING AND SPONSORSHIP

Products should be sold in plain packaging with warnings about risks of use.

SET A MINIMUM AGE

Sales or supply of cannabis products to underage individuals should be penalized.

CAMH offers **10 basic principles** to guide regulation of legal cannabis use.

PRODUCT INFORMATION SHOULD BE CLEARLY DISPLAYED

In particular, products should be tested and labelled for THC and CBD content.

LIMIT AVAILABILITY

Place caps on retail density and limits on hours of sales.

CURTAIL HIGHER-RISK PRODUCTS AND FORMULATIONS

This would include higher-potency formulations and products designed to appeal to youth.

ADDRESS & PREVENT CANNABIS-IMPAIRED DRIVING

Develop a comprehensive framework that includes prevention, education and enforcement.

CURB DEMAND THROUGH PRICING

Pricing policy should curb demand while minimizing the continuation of black markets.

INVEST IN EDUCATION AND PREVENTION

Need both general and targeted initiatives for specific groups e.g. adolescents, people with a history of mental illness.

ENHANCE ACCESS TO TREATMENT AND EXPAND TREATMENT OPTIONS

Include a spectrum of options from brief interventions for at-risk users to more intensive interventions.

Figure 6.2   CAMH cannabis policy framework.
Centre for Addiction and Mental Health, 2014.

To reduce harm, legalization of cannabis is a necessary – but not a sufficient – condition. It must include effective controls on availability and regulations that steer users towards less harmful products and practices. It must be embedded in a comprehensive strategy with a strong prevention focus and a range of interventions aimed at groups at higher risk of harm, such as youth and people with a personal or family history of mental illness.[38]

Note the reference to "effective controls." Decades of research in the field of alcohol have produced solid evidence about the types of controls that reduce harm.[39] These lessons from alcohol control

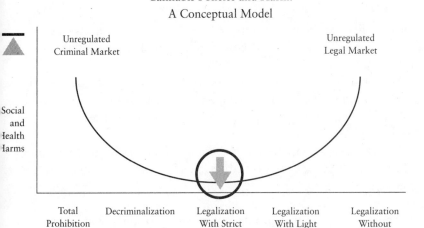

Figure 6.3 "The paradox of prohibition."

Table reproduced from CAMH, "Cannabis Policy Framework," 11. Original in Marks, "The Paradox of Prohibition," 77.

provide a useful model for a public health approach to cannabis regulation, and they were adapted for this purpose in 2014 by the Centre for Addiction and Mental Health (see Figure 6.2).[40]

Jurisdictions that implement these controls do better at mitigating alcohol-related harm than those that do not. And on one point, the evidence is quite clear: these policies are most effectively implemented when a public entity controls distribution and sales.[41] Government monopolies may seem antiquated but, being more resistant to commercialization, they have been shown to mitigate alcohol-related harms. Conversely, alcohol privatization has been shown to substantially increase them.[42] This is very likely to hold true for cannabis.[43]

Many of these principles are evident in many aspects of Bill C-45 and its associated regulations, notably those on minimum age, product packaging, and impaired driving, which have set certain minimum requirements for the provinces and territories. However, from a public health perspective, concerns remain.

LEGALIZE IT... BUT DON'T ADVERTISE IT

Drug policy can be pictured as existing on a continuum, with criminalization on one end and commercialization on the other[44] (see Figure 6.3).

We have discussed the health and social harms of cannabis criminalization, but the other extreme – commercialization – is harmful as well. The goal of a public health approach is to land somewhere in the middle.

Under legalization, cannabis production and distribution will take place in a for-profit context, and this poses certain challenges from a public health standpoint.

> There is concern that profit-maximizing marijuana companies will target heavy users. Since 80 per cent of marijuana consumption is by daily or near-daily users, roughly 80 per cent of marijuana companies' profits would come from marketing to such heavy users, about half of whom currently meet clinical criteria for having substance-use disorders... Thus, like the alcohol industry, the private marijuana industry will likely seek to serve and develop a market of heavy users.[45]

In the world of alcohol control it is often stated that alcohol is "no ordinary commodity": since it is not a benign product, it should not be sold like one.[46] The same is true of cannabis. As economist Milton Friedman pointed out long ago, the purpose of business – in fact, its sole responsibility – is to increase its profits.[47] A public health approach, *by definition*, makes considerations of profit subsidiary to those of health. So since we know, for example, that youth who view alcohol and tobacco advertising are more likely to consume those substances and experience related harms,[48] those substances should not be advertised. And neither should cannabis. For legalization to be a benefit to society in terms of health, commercialization must be avoided to the greatest extent possible.

IN CONCLUSION

Researchers will be closely watching for the health impacts of cannabis legalization – as will politicians, the media, and the public. Some harm indicators will be obvious: cannabis-associated motor vehicle accidents, for instance, and cases of cannabis use disorder. It will be important to keep in mind that just as cannabis use does not automatically entail harm, an increase in cannabis prevalence would not necessarily be evidence of an increase in cannabis-related harm. More important will be changes in the modes (smoking, vaping, etc.) and patterns (e.g., frequency, age of onset) of use.[49] To truly understand the health impact of cannabis legalization, we will also, to the extent possible, need to understand trends in the use of other drugs. What impact does cannabis legalization have on patterns of alcohol use? Will people with chronic pain who currently rely on opioids turn to cannabis instead? Social harms must be monitored as well. Bill C-45 creates a number of new cannabis offences, especially for youth. Could cannabis legalization actually lead to more cannabis arrests?[50]

It is worth repeating that a public health approach to cannabis can be implemented only when a substance is legal. Legalization removes the social harms of criminalization, but it is only the first step; to properly address and mitigate cannabis-related health harms, governments must avail themselves of this opportunity to regulate, and implement evidence-based regulation.

NOTES

1   Peter Tosh, "Legalize It," Columbia Records, PC 34253, 1976.
2   *Reefer Madness*, directed by Louis J. Gasnier, Motion Picture Ventures, 1936.
3   Task Force on Marijuana Legalization and Regulation, *Toward the Legalization, Regulation and Restriction of Access to Marijuana: Discussion Paper* (Ottawa: Government of Canada, 2016), https://www.canada.ca/content/dam/hc-sc/healthy-canadians/migration/health-system-systeme-sante/consultations/legalization-marijuana-legalisation/alt/legalization-marijuana-legalisation-eng.pdf; also see Government of Canada, "Health Canada Launches Public Consultation on Proposed Approach to the Regulation of Cannabis," *Health Canada*, 21 November 2017, https://www.canada.ca/en/healthcanada/news/2017/11/health_canada_launchespublicconsultationonproposedapproachtother.html.; Government of Canada, "Health Canada Releases Summary of Comments from Cannabis Regulatory Consultations," *Health Canada*, 19 March 2018, https://www.canada.ca/en/health-canada/news/2018/03/health-canada-releases-summary-of-comments-from-cannabis-regulatory-consultations.html.

4   Task Force on Marijuana, *Discussion Paper*, 25–7; Tonda MacCharles, "Bill Blair and the Politics of Being Joint Chief," *Toronto Star*, 2 February 2017, https://www.thestar.com/news/canada/2017/04/02/bill-blair-and-the-politics-of-being-joint-chief.html; Meagan Campbell, "How Senator Tony Dean Saved Trudeau's Pot Law," *Maclean's*, 23 March 2018, https://www.macleans.ca/politics/ottawa/the-senator-who-lived-and-breathed-the-pot-bill-to-get-it-passed.

5   For a discussion of what a public health approach to cannabis is – and is not – see Jean-François Crépault, "Cannabis Legalization in Canada: Reflections on Public Health and the Governance of Legal Psychoactive Substances," *Frontiers in Public Health* 6 (August 2018): 220. On misuse of the term "public health approach" in drug policy deliberations at the United Nations, see Joanne Csete and Daniel Wolfe, "Seeing Through the Public Health Smoke-Screen in Drug Policy," *International Journal of Drug Policy* 43 (2017): 491–5.

6   Geoffrey Rose, "Sick Individuals and Sick Populations," *International Journal of Epidemiology* 30, no. 3 (2001): 427–32.

7   Jacques Derrida, *Points de suspension : Entretiens*, (Paris: Galilée, 1992), 241–68. Of course, the concept of addiction is also socially constructed, and for that matter, so is the concept of health. See Matilda Hellman et al., *Concepts of Addictive Substances and Behaviours across Time and Place* (Oxford: Oxford University Press, 2016), as well as Alan Petersen and Robin Bunton, *Foucault, Health and Medicine* (London: Routledge, 1997).

8   Toby Seddon, "Inventing Drugs: A Genealogy of a Regulatory Concept," *Journal of Law and Society* 43, no. 3 (2016): 393–415.

9   P.J. Giffen, Shirley Endicott, and Sylvia Lambert, *Panic and Indifference: The Politics of Canada's Drug Laws* (Ottawa: Canadian Centre on Substance Abuse, 1991), 179; Catherine Carstairs, *Jailed for Possession: Illegal Drug Use, Regulation, and Power in Canada, 1920–1961* (Toronto: University of Toronto Press, 2006), 31. (Scholars tend to agree that this legislation, like its predecessors the *Opium Act* of 1908 and the *Opium and Drugs Act* of 1911, were rooted in racially based drug panics – specifically, anti-Chinese racism. However, the inclusion of cannabis remains a mystery.)

10 Carstairs, *Jailed for Possession*, 189.

11 Giffen, Endicott, and Lambert, *Panic and Indifference*, 182.

12 Carstairs, *Jailed for Possession*, 158.

13 Benedikt Fischer, Kari Ala-Leppilampi, Eric Single, and Amanda Robins, "Cannabis Law Reform in Canada: Is the 'Saga of Promise, Hesitation

and Retreat' Coming to an End?" *Canadian Journal of Criminology and Criminal Justice* 45, no. 3 (2003): 270.

4   Senate Special Committee on Illegal Drugs, *Cannabis: Our Position for a Canadian Public Policy* (Ottawa: Canada Senate, 2002): 35.

5   "The saga of promise, hesitation, and retreat" is how Giffen, Endicott, and Lambert (*Panic and Indifference*, 571) described the federal government's indecision and inertia around cannabis policy in the 1970s and 80s.

6   Penny F. Whiting et al., "Cannabinoids for Medical Use: A Systematic Review and Meta-Analysis," *Journal of the American Medical Association* 313, no. 24 (2015): 2456–73.

7   For a discussion, see Benedikt Fischer, Sharan Kuganesan, and Robin Room, "Medical Marijuana Programs: Implications for Cannabis Control Policy – Observations from Canada," *International Journal of Drug Policy* 26, no. 1 (2015): 15–19.

8   Government of Canada, "Authorized Licensed Producers of Cannabis for Medical Purposes," *Health Canada*, 10 August 2018, https://www.canada.ca/en/health-canada/services/drugs-health-products/medical-use-marijuana/licensed-producers/authorized-licensed-producers-medical-purposes.html; John Daly, "Canada's Great Pot Boom Could Be Headed for a Giant Bust – For Investors and Consumers," *The Globe and Mail*, 26 June 2018, https://www.theglobeandmail.com/business/rob-magazine/article-canadas-great-pot-boom-could-be-headed-for-a-giant-bust-for-2.

9   *The Globe and Mail*, "By the Numbers: Canada's Medical Marijuana Use," *The Globe and Mail*, 3 October 2013, https://www.theglobeandmail.com/news/national/by-the-numbers-canadas-medical-marijuana-use/article14694389; Government of Canada, "Cannabis for Medical Purposes (FY 2017–18) – Licensed Producers: Monthly Data," *Health Canada*, 13 July 2018, https://www.canada.ca/en/health-canada/services/drugs-medication/cannabis/licensed-producers/market-data.html.

10 Fischer, Kuganesan, and Room, "Medical Marijuana Programs," 17.

11 Centre for Addiction and Mental Health, *Cannabis Policy Framework* (Toronto: CAMH, 2014); Liberal Party of Canada, "Liberals welcome CAMH call for marijuana legalization," *Liberal Party of Canada*, 9 October 2014, retrieved from https://www.liberal.ca/liberals-camh-call-marijuana-legalization; Justin Trudeau (@JustinTrudeau), "Welcome call from @CAMHnews for a regulated, legal system for marijuana access, which will help keep drugs out of our kids' hands," Twitter, 9 October 2014, https://twitter.com/justintrudeau/status/520296302291075072.

22 For a detailed review see Benedikt Fischer et al., "Lower-Risk Cannabis Use Guidelines: A Comprehensive Update of Evidence and Recommendations," *American Journal of Public Health* 107, no. 8 (2017): 1277–89.

23 Dirk W. Lachenmeier and Jürgen Rehm, "Comparative Risk Assessment of Alcohol, Tobacco, Cannabis and Other Illicit Drugs Using the Margin of Exposure Approach," *Scientific Reports* 5 (2015): 8126; David J. Nutt, Leslie A. King, and Lawrence D. Phillips, "Drug Harms in the UK: A Multicriteria Decision Analysis," *The Lancet* 376, no. 9752 (2010): 1558–65.

24 Benedikt Fischer, Sameer Imtiaz, Katherine Rudzinski, and Jürgen Rehm, "Crude Estimates of Cannabis-Attributable Mortality and Morbidity in Canada: Implications for Public Health Focused Intervention Priorities," *Journal of Public Health* 38, no. 1 (2016): 183–8.

25 Canadian Research Institute on Substance Misuse, "'Lower-Risk Cannabis Use Guidelines' (LRCUG) – Update and Revisions," CRISM, last modified 2017, http://crismontario.ca/research-projects/lower-risk-cannabis-use-guidelines.

26 Canadian Public Health Association, *A New Approach to Managing Illegal Psychoactive Substances in Canada*, (Ottawa: CPHA, 2014); Peter Anderson et al., *The New Governance of Addictive Substances and Behaviours* (Oxford: Oxford University Press, 2017); Caitlin Elizabeth Hughes and Alex Stevens. "A Resounding Success or a Disastrous Failure: Re-Examining the Interpretation of Evidence on the Portuguese Decriminalisation of Illicit Drugs." *Drug and Alcohol Review* 31, no. 1 (2012): 101–13.

27 UNICEF Office of Research, *Child Well-Being in Rich Countries: A Comparative Overview* (Florence: UNICEF, 2013).

28 Michael T. Lynskey, Chandni Hindocha, and Tom P. Freeman, "Legal Regulated Markets Have the Potential to Reduce Population Levels of Harm Associated with Cannabis Use," *Addiction* 111, no. 12 (2016): 2091–92.

29 Centre for Addiction and Mental Health, *The Legal Sanctions Related to Cannabis Possession/Use* (Toronto: CAMH, 2000): 3; also see Michael T. Lynskey and Arpana Agrawal, "Denise Kandel's Classic Work on the Gateway Sequence of Drug Acquisition," *Addiction* (2018).

30 Patricia G. Erickson and Elaine Hyshka, "Four Decades of Cannabis Criminals in Canada: 1970–2010," *Amsterdam Law Forum* 2, no. 4 (2010): 172–9; Robert Solomon, Eric Single, and Patricia G. Erickson, "Legal Considerations in Canadian Cannabis Policy," *Canadian Public Policy* 9, no. 4 (1983): 419–33; John Howard Society of Ontario, *Help*

Wanted: Reducing Barriers for Ontario's Youth with Police Records (Toronto: JHSO, 2014).

31   Craig Offman and Ann Hui, "Where in Canada You're Least Likely to Be Charged for Pot Possession," *The Globe and Mail*, 16 January 2014. http://www.theglobeandmail.com/news/politics/canadas-patchwork-pot-policy-how-possession-charges-vary-from-city-to-city/article16377021.

32   Jim Rankin, Sandro Contenta, and Andrew Bailey, "Toronto Marijuana Arrests Reveal 'Startling' Racial Divide," *Toronto Star*, 6 July 2017, https://www.thestar.com/news/insight/2017/07/06/toronto-marijuana-arrests-reveal-startling-racial-divide.html; also see Scot Wortley and Akwasi Owusu-Bempah, "Race, Ethnicity, Crime and Criminal Justice in Canada," in *Race, Ethnicity, Crime and Criminal Justice in the Americas*, ed. Anita Kalunta-Crumpton (London: Palgrave Macmillan, 2012), 11–40.

33   Robin Room et al., *Cannabis Policy: Moving Beyond Stalemate* (Oxford: Oxford University Press, 2010), 15.

34   Global Commission on Drug Policy, *Advancing Drug Policy Reform: A New Approach to Decriminalization* (Geneva: GCDP, 2016); Rebecca Jesseman and Doris Payer, *Decriminalization: Options and Evidence* (Ottawa: CCSA, 2018).

35   CAMH, *Cannabis Policy Framework*, 9; also see Benedikt Fischer, Jürgen Rehm, and Jean-François Crépault, "Realistically Furthering the Goals of Public Health by Cannabis Legalization with Strict Regulation: Response to Kalant," *International Journal of Drug Policy* 34 (2016): 14–15.

36   Jean-François Crépault, Jürgen Rehm, and Benedikt Fischer, "The Cannabis Policy Framework by the Centre for Addiction and Mental Health: A Proposal for a Public Health Approach to Cannabis Policy in Canada," *International Journal of Drug Policy* 34 (2016): 1–4.

37   See Lachenmeier and Rehm, "Comparative Risk Assessment of Alcohol, Tobacco, Cannabis and Other Illicit Drugs" in *The New Governance of Addictive Substances and Behaviours*, eds. Anderson et al. (Oxford: Oxford University Press, 2017).

38   CAMH, *Cannabis Policy Framework*, 16.

39   Thomas F. Babor et al., *Alcohol, No Ordinary Commodity: Research and Public Policy*, 2nd ed. (Oxford: Oxford University Press, 2010); Anderson et al., *The New Governance of Addictive Substances and Behaviours*.

40   Crépault, Rehm, and Fischer, "The Cannabis Policy Framework," 1–4.

41   Babor et al., *Alcohol: No Ordinary Commodity*; Anderson et al., *The New Governance of Addictive Substances and Behaviours*.

42 Tim Stockwell et al., "Impact on Alcohol-Related Mortality of a Rapid Rise in the Density of Private Liquor Outlets in British Columbia: A Local Area Multi-Level Analysis," *Addiction* 106, no. 4 (2011): 768–76.

43 Wayne Hall and Michael Lynskey, "Evaluating the Public Health Impacts of Legalizing Recreational Cannabis Use in the United States," *Addiction* 111, no. 10 (2016): 1764–73; Rosalie Liccardo Pacula et al., "Developing Public Health Regulations for Marijuana: Lessons from Alcohol and Tobacco," *American Journal of Public Health* 104, no. 6, 1021–28.

44 John Marks, "The Paradox of Prohibition," in *Treatment Options in Addiction: Medical Management of Alcohol and Opiate Use*, ed. Colin Brewer (London: Gaskell, 1993) 77–85.

45 Jonathan P. Caulkins et al., *Options and Issues Regarding Marijuana Legalization* (Santa Monica: RAND Corporation, 2015), 5.

46 Babor et al., *Alcohol: No Ordinary Commodity*.

47 Milton Friedman, *Capitalism and Freedom* (Chicago: University of Chicago Press, 1964).

48 Crépault, "Cannabis Legalization in Canada," 4.

49 Benedikt Fischer et al., "Assessing the Public Health Impact of Cannabis Legalization in Canada: Core Outcome Indicators towards an 'Index' for Monitoring and Evaluation," *Journal of Public Health* xx, no. 10 (2018): 1–10.

50 Tara Marie Watson and Patricia G. Erickson, "Cannabis Legalization in Canada: How Might 'Strict' Regulation Impact Youth?," *Drugs: Education, Prevention and Policy* (2018).

PART THREE

Law

7

Is Legalization a War on Drugs by the Back Door?

JACOB STILMAN

The *Cannabis Act*,[1] which has now come into force, represents a seismic shift in drug policy in Canada. The new regime in Canada permits the legal consumption and production of cannabis for both recreational and medicinal purposes. Until its passage, the legal consumption and production of cannabis could only occur under the auspices of cumbersome and largely ineffectual regulatory schemes, which previous governments had adopted in response to judicially mandated reforms of our marijuana laws, the most recent of which was known as the *Access to Cannabis for Medical Purposes Regulations*.[2] These (now moot) regulations addressed the need for a rational and enforceable regulatory scheme in response to judicial interventions that had determined that the denial of access to marijuana for medical purposes constituted a Charter violation. Beginning with the Parker[3] decision, the government has been judicially compelled to put into place a scheme to allow for the access and production of cannabis for medical purposes, while still maintaining laws that prohibited the distribution and consumption of cannabis for recreational purposes under the *Controlled Drugs and Substances Act* (CDSA).[4]

The regulatory approach to the control of medicinal marijuana was rife with abuse, legal ambiguity, and arbitrariness. Individuals seeking access to marijuana for purposes other than legitimate medical needs could easily acquire production and/or possession licenses by tapping into a network of compliant doctors who would liberally issue marijuana authorizations to be acted upon by Health Canada. Frequently such licenses would authorize the production of a number of cannabis plants far in excess of the realistic medicinal needs of any patient, and further permit the possession of dried cannabis end-product in multi-kilogram quantities.[5] Unscrupulous individuals intent on trafficking could partner with individuals who held "personal production licenses," which would assure such traffickers of a reliable and quasi-legal supply of product.[6] Meanwhile, a grey-area network of storefront marijuana dispensaries proliferated, which operated openly by providing dubious licenses to any "patients" who walked in off the street. While individual abusers were sometimes prosecuted for the illegal production and trafficking of marijuana under the guise of medical distribution, it is not difficult to appreciate how the regulatory scheme, which was instituted to address the legitimate medical marijuana issue, devolved into something of a farce that served ultimately to drive the political agenda of the current government, culminating in the legalization of recreational cannabis under the new Act.

Ground-up pressures aside, advocates for a liberalized approach to our cannabis laws have long pointed out the contradictions of cannabis prohibition, even as it came to be moderated in the post-Parker era. The criminalization of a relatively benign substance saddled untold thousands of Canadians with criminal records for the victimless offence of possession. This, despite abundant evidence that cannabis represents a lower overall risk to health than do alcohol, tobacco, and a host of legal prescription medications.[7] In view of the ubiquity of cannabis, and evidence as to the limited risk that comes with moderate consumption levels in most circumstances, its status as an illegal substance could no longer be sustained as a cogent drug policy.

Nonetheless, despite the compelling arguments in favour of legalizing cannabis, both from a practical/legal standpoint and a scientific/harm-analysis one, legalization is bound to usher in collateral societal risks. Leaving aside the fact that long-term abuse of any substance can produce detrimental health effects, and that studies have indicated that abuse amongst teens in particular can be linked to an augmented risk of psychiatric illness,[8] the most pressing concern to accompany legalization is in the realm of highway safety. This is because it is reasonable to assume that with legalization will come augmented consumption rates, as well as a more casual and accepting attitude towards cannabis use generally. As the legal barriers to recreational use are eliminated, and the stigma of open consumption reduced, the law of averages dictates that there will be a much higher incidence of people operating motor vehicles while high.[9] This new reality presents complex legal challenges. Hence, in conjunction with the legalization scheme brought in under the *Cannabis Act* (Bill C-45), the government has attempted to address the concern over highway safety with an overhaul of the Impaired Driving laws by simultaneously enacting Bill C-46.[10]

The government's legislative response attempts to address public safety concerns that will be attendant with the increased availability of marijuana. However, as Parliament is navigating largely uncharted waters, there are a host of questions and concerns which have yet to be fully resolved. In the next few years these issues are bound to percolate up through the courts, and we can expect legal, procedural, and constitutional questions to be resolved through the jurisprudence. However, while lawyers and judges will have their hands full with the inevitable litigation that will ensue, the basic premises and mechanisms of the new drug-impairment law need to be assessed. As a starting point, what is the scientific rationale for the proscribed THC levels set out in C-46, and to what extent are the tools that law enforcement is being equipped with effective, appropriate, and Charter-compliant?

I: THE NEW IMPAIRED-BY-DRUG PROVISIONS, EXPLAINED

The "business end" of Bill C-46 modifies the Criminal Code sections dealing with the offence of Impaired Driving by adding section 253(3) to the existing provisions.[11] This new section specifically addresses cannabis impairment and driving by making it an offence to have, within two hours of ceasing to operate a motor vehicle, a "blood drug concentration that is equal to or exceeds the blood drug concentration for the drug that is prescribed by regulation," as well as "a blood alcohol and a blood drug concentration that is equal to or exceeds the (drug and alcohol) concentration prescribed by regulation for instances where alcohol and that drug are combined."[12] This new section mirrors the "Over 80" provisions contained in s 253(1)(b), which makes it illegal to have a blood alcohol concentration greater than 80 milligrams of alcohol in 100 millilitres of blood.[13] However, unlike the previous provisions of the Criminal Code, which established the legal limit for blood alcohol concentration within the direct wording of the statute, the new legislation defers to government regulation in determining the lawful THC level.[14] This is potentially a progressive step. Presumably, as more knowledge is gained as to the impairing (or benign) effects of cannabis, the government will be able to more efficiently adapt to changes within the body of scientific knowledge by tweaking the proscribed levels through regulation,[15] and avoiding the need to amend the Criminal Code itself.

The regulations prescribe that a level of between 2 nanograms of THC up to 5 ng/1 millilitre of blood or more constitutes a Summary offence pursuant to the new section 253(3)(b). A level of 5 ng or greater constitutes a Hybrid offence under s 253(3)(a) (meaning that it can proceed either by way of Summary or Indictable proceeding, thereby attracting a higher potential sentence and consequences). As for s 253(3)(c), which makes it an offence to operate a vehicle while combining drugs and alcohol, the regulations prescribe a THC level of 2.5 ng/ml, in combination with a blood alcohol concentration of 50 mg/100 ml. This new provision reflects the scientific consensus that the combination of THC and alcohol potentiates the impairing effects of both substances. In arriving at these prescribed THC and THC/alcohol limits, the government relied on the recommendations of the Drugs and Driving Committee (DDC) of the Canadian Society of Forensic Science.[16]

II: ENFORCEMENT MECHANISMS

Having statutorily enacted a permissible limit for blood-THC concentration, the second significant element to the legislation addresses the need for a novel detection and enforcement mechanism. In the case of alcohol, the detection and enforcement mechanism under the existing legislation empowers police to demand that a driver suspected of operating a motor vehicle with alcohol in their system submit to a screening test conducted with an approved instrument. The Approved Screening Device typically operates on a "pass-warn-fail" basis, with a "fail" result presumptively indicating that the driver is over the lawful alcohol limit, thereby entitling the police to arrest them. After the driver is arrested, a further series of tests are conducted using a more sophisticated breath analysis instrument, which produces a verifiable and Charter-compliant result.[17] The laws also permit police to forgo the screening device test in cases where the driver exhibits clear signs of alcohol impairment. In such a case, police may arrest the driver directly for impaired operation, and they are still subjected to the breath analysis tests to accurately determine their blood alcohol level.

The new drug-related provisions largely incorporate and reflect the alcohol detection provisions, but also establish a new drug-specific roadside screening mechanism. Under the modified provisions, s 254(2) now entitles an officer to require a motorist suspected of operating a vehicle "with alcohol or a drug in their body" to submit to physical coordination tests at the roadside, or to provide a bodily sample into an approved drug-screening device. The devices contemplated are to be set by regulation,[18] and are purported to be able to screen for THC levels through a saliva sample. The efficacy and reliability of these devices will no doubt be an area of concern and controversy; this is addressed below.

III: COMPULSORY STANDARD FIELD SOBRIETY TESTS (SFSTS): A LICENSE TO PERSECUTE

The compulsory roadside coordination tests mandated under s 254(2)(a) were already in existence under the previous law,[19] while the screening mechanism under the new s 254(2)(c) is virtually identical in form and substance to the screening provision for alcohol under s 254(2)(b). However, while on its surface this provision hews to the traditional alcohol detection and enforcement approach, there are a number of concerns that merit comment. There can be little dispute that detection and assessment of drug impairment is inherently more ambiguous than it is for alcohol. Alcoholic drinks exhibit an odour that is easily identifiable, and the signs of alcohol impairment are consistent within the population at large, and therefore readily identifiable.[20] By contrast, cannabis, unless very recently consumed, is unlikely to produce the same olfactory cues, and outwardly visible indicators of consumption and impairment may be much more discreet and variable within the population. Thus, there is a significant concern for police overreach and mis-evaluation in the case of cannabis impairment, since the capacity of a police officer to objectively evaluate a subject's performance on physical evaluative roadside tests in the best of conditions is going to be questionable. This problem may be compounded given the level of drug-effect naivete amongst large sectors of law enforcement.[21] Furthermore, the assessment of field sobriety test results is highly vulnerable to confirmation bias. A police officer demanding that a subject perform SFSTs will already have formed a not insignificant measure of suspicion that the driver has consumed drugs. From the officer's biased perspective it is likely that any deviation from the so-called norm will lead to a conclusion of drug impairment. Finally, the three SFSTs authorized under the regulations may not fully account for baseline variability within the population. How well would a person with a severe sciatic condition do on a heel-to-toe or a balance test? Or someone with arthritis, an inner ear problem, or perhaps just advanced age?

The risk of a false positive arising from the implementation of SFSTs aside, an increased reliance on such tests is likely to usher in more intrusive and arbitrary police practices. Indeed, this may prove to be one of the biggest sources of police overreach under the new legislation. In the case of alcohol, a police officer's "reasonable suspicion" that a driver has alcohol in his system can be assessed against objectively verifiable evidence. No officer can justify an alcohol-screening demand without first either detecting the odour of alcohol, obtaining an admission of recent alcohol consumption, or making observations consistent with recent alcohol ingestion (such as witnessing the car leaving a licensed establishment, seeing an open liquor container in the vehicle, etc.). With cannabis, these objectively verifiable indicators will frequently be absent. However, a police officer whose "Spidey senses" are "tingling" could resort to the "reasonable suspicion" standard contained in the new s 254(2) to investigate an individual in almost any circumstance, on the pretext that they had a genuine belief that a driver was operating with "drugs in their body."[22] Such an assertion would be almost unchallengeable, since the officer need not assert actual drug impairment, but merely the "presence of a drug in the body." If an individual is known to the police as a regular cannabis consumer, even if only under the auspices of a medical licence, the officer could assert having "grounds to reasonably suspect" that the person is driving "with drugs in their system" and stop them virtually each time they are observed to be driving. People residing in smaller towns or suburban bedroom communities, where police tend to have more time on their hands or may be personally familiar with the "local undesirables," may find themselves unduly targeted by this broad and poorly defined new investigative power.

As a corollary, an improper resort to this provision could be used as a pretext for stopping all manner of individuals who appear suspicious to the police, and could provide cover for the profiling of identifiable groups or racialized individuals. The potential for this sort of abuse is particularly insidious, since once a vehicle is stopped, police have ample opportunity to justify more extensive questioning and searches of the vehicle's occupants. It will be interesting to see how many s 254(2) "drug suspicion" stops result in the "incidental" finding of firearms, illegal drugs, and other forms of contraband that just happen to be located during the vehicle stops.

IV: DRUG SCREENING TESTS – SPIT IT OUT!

In addition to authorizing compulsory physical roadside sobriety tests, the enforcement apparatus under s 254(2) also authorizes police to demand the motorist to provide a bodily sample into "approved drug screening equipment."[23] This provision is similar to the existing legislation, which has long authorized resort to an approved alcohol-screening device. Thus far the government has approved one drug-screening device that will test for blood-THC levels by measuring its presence in saliva.[24] However, the reliability of this device has yet to be fully determined. The scientific literature has pointed out at least two significant areas of concern. For one thing, many drugs, cannabis included, can produce a dry mouth, which would have the effect of limiting an individual's capacity to produce an adequate saliva sample at all. It is not difficult to conceive of a scenario wherein a motorist, under the nervous pressure of a police demand compounded by mouth dryness due to cannabis consumption, is unable to produce enough saliva to provide an adequate sample. But since the failure to provide a sample is in and of itself a discreet offence under the legislation,[25] overzealous policing could result in the charging of persons who are simply incapable of producing enough saliva to be analyzed in the device.

A second concern is that, although saliva samples have been shown to correlate to blood-drug concentrations, when cannabis has been introduced by inhalation (the most common mode of consumption) it will result in an elevated concentration of THC within the subject's oral cavity for some period. In such circumstances a saliva test would produce a false positive,[26] resulting in the unnecessary arrest and excessive interference with a person's liberty and bodily integrity (since, upon arrest following the failure of a roadside test, the subject will be compelled to provide more invasive bodily samples, including blood and/or urine).

V: PER SE LIMITS AND CANNABIS IMPAIRMENT: "BUT I DRIVE BETTER WHEN I'M STONED"

While an analogy can be made between impairment by cannabis and impairment by alcohol, there are significant distinctions between the two. Alcohol impairment in the context of driving has been extensively studied, such that there is universal consensus within the field of forensic toxicology that a person's ability to operate a motor vehicle is impaired if their blood-alcohol concentration (BAC) is above 50 mg/100 ml.[27] Thus, the per se limit of 80 BAC is not disputed as being unreasonable – in fact, many in the field believe that it is too high and should be lowered to 50 BAC.[28] Regardless of what level the per se limits are set to, the correlation between alcohol consumption and increased risk to highway safety is indisputable.

There is certainly plenty of data to establish that drug-impaired driving represents a real risk to the public, and that also suggests that the incidence of drug impaired–driving accidents is overtaking that of alcohol-related car crashes.[29] However, despite a positive correlation between cannabis and driving incidents, the cannabis 2 ng/ml per se blood-drug limit is controversial. For one thing, the data collection techniques used to evaluate the incidence of cannabis use in car crashes worldwide are quite variable and inconsistent, such that the Drug and Driving Committee of the Canadian Society of Forensic Sciences, whose mandate is to advise the government on the proposed changes to the legislation, itself sounded a note of caution.

The application of such case-control methods to the study of crash risks for drivers using drugs is somewhat more complex than for those using alcohol. In comparison to alcohol, the testing for drugs, both among the cases and the controls, is more difficult. Analysis for drugs occurs in a laboratory setting rather than at roadside or at a police station. Ideally, blood for drug analysis should be obtained from both cases and controls, but obtaining the needed compliance from controls can be difficult. Consequently, testing rates are often low, and attributing meaning to the data is problematic. Among cases, similar problems are experienced unless the individual has gone to hospital, where a blood sample has been taken, or in fatalities in which post mortem blood is available. The net result is that the estimates of risk are often of questionable validity and reliability.[30]

Throughout its report, the Drug and Driving Committee is careful to point out that over-representation of a substance in car crash cases may merely be evidence of an association, rather than proof positive that it is a contributing factor.[31] Ultimately, however, the Committee concludes that "the weight of evidence suggests that cannabis use is associated with increased risk of car crash involvement"[32]

The Committee went on to identify a number of problems with the per se limit approach in the new law. Once cannabis is introduced into the body, blood-THC levels drop off quite rapidly, but the drug's subjective effects on the brain persist, and may endure for up to six hours after consumption. Oral ingestion produces a different absorption rate than smoking, resulting in a slower onset of psychoactive effects and a lower overall blood-THC level, but the effects last longer. A further problem is that because blood-THC levels drop off quite rapidly after cannabis consumption, by the time a blood sample is actually seized the subject may be below the lawful per se level, even though they were factually impaired by cannabis at the time of driving.[33] Finally, amongst chronic users, there is a real risk of testing above the legal per se limit long after they have ceased smoking, due to the buildup of THC in their fatty tissues, despite the fact that the acute intoxication and impairment caused by cannabis in such circumstances would have long since subsided.[34]

The above concerns demonstrate that the offence of violating the per se THC limit, which will likely be the most commonly laid charge under the new provisions, carries with it a real risk of both under-charging individuals who were in fact over the limit at the relevant time, and over-charging others who are chronic or medicinal users of cannabis. The per se limit of 2 ng/ml, while purportedly establishing a reasonable standard for road safety, also fails to adequately take into account the wide level of variability of individual tolerance for cannabis. A habitual or chronic user may be over the blood-THC limit yet not be suffering from acute intoxication or its impairing effects.[35] Thus, there is a real concern that too blunt an instrument is being applied, and that conduct which really does not represent a road-safety hazard will still attract full criminal liability. Finally, per se limits aside, the physical evaluative tests designed to determine whether the driver is factually impaired, which are to be conducted under the auspices of s 254(3.1) by a qualified evaluating officer or DRE (Drug Recognition Expert)[36] carry with them a significant risk of over-charging. Greater reliance on the evidence of DREs will result in more prosecutions of individuals who may be only marginally affected by cannabis, but who simply perform

poorly on physical tests. Also, as discussed earlier in the context of
SFST screening, the risk of confirmation bias having an impact on
an evaluating officer's conclusion is a real issue, and any opinion
evidence from police in this area should be taken with a healthy
dollop of salt.

CONCLUSION

Legalization of marijuana will almost certainly produce the unwel-
come effect of more drug-impaired drivers on the road. With new
powers granted to the police will come the potential for abuse and
overreach. Police officers will be granted new investigative authority
with few guarantees that they are adequately qualified to carry it out
effectively or fairly.

While the public ought to be concerned about the risks of marijuana
use as it relates to highway safety, we should not lose sight of the fact
that with the loosening of one set of laws will come the potential for
greater police and state intrusion into other aspects of our lives. The
cannabis-related highway safety laws contained in Bill C-46 create the
potential for over-reach by charging people who do not constitute a
public safety hazard, empower police to investigate almost anyone on
the vaguest of pretexts, and could easily result in the over-prosecution
of factually innocent individuals. At the same time, the inherent limitations attendant with the creation of prescribed per se THC levels, in
terms of the technological limitations for effective detection, the potential for police abuse and overreach, and concern that detected THC
levels may not correlate very well to actual impairment, could lead to
both over-charging of the innocent and under-charging of the guilty.

For this reason it is suggested that a flexible and evidence-based
approach be adopted in order to enable the government to address
shortcomings in the legislation that are bound to arise in the first years
of its implementation. In at least one respect, the current legislation has
accommodated this concern, by leaving the per se THC limit to be set
by regulation rather than enacted directly in the statute. Similarly, as
technologies evolve and new devices are introduced to the market, the
legislation can adapt, since drug detection devices are set by regulation.

However, the government would be well-advised to formalize the
review process by creating a standing, arms-length advisory committee of independent experts to oversee the implementation of
the legislation and monitor its effectiveness. Such a body should be

comprised of experts in the field of forensic toxicology, as well as from the legal arena. While the government has long consulted with the Canadian Society of Forensic Sciences with respect to alcohol-driving issues, extreme vigilance will be required as the new cannabis regime comes into effect. The development of workable and consistent parameters for the determination of driving impairment by cannabis remains a significant challenge. A better mechanism for evaluation must be developed – one that is not vulnerable to confirmation bias, arbitrariness, or the baseline physical limitations of the test subject. Additional resources should be dedicated to the development of more scientific drug-evaluation techniques that are both reliable and minimally intrusive.

Furthermore, it will not be sufficient for the government to consult only with the scientists. Due to the potential for abuse in the day-to-day implementation of the new laws, the government needs to monitor the changing legal landscape in real time. Court decisions, including those – indeed especially those – from trial courts should be aggregated and assiduously reviewed by independent legal experts so as to assess whether the present standards are workable, are being fairly applied, and are Charter-compliant. Under the auspices of such a legal review, the government would be well-advised not to regard court rulings that are critical of the new laws as a rebuke to its legislative efforts, thereby triggering knee-jerk appeals to higher courts, but rather as a challenge to improve the legislation and make it more workable and effective. It should also be within the mandate of this committee to produce an annual compendious report so that the public can see for itself, without the distorting effects of government spin, whether the new laws are effective and just. In time, hopefully, through feedback and transparency, these untested laws will be refined and accepted by the public.

NOTES

1   The *Cannabis Act*, SC 2018, c 26.

2   SOR/2016-23 (this regulation's predecessors included the *Marihuana for Medical Purposes Regulations* (MMPR) SOR/2013-119 and the *Marihuana Medical Access Regulations* (MMAR) SOR/2001-227).

3   *R v Parker*, [2000] OJ No. 2787, 49 OR (3rd) 481; other court rulings that helped move the dial are *R v Malmo-Levine*, 2003 SCC 74, which was a

challenge to the law against marijuana possession outside of the medical arena wherein in a split decision the laws were upheld, but with strong dissents. Other government policies were successfully challenged in *Canada (AG) v PHS Community Health Services*, 2011 SCC 44, which prevented the Harper government from closing down the safe injection clinic in Vancouver, and *R v Smith*, 2015 SCC 34, which found that the ban on cannabis edibles under the medical marijuana regulations constituted a Charter violation.

4　*Controlled Drugs and Substances Act*, SC 1996, c 19, s 4 (prohibits possession of scheduled substances, which includes cannabis); s 5 (addresses trafficking), and s 7 (prohibits production; i.e., growing).

5　A typical case in which I was involved authorized the production of 171 plants, along with the storage of 7.6 kg of dried product, and the personal (carrying) possession of over 1 kg of dried product. All of this was pursuant to Health Canada–issued licenses, which had been signed off on by a doctor, and was ostensibly for personal medical use. It would be difficult to conceive of any patient requiring this amount of product for any purpose other than commercial production and trafficking.

6　Again, I am speaking from personal experience as a defence counsel, as well as from anecdotal knowledge of other cases.

7　A comparative analysis contrasting the effects of alcohol, tobacco, and psychoactive prescription medications such as the benzodiazepine family is beyond the scope of this paper. The detrimental effects of cannabis are acknowledged and well-documented, and easily researchable. See for example Heather Ashton, "Pharmacology and the Effect of Cannabis: A Brief Review," *British Journal of Psychiatry* 178, no. 2 (February 2001): 101–6.

8　There are extensive studies showing linkage between adolescent cannabis use and psychotic illnesses such as schizophrenia. Again, this subject is beyond the scope of this paper.

9　See Mike Hager, "One in Seven Cannabis Users Admits They Consumed Drug Then Drove, Statscan Says," *The Globe and Mail*, 9 August 2018, https://www.theglobeandmail.com/cannabis/article-statscan-survey-shows-about-one-in-seven-cannabis-users-admit-to/ (according to this survey, users of cannabis self-report a much higher incidence of driving following consumption of cannabis than drinkers of alcohol – three times higher).

10　*An Act to amend the Criminal Code (offences relating to conveyances) and to make consequential amendments to other Acts*, SC 2018, c 21.

11　Up until the passage of Bill C-46, it was an offence to operate a motor vehicle while impaired "by alcohol or drug," which implicitly included cannabis, but there was no legal limit placed on the blood concentration for any other substance other than alcohol.

12 Act to amend the Criminal Code, SC 2018, c 21, s 1.

13 Criminal Code of Canada, RSC 1985, c 46, s 253(1)(b) (the "per se" legal limit of 80 mg/100 ml blood alcohol concentration was implemented in 1969 and a conviction for Over 80 has the identical punitive consequences, as does a conviction for Impaired Operation).

14 The regulation contains a menu of common recreational drugs, of which cannabis is now the only legal substance, all others being prohibited under the CDSA. Unsurprisingly, in the case of every other listed substance – e.g., LSD, Psilocybin, Ketamine, cocaine, etc. – it is unlawful to have any detectable level.

15 SOR/2018-148.

16 Amy Peaire et al, *Report on Drug per se Limits* (Ottawa: Canadian Society of Forensic Sciences Drugs and Driving Committee, 2017).

17 Under s 254(3)(a)(ii) the subject can also be required to provide blood samples if, in the opinion of the police officer, they are incapable of providing breath samples. This usually occurs in the case of injury to the subject following an accident.

18 See Approved Drug Screening Equipment Order, (2018) C Gaz I.

19 There are three Standard Field Sobriety Tests, which are prescribed by regulation: the horizontal gaze nystagmus, which assesses jerky eye movements while tracking a slow-moving objects across the subject's field of vision; the walk and turn test, in which the subject takes nine heel-to-toe steps on a straight line, turns, and walks back; and the one-foot balance test, in which the subject balances on one foot and counts down 30 seconds.

20 In alcohol impairment cases officers will typically testify to some or all of these indicia: red/bloodshot eyes, slow or slurred speech, strong odour of alcohol issuing from the breath, noticeably poor balance, and poor fine-motor skills.

21 A comical personal anecdote that demonstrates the problem of police naivete: A client was investigated for erratic driving and was then subjected to SFSTs. When asked to take the heel-to-toe steps, the client did not proceed as instructed, but engaged in increasingly bizarre behaviour, such as crouching down on the road. The client advised me that he was under the influence of LSD, but had had the good sense not to divulge this to the police. Rather than recognizing that this behaviour was symptomatic of a psychedelic trip, which would have fully justified the charge of "impaired operation by drug," the police officer charged him with "refusal of SFST." Charges were ultimately withdrawn.

22 NB: in order to trigger the SFST or screening sample authority under this section, the officer need not suspect actual impairment by drug, but merely "consumption." Hence, a police officer might easily detain any carload of young people on a typical weekend night, even if observable indicators of consumption are absent. Such random and intrusive detentions would be far less likely if the justification were only for alcohol.

23 Criminal Code, RSC 1985, c C-46, s 254(2)(c).

24 Approved Drug Screening Equipment Order, (2018) C Gaz I (the device is the Drager Drug Test 5000, and while blood-THC levels do correspond to concentrations found in saliva, the technology is relatively new).

25 S 254(5), which is unaffected by Bill C-46, makes it an offence to refuse a demand for a breath test, bodily sample, or SFST, and the punitive consequences upon conviction are identical to those of the substantive offences.

26 See Olaf Drummer, "Drug Testing in Oral Fluid," *Clinical Biochemist Reviews* 27, no. 3 (August 2006).

27 Numerous empirical studies have been conducted since the 1950s, using test subjects either in laboratory simulations of driving tasks, or on closed courses. Almost every study has found that one or more faculties required for the safe operation of a motor vehicle (divided attention tasks, reaction times, visual perception and processing, physical dexterity, etc.) will be impaired even at a low blood-alcohol concentration, and that above 50 BAC there is significant degradation.

28 See "Drunk driving law by country," Wikipedia, last modified 24 August 2018, https://en.wikipedia.org/wiki/Drunk_driving_law_by_country#Europe (Canada and all states in the USA have a BAC limit of 80, but many nations in Europe have set the limit at 50 or lower, and some countries have a limit of zero).

29 See for example "Alcohol and/or Drugs among Crash Victims," MADD, last modified April 2018, https://madd.ca/pages/impaired-driving/overview/statistics/ (showing that more fatalities in 2014 were positive for drugs, although not necessarily cannabis, than alcohol).

30 Peaire et al, *Report on Drug Per se Limits*, 9.

31 Peaire et al, *Report on Drug Per se Limits*, 10.

32 Peaire et al, *Report on Drug Per se Limits*, 11.

33 Peaire et al, *Report on Drug Per se Limits*, 14 (While in the case of alcohol, a driver's BAC may also be under the lawful limit by the time of testing, there is a very simple calculation by which the BAC can be back-extrapolated in order to determine its level at the time of driving, since alcohol is eliminated from the body at a predictable rate once ingested: roughly 15 mg/ml per hour. The same is not true for cannabis,

due to the high variability in absorption, distribution, and elimination kinetics of THC within the population).

34   Peaire et al, *Report on Drug Per se Limits*, 16.

35   See Andrew Sewell, James Poling, and Mehmet Sofuoglu, "The Effect of Cannabis Compared with Alcohol on Driving," *American Journal on Addictions* 18, no. 3 (May–June 2009) (The impairing effects of THC in the driving context, while real, do not necessarily analogize directly with those of alcohol. The authors note that frequently, drivers impaired by cannabis tend to have better insight into their condition and as a result are over-cautious, drive more slowly, and generally compensate behaviourally in a way that reduces their risk to road safety, as opposed to drivers under the influence of alcohol, who take increased risks and constitute a much more acute hazard to the public).

36   An evaluating officer (or DRE – Drug Recognition Expert) is a specially accredited police officer trained to evaluate a subject to determine their level of drug impairment. While the DRE designation has been in existence for some time, it is not frequently resorted to. This is likely to change once the full impact of cannabis legalization has taken effect and there is an uptick in drug-impaired driving charges, as well as a perceived need for more accredited DREs on police forces.

8

Unequal Justice: Race and Cannabis Arrests in the Post-Legal Landscape

AKWASI OWUSU-BEMPAH, ALEX LUSCOMBE,
AND BRANDON M. FINLAY

It is widely acknowledged that the American war on drugs is heavily racialized. Indeed, despite relatively similar rates of drug use across racial groups, a substantial proportion of individuals arrested and prosecuted for drug possession in the United States are Black and Latino.[1] The enforcement of drug laws generally, and their unequal application in particular, have been credited with fuelling America's racialized mass incarceration problem. While certain racialized groups are over-represented in Canada's prison system (notably Indigenous peoples and African Canadians), a lack of racially disaggregated criminal justice data means that very little is known about how racialized communities in Canada have been affected by our own war on drugs.[2]

Although the Canadian government is now being celebrated in many progressive circles for having legalized the recreational use of cannabis, Canada once stood at the vanguard of international drug prohibition with the implementation of the *Opium Act* of 1908. Indeed, few people recognize that Canada has been waging its own war on drugs since the 1980s.[3] In order to examine the extent to which Canadian drug law enforcement has also been racialized, we provide a first look at cannabis arrest data obtained from police agencies in five Canadian cities. Our analysis of these data demonstrates that race is also an important factor influencing arrest rates for simple cannabis possession in Canada. We find that Indigenous people and African Canadians have been disproportionately affected by cannabis prohibition.

Our paper proceeds as follows. In the first section we provide a brief history of drug prohibition in Canada, highlighting the key role that racial anxieties played in the development of early drug laws. The second section of the paper provides a multi-jurisdictional examination of Canadian cannabis law enforcement using arrest data obtained from Canadian police agencies in Toronto, Vancouver, Calgary, Regina, and Halifax. In the third section we consider what might happen in Canada post-legalization drawing on data from American jurisdictions where cannabis has been legalized or decriminalized. Our paper concludes with measures to reduce racial disparities in cannabis arrests post-legalization and to repair the harms caused to racialized communities by a near century of prohibition.

CANADA'S WAR ON CANNABIS

Constructing an Anti-Drug Framework

Although cannabis was first prohibited in Canada in 1923, the classist and racialized logic of its prohibition and control over the next ninety-five years can be understood only when situated in a longer historical time-frame dating back to the 1908 *Opium Act*. Prior to 1908, the control and criminalization of "altered states of consciousness" had not been a matter of state or public interest in Canada.[4] The *Opium Act* and its moral crusaders set in motion a much larger "drug scare" that fizzled out in the early 1920s but saw through the eventual prohibition of cannabis alongside cocaine, morphine, and a variety of other drugs between 1908 and 1923.[5]

Growing racial tensions and social anxieties over Asian immigration and settlement in Canada provided the main impetus for the passage of the *Opium Act*. Beginning in the 1880s, with the completion of railroad projects and a declining gold rush, Chinese immigrants were increasingly viewed as economic competition and a threat to White settler Canadians.[6] With a sudden increase in Japanese immigration to Canada in the early 1900s, anti-Asian sentiment amplified, culminating in the Vancouver "Anti-Oriental" Riots of 1907. Deputy Minister of Labour Mackenzie King travelled to British Columbia in the wake of the riots and, after interviewing two opium dealers in Vancouver, opted to make the eradication of the opium trade in Canada one of his top concerns.[7] The *Opium Act* received royal assent shortly thereafter.

Canada's Asian population was disproportionately affected by the 1908 *Opium Act*, the *Opium and Drugs Act* of 1911, and its later iterations.[8] For decades, the enforcement of the anti-opium law was heavily targeted at Canada's lower-class Chinese population, who were treated much more harshly than their White, middle- and upper-class counterparts. In her history of anti-drug law in 1920s English Canada, Catherine Carstairs highlights numerous possible causes behind the ensuing drug scare.[9] Among all the possible factors, however, from addicted soldiers to alcohol-prohibition law, she argues that anti-Asian racism had the greatest influence.[10] As Carstairs notes, anti-drug discourse in 1920s Canada was never politically neutral, but rather mirrored existing "social prejudices and practices and reinforced them in new ways."[11] The creation of these initial anti-drug laws and supporting moral tropes paved the way for the eventual criminalization of cannabis.

The Unexpected Criminalization of Cannabis

Cannabis was added to the schedule of restricted drugs in Canada in 1923, criminalizing simple possession, production, and supply.[12] Though the anti-drug campaign in Canada gained a great deal of momentum throughout the 1920s, the addition of cannabis to anti-drug law is not easily explained: psychotropic usage of cannabis among Canadians was low; there was no strong evidence in favour of banning cannabis; news media and anti-drug campaigners rarely if ever discussed it; it was never debated in parliament; and both domestic and international political pressure to include the drug in the law seemed non-existent at the time.[13] In the absence of any clear evidence, the unexpected addition of cannabis to anti-drug laws has been aptly characterized as a "solution without a problem."[14]

In 1929, the major revisions made to the *Opium and Drugs Act* between 1921 and 1927 were consolidated in the *Opium and Narcotic Drug Act*.[15] According to Carstairs, the parliamentary debate over the law's consolidation was absent of any discussion of race, though panic over Asian immigration and opiate drug use remained strong in the news media.[16] Anti-Asian panic had generally receded throughout Canadian society, but more importantly, was no longer necessary to push new, punitive drug laws. The image of the illicit drug user and trafficker as dangerous and in need of punishment and control was now simply a taken-for-granted truth in the overarching narrative.

A Surge in Enforcement

Further attesting to the curiousness of Canada's prohibition of can-nabis in 1923, making cannabis illegal and expanding Canada's drug enforcement network did little to change the actual patterns of enforcement until the 1960s.[17] Indeed, the first seizure of cannabis by police was not made until 1932, and the first cannabis arrest was not made until 1947.[18] The focus remained on Chinese opium users until about the mid-1930s, shifting to morphine and heroin users in the 1940s and 1950s.

Three major developments in the 1960s put the latent law against cannabis into action.[19] First was the passing of the new *Narcotic Control Act* in 1961, which at the time made cannabis a schedule 1 offence, punishable by seven years of imprisonment for possession and up to life for supply and other trafficking-related offences. Second, the growing counter-culture movement of the 1960s pop-ularized the use of the drug by a large population that went against existing drug-user stereotypes and made minimal efforts to keep their use hidden. Third, backed by the growth of a new "addic-tion science," a new set of discourses emerged solidifying the links between cannabis and its imagined harms on personality, mental health, productivity, and rates of crime. Despite lacking validity, this developing science on the so-called deleterious effects of cannabis was uncritically embraced by the Canadian news media and law enforcement agencies that now had the discursive lens necessary to see cannabis as a "public evil."[20]

The Le Dain Commission and Beyond

Throughout the 1960s, law enforcement agencies in Canada began cracking down on cannabis offences in an increasingly repressive manner.[21] Cannabis became law enforcement's core drug of concern, a shift that culminated in thousands of arrests each year.[22] Given the white, educated, and predominantly middle-class make-up of the typical offender at the time, many of whom were now receiving criminal records, the working consensus about the alleged dangers of cannabis broke down.[23] Public opinion data at the time provided further reason to be skeptical of the increasing repressiveness: most Canadians in the 1960s reported being *against* the criminalization of simple cannabis possession.[24] It was in response to this increasing

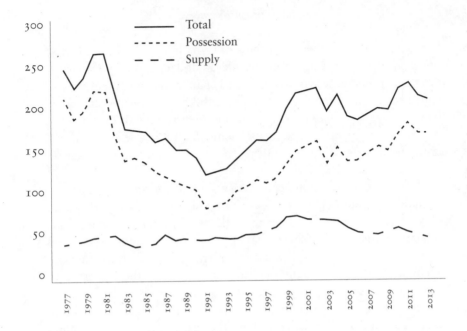

Figure 8.1: Police-reported cannabis offences in Canada, by type of offence, 1977–2013.

Graph reproduced using data from Cotter et al. (2015). Reproduced in Excel using Statistics Canada data available at: http://www.statcan.gc.ca/pub/85-002-x/2015001/article/14201/c-g/desc/desc03a-eng.htm.

public discord around the framing and treatment of cannabis users that in 1968 the federal government launched the Commission of Inquiry into the Non-Medical Use of Drugs, better known as the Le Dain Commission.[25] The commission agreed that cannabis law in Canada was overly repressive and called for a number of reforms with regards to its criminalization.[26] The Le Dain Commission's recommendations on cannabis law reform, however, failed to materialize, and a decade-and-a-half later in 1986, then–prime minister Brian Mulroney formally pronounced a Canadian "war on drugs."[27]

In 1996, the *Narcotic Control Act* was replaced by the much more repressive and punitive *Controlled Drugs and Substances Act* (CDSA).[28] Reflecting on this legislative change, Patricia Erickson wrote: "the new drug law ensconced the severe maximum penalties and extensive police powers found in the previous *Narcotic Control Act*, and added resources to aid even more efficient arrest and prosecution of illicit drug users and sellers. Canada's allegiance to criminalization was affirmed."[29] Despite the more liberal attitude toward cannabis and other illicit drugs in Canada compared to the United States, strict enforcement of existing anti-drug laws continued.[30]

Starting in 1991, Canada's crackdown on the possession and trafficking of illicit drugs, cannabis included, intensified dramatically. In 1995, of 63,851 total drug offences, 45,286 (70 per cent) involved cannabis, and nearly half (49 per cent) of the offences were for simple possession of cannabis, usually involving small, personal amounts.[31] From 1991 to 2002, the national rate per 100,000 population for total police-reported cannabis offences rose from 119 to 222 (Figure 8.1). By the late 1990s, over 600,000 Canadians had been given criminal records resulting from possession of cannabis offences.[32]

While the commitment to prohibition "weakened" with the introduction of a medical cannabis program in 2001 (then called the Medical Marijuana Access Regulation), Canada's punitive control of cannabis and other illicit drugs was far from over. In 2007, the then-Conservative majority under prime minister Stephen Harper passed its *National Anti-Drug Strategy*. The new national strategy removed the government's commitment to harm reduction, emphasized law enforcement over treatment and prevention, and promised to introduce mandatory minimum sentencing for cannabis and other drug-related offences under the CDSA. In 2012, the Harper government passed its controversial omnibus crime bill, Bill C-10: *The Safe Streets and Communities Act*, which included, alongside eight other measures, a bill amending certain sections of the CDSA. As promised in its strategy, this bill added mandatory minimum sentencing for certain drug-related offences, including trafficking, importing, exporting, and producing cannabis.[33]

Looking at the most recent uniform crime-report data available, it is clear that the impact of the war on drugs on cannabis users was as strong as ever under Harper's National Anti-Drug Strategy. In 2013, of 109,000 CDSA violations reported by police, cannabis was involved in two-thirds (67 per cent) of the cases, while cannabis possession alone made up more than half of these offences (54 per cent).[34] In 2013, of the total 73,000 cannabis-related offences reported by police, 59,000 (80 per cent) were for possession.

In light of the racial underpinnings of Canada's first drug laws, and a growing body of literature documenting the racialized nature of policing in Canada, we might expect our drug law enforcement to be similarly racialized – that is, for certain racial groups to have been disproportionately affected by the war on drugs. However, given a lack of systematic access to racially disaggregated criminal justice data in Canada, it has been difficult to support or refute such an assertion.[35] Indeed, until very recently Canadians have known almost nothing about how race has influenced the enforcement of drug laws. Below, we briefly highlight the findings of a *Toronto Star* analysis of Toronto Police Service (TPS) cannabis arrest data. We then provide a detailed analysis of newly obtained racially disaggregated cannabis arrest data from several jurisdictions across the country.

MULTI-JURISDICTIONAL ANALYSIS OF CANNABIS ARRESTS IN CANADA

Toronto Star *Findings*

Until very recently, the only official documentation of racial disparities in cannabis arrests in Canada to date came from the work of journalist Jim Rankin and colleagues at the *Toronto Star*. Using freedom of information (FOI) law, Rankin obtained and analyzed cannabis arrest and charge data from the Toronto Police Service for the years 2003–13. Over this period, the TPS arrested 27,635 people for cannabis possession and possession for the purpose of trafficking offences. Looking only at cases of simple cannabis possession (under 30 grams of dried cannabis or 1 gram of hashish) where the subject had no prior criminal record, the *Star*'s analysis showed that Black people were greatly over-represented in arrests for cannabis possession offences. Whereas Black people represented 8.4 per cent of Toronto's population during this time, they accounted for 25.2 per cent of those arrested for cannabis possession – three times their representation in the general population. By contrast, White and "Brown"[36] Torontonians were arrested at rates relatively similar to their representation in the general population. Whites made up 53.1 per cent of the population and 52.8 per cent of those arrested, while Brown people accounted for 14.7 per cent of the population and 15.7 per cent of those arrested.[37]

These findings are informative and align well with other data on racial disparities in policing published by the *Star*.[38] However, the data are from just one jurisdiction, and due to limits in TPS record keeping, they provide no insight into the experiences of Canada's Indigenous population. This shortcoming is significant given the over-representation of Indigenous people in other criminal justice outcomes, notably their gross over-incarceration.[39] Below, we provide an examination of more inclusive data from Vancouver, Calgary, Regina, Ottawa, and Halifax.

Data and Methods

In the summer of 2017, we began working with a senior reporter at *Vice News* to collect and analyze cannabis arrest data from a number of jurisdictions across Canada. Below, we present our analysis of rates of arrest by race for simple cannabis possession in five cities for the year 2015: Vancouver, Calgary, Regina, Ottawa, and Halifax. We counted simple cannabis possession as arrests for which possessing under 30 grams of dried cannabis or 1 gram of hashish was the sole offence. We focus on these minor cannabis-related offences, on the assumption that officers can exercise a large amount of discretion, thereby heightening the potential influence of race on decision-making. Data were released using respective freedom of information laws in each province and analyzed in SPSS. We used publicly available census metropolitan-area data from 2016 in order to compare the racial make-up of arrestees in a given jurisdiction to the racial composition of the city population. Although not without its limitations, this type of census benchmarking can provide insight into the existence of racial disparities in a jurisdiction.

Findings

Table 8.1 provides descriptive information about the sample and compares the representation of each racial group in the cannabis arrest data to their representation in the local population. In 2015, the vast majority of arrestees across the cities were male (86.7 per cent), and the median age for the sample was 25. In line with the previously published findings from Toronto, our data demonstrate that African Canadian and Indigenous peoples are over-represented in cannabis arrests across Canada.

Table 8.1: Racial breakdown of 2015 cannabis arrests across Canadian jurisdictions.

City	Total Arrests	Total Arrests (% of total)			2016 CMA Population Data (% of total)			Rate per 10,000		
		Indigenous	Black	White	Indigenous	Black	White	Indigenous	Black	Wh
Vancouver	839	132 (15.7)	38 (4.5)	370 (44.1)	61,455 (2.5)	29,830 (1.2)	1,179,100 (48.6)	21.5	12.7	3
Calgary	454	39 (8.6)	51 (11.2)	274 (60.4)	42,645 (3.0)	54,190 (3.9)	869,555 (63.3)	9.1	9.4	3
Regina	383	120 (31.3)	22 (5.7)	133 (34.7)	21,650 (9.3)	6,470 (2.8)	169,735 (73.0)	55.4	34.0	7
Ottawa	771	52 (6.7)	163 (21.1)	383 (48.7)	25,035 (2.6)	60,975 (6.3)	705,190 (72.5)	20.8	26.7	5
Halifax	110	3 (2.7)	17 (15.5)	88 (80)	15,815 (4.0)	15,090 (3.8)	336,525 (84.6)	1.9	11.3	2

In Vancouver in 2015, Indigenous and Black people were arrested at a rate of 21.5 and 12.7 per 10,000 people, while White people were arrested at a much lower rate of 3.1 per 10,000. Indigenous people were thus nearly seven times more likely than White people to be arrested for the same crime.

In Calgary, White people constituted 63 per cent of the city's population and were under-represented in cannabis arrests in 2015, accounting for 60.4 per cent of those arrested for minor cannabis possession. Conversely, Aboriginal people represented 3 per cent of Calgarians but 8.6 per cent of those arrested. Indigenous and Black people were arrested at similar rates to one another, at 9.1 and 9.4 per 10,000 population, roughly three times more than Whites, who were arrested at a rate of 3.2 per 10,000.

Data from Regina indicate that the city has some of the starkest racial differences in cannabis possession arrests among the jurisdictions examined here. These disparities were most pronounced for Aboriginals, who were greatly over-represented in arrests, whereas White people in the city were greatly under-represented. Indigenous and Black people were arrested at a rate of 55.4 and 34 per 10,000, seven and five times more than White people (7.8 per 10,000) respectively. In the nation's capital, Indigenous people were arrested at a rate of 20.8 per 10,000, Blacks at a rate of 26.7 per 10,000, and Whites at a rate of 5.4 per 10,000.

Finally, in Halifax, though the overall number of cannabis arrests was low compared to the other jurisdictions (n=169), there was a clear racial disparity between Black and White people. In 2015, 24 per cent of the people arrested for possession were Black, although they comprised only 3.6 per cent of the city's population. Black people were arrested a rate of 11.3 per 10,000, versus 2.6 per 10,000 for White people. Along with Indigenous people in Regina, Blacks were over-represented in Halifax cannabis possession arrests; the rates for these two groups were the most disparate in the country.

Clearly, Canada's cannabis laws have had a disparate impact on Black and Indigenous people. In line with previous American research, the limited available data from Canada indicate that rates of cannabis use are similar across racial groups, providing support for the notion that drug law enforcement is biased.[40] Unfortunately, our data do not allow us to examine whether the observed disparities can be explained by racial differences in other factors such as previous criminal record or rates of public consumption.

RACE AND CANNABIS ARRESTS AFTER LEGALIZATION: EVIDENCE FROM THE UNITED STATES

Although drug law enforcement has been a key driver of racial disparities in policing outcomes, evidence from the American jurisdictions that have legalized or decriminalized cannabis demonstrate that Black and Brown people continue to be disproportionately targeted despite relatively similar rates of cannabis use across racial groups.[41] Here we review evidence from Colorado and Alaska, where cannabis has been legalized at the state level.[42] We also present data from Chicago, where possession of small quantities of cannabis was decriminalized in 2012; and New York City, where overall numbers of cannabis arrests have been declining since 2011. The data available show that while the legalization and decriminalization of cannabis have substantially reduced the number of Black and Latinx people arrested for cannabis offences, they have not eliminated the forces that contributed to the disparities in the first place.[43] As a result, although there are fewer arrests overall, the racial disparities persist.

In Colorado between 2012 and 2014, there was a 51 per cent decrease in cannabis arrests of White people, compared to a 33 per cent decrease for Latinx and a 25 per cent decrease for Blacks. The cannabis arrest rate for African Americans (348 per 100,000) in Colorado was almost triple that of Whites (123 per 100,000) in 2014.[44] The situation appears to be more troubling for racialized youth; whereas the cannabis arrest rate for White 10- to 17-year-olds decreased by almost 10 per cent between 2012 and 2014, the rate for Latinx and Black youth actually increased by more than 20 per cent and 50 per cent, respectively, over this period.[45] As was the case in Colorado, overall arrests for cannabis-related offences decreased dramatically for both Black and White people in Alaska following legalization. Nevertheless, the racial disparities in arrests remain. In 2016, the cannabis arrest rate for Black people (17.7 per 100,000) was ten times greater than that of White people (1.8 per 100,000).[46] Racial disparities in arrests also persist post-legalization in the state of Washington and in Washington, D.C.[47]

The "decriminalization" of cannabis in Chicago and New York City has also failed to eliminate racial disparities in cannabis arrests. Chicago provides a clear example of this. On 4 August 2012, the Alternative Cannabis Enforcement program came into effect, allowing police officers to ticket individuals for simple possession of 15 grams or less of cannabis. As Mick Dumke of the *Chicago Reader* demonstrated in 2014, the "racial grass gap," as he called it, was still present in Chicago following the change in policy. Indeed, between 4 August 2012 and February 2014, Black Chicagoans accounted for 78 per cent of those arrested (rather than ticketed) for possession of cannabis, the same percentage as between 2009 and 2010, before the new policy was introduced.[48] As of 2016, despite a major reduction in the overall number of arrests, Blacks still accounted for 76 per cent of cannabis possession arrestees in Chicago.[49]

New York City saw a drastic increase in cannabis possession arrests in the late 1990s and into the 2000s under mayors Giuliani and Bloomberg. Overall arrests have declined under the current leadership of Mayor Bill de Blasio (from 2014 to the present). However, as with the cases above, the racial gap in cannabis arrests has not decreased along with this overall decline. Indeed, Blacks and Hispanics in New York continue to face arrest rates nearly ten times greater than those of Whites in the city. Whereas Black people accounted for 52 per cent of arrests in 2011, they made up 48 per cent in 2017. Similarly, Hispanics accounted for 32 per cent of arrestees in 2011; this figure increased to 38 per cent in 2017.[50]

DISCUSSION

In both Canada and the United States, the move towards drug legalization has been touted as a means of promoting racial justice.[51] Given the crucial role that drug laws have played in criminalizing Black and Indigenous people, an overall reduction in arrests will be an improvement over the status quo. However, the fact remains that racial disparities in arrests for drug offences are the result of broader policing practices that are themselves heavily racialized. The racial profiling of specific groups on the basis of stereotypes, rather than evidence of criminal activity, is at least partly to blame. We know, for example, that cannabis possession arrests in Toronto increased in tandem with the practice of "carding" (a form of police intelligence-gathering named after the "contact cards" that officers fill out in the course of their duties). Because carding is itself heavily racialized, Black and Brown people are more likely to be stopped, searched, and subsequently arrested for drug possession. There is also evidence to suggest that the police exercise discretion differently across racial groups, giving some people a break while choosing to arrest and charge others for the same activities.[52]

The evidence provided above demonstrates that some of Canada's most vulnerable populations have had their ability to participate fully in Canadian society eroded by criminal records received as a result of the war on drugs. Indeed, people with a criminal record have a harder time securing employment, which restricts their ability to make a living salary and the financial contributions they can make to their families and communities. Minor cannabis offences can also serve as a "gateway" into the criminal justice system for people who become "known to police," which increases their chances of further criminalization and social marginalization.

It is important to note that cannabis legalization does not mean an end to law and its enforcement; there are now more laws regulating cannabis following "legalization" than under prohibition. The increased focus on, and enhanced penalties for, cannabis-impaired driving, possession of "illicit cannabis," trafficking to young people, and youthful possession – which will come as a result of legalization – may just as easily reproduce existing racial disparities in the Canadian post-legal landscape.

As such, drug legalization will amount to racial justice only if the broader forces that promote injustice in Canada's law enforcement apparatus are addressed. Effective oversight of police stop-and-search activities in general, and of drug-law enforcement in particular, are fundamental. This requires access to meaningful and reliable data that should be proactively released to the public by police and governmental agencies. Efforts should also be made to rectify the harm done to racialized populations by cannabis prohibition. We suggest a three-pronged approach, based largely on a model that is developing in the United States, to do just that. Some American jurisdictions that have legalized cannabis are working to incorporate reparations and equity measures into law, policy, and practice. Below are three main areas that should be addressed in Canada.

Federal Legislation – Expungement of Criminal Convictions

In the case of expungement, we should follow the example provided in Bill C-66, where the government is working to erase the criminal records of LGBTQ Canadians convicted of activities that are no longer illegal. In the case of cannabis, this expungement should be automatically granted by the federal government and should extend to any subsequent charges stemming from an original cannabis-related charge (failure to comply with the conditions of a probation order, for example). The latter are important because they serve to unnecessarily pull individuals further into the criminal justice system.

The Redistribution of Cannabis Tax Revenue

The government should commit to reinvesting a portion of tax revenue from the legal sales of cannabis to improve the circumstances of individuals and communities most harmed by prohibition. Canada's three levels of government have long committed tax dollars to help police agencies enforce cannabis laws. Some of the tax revenue generated from the legal industry should be directed to those individuals and communities most affected by drug-law enforcement. Such measures could include targeted funding allocations to schools, community centres, and job-training programs in the affected neighbourhoods, and grant and funding opportunities for formally criminalized people.

Enhancing Cannabis Industry Participation

Government and private corporations should ensure that those racialized and otherwise marginalized populations most impacted by cannabis prohibition are given the opportunity to participate in the licit cannabis industry. These populations should not be both targeted by drug-law enforcement and subsequently excluded from working in the legal cannabis economy. This would serve as a double punishment. Both government and private corporations can work to broaden industry participation in a number of ways. For example, all levels of government should implement tiered licencing systems to foster small business development and provide specialized loans to help these businesses grow. Private corporations can also help by implementing recruiting and human resource strategies that foster inclusion in the industry. Pairing industry insiders with potential cannabis entrepreneurs in targeted mentoring programs would also prove useful. Those provinces that have declared a monopoly over sales should implement the same strategies suggested for private industry.

We conclude by reminding readers that Canada stood at the vanguard of international drug law with its adoption of the *Opium Act*. This law, and many that followed, have had a detrimental impact on the very groups that their proponents so often purported to help. At a time when Canada once again stands at the forefront of international drug law, the nation should set an international example by providing redress for the innumerable harms that have been inflicted by the war on drugs.

NOTES

1   Michelle Alexander, *The New Jim Crow: Mass Incarceration in the Age of Colorblindness* (New York: The New Press, 2012).

2   Akwasi Owusu-Bempah and Scot Wortley, "Race, Crime, and Criminal Justice in Canada," in *The Oxford Handbook of Ethnicity, Crime, and Immigration*, eds. Sandra Bucerius and Michael Tonry (New York: Oxford University Press, 2014), 281–320.

3   Akwatu Khenti, "The Canadian War on Drugs: Structural Violence and Unequal Treatment of Black Canadians," *International Journal of Drug Policy* 25, no. 2 (March 2014): 190–5.

4   Neil Boyd, "The Origins of Canadian Narcotics Legislation: The Process of Criminalization in Historical Context," *Dalhousie Law Journal* 8, no. 1 (1984): 102, 104.

5   Craig Reinarman, "The Social Construction of Drug Scares," in *Constructions of Deviance: Social Power, Context, and Interaction*, eds. Patricia Adler and Peter Adler (Belmont: Wadsworth Publishing, 1994), 155–65.

6   Robert Solomon and Melvyn Green, "The First Century: The History of Non-Medical Opiate Use and Control Policies in Canada, 1870–1970," in *Illicit Drugs in Canada: A Risky Business*, eds. Judith Blackwell and Patricia Erickson (Scarborough: Nelson, 1988), 88–104.

7   Solomon and Green, "First Century."

8   Catherine Carstairs, *Jailed for Possession: Illegal Drug Use, Regulation, and Power in Canada, 1920–1961* (Toronto: University of Toronto Press, 2006); Barbara Macrae "Drug Policy in Canada: War if Necessary but not Necessarily War," in *Perspectives on Canadian Drug Policy* vol. 1, ed. Graham Stewart (Kingston: The John Howard Society of Canada, 2003), http://johnhoward.ca/wp-content/uploads/2016/12/Perspective-on-Canadian-Drug-Policy-Volume-1.pdf.

9   Catherine Carstairs, "Innocent Addicts, Dope Fiends, and Nefarious Traffickers: Illegal Drug Use in 1920s English Canada," *Journal of Canadian Studies* 33, no. 3 (Fall 1998): 145–62.

10 Carstairs, "Innocent Addicts," 148.

11 Ibid., 145.

12 P.J. Giffen, Sylvia Boorman, and Shirley Jane Endicott, *Panic and Indifference: The Politics of Canada's Drug Laws: A Study in the Sociology of Law* (Ottawa: Canadian Centre on Substance Abuse, 1991).

13 Carstairs, *Jailed for Possession;* Benedikt Fischer et al., "Cannabis Law Reform in Canada: Is the 'Saga of Promise, Hesitation and Retreat'

Coming to an End?," *Canadian Journal of Criminology and Criminal Justice* 45, no. 3 (July 2003): 265–98; Giffen, Boorman, and Endicott, *Panic and Indifference;* Clayton James Mosher, *Discrimination and Denial: Systemic Racism in Ontario's Legal and Criminal Justice Systems: 1892–1961* (Toronto: University of Toronto Press, 1998).

14   Giffen, Boorman, and Endicott, *Panic and Indifference,* 182.

15   Robert M. Solomon and S.J. Usprich, "Canada's Drug Laws," *Journal of Drug Issues* 21, no. 1 (January 1991): 20.

16   Carstairs, *Jailed for Possession,* 33.

17   Fischer et al., "Cannabis Law Reform in Canada," 265–98.

18   Daniel Schwartz, "Marijuana Was Criminalized in 1923, but Why?," CBC *News,* 3 May 2014, http://www.cbc.ca/news/health/marijuana-was-criminalized-in-1923-but-why-1.2630436; Giffen, Boorman, and Endicott, *Panic and Indifference.*

19   Fischer et al., "Cannabis Law Reform in Canada," 265–98.

20   Melvyn Green, "A History of Canadian Narcotics Control: The Formative Years," *University of Toronto Faculty of Law Review* 37 (1979): 47.

21   Fischer et al., "Cannabis Law Reform in Canada," 265–98; Reginald Whitaker, *Drugs & the Law: The Canadian Scene* (Toronto: Methuen Publishing, 1969).

22   Neil Boyd, *High Society: Legal and Illegal Drugs in Canada* (Toronto: Key Porter, 1991); Michael C. Bryan, "Cannabis in Canada: A Decade of Indecision," *Contemporary Drug Problems* 8 (1979): 169–92.

23   Benedikt Fischer, Sharan Kuganesan, and Robin Room, "Medical Marijuana Programs: Implications for Cannabis Control Policy – Observations from Canada," *International Journal of Drug Policy* 26, no. 1 (2015): 16.

24   Fischer et al., "Cannabis Law Reform in Canada," 271.

25   *Bill C-45: An Act* respecting *cannabis and to amend the Controlled Drugs and Substances Act, the Criminal Code and other Acts.* Ottawa, ON: Parliament of Canada. http://www.parl.ca/LegisInfo/BillDetails.aspx?billId=8886269&View=0. (2018).

26   Patricia G. Erickson and Reginald Smart, "The Le Dain Commission Recommendations," in *Illicit Drugs in Canada: A Risky Business,* eds. Judith C. Blackwell and Patricia G. Erickson (Scarborough: Nelson, 1988).

27   Patricia G. Erickson, "Recent Trends in Canadian Drug Policy: The Decline and Resurgence of Prohibitionism," *Daedalus* 121, no.3 (1992): 239–67.

28   Macrae, "Drug Policy in Canada," 47; Akwatu Khenti, "The Canadian War on Drugs: Structural Violence and Unequal Treatment of Black

Canadians," *International Journal of Drug Policy* 25, no. 2 (2014): 190–5.

29   Patricia G. Erickson, "A Persistent Paradox: Drug Law and Policy in Canada," *Canadian Journal of Criminology* 41 (1999): 275.

30   Patricia. G. Erickson and David L. Haans, "Drug War, Canadian Style," in *Drug War American Style: The Internationalization of Failed Policy and Its Alternatives*, eds. Jurg Gerber and Eric L. Jensen (New York: Garland Publishing, 2001).

31   Benedikt Fischer et al., "Cannabis Use in Canada: Policy Options for Control," *Policy Options* 19 (October 1998): 34–8.

32   Neil Boyd, "Rethinking Our Policy on Cannabis," *Policy Options* 19 (October 1998): 31–3.

33   Laura Barnett et al., *Legislative Summary of Bill C-10: An Act to enact the Justice for Victims of Terrorism Act and to amend the State Immunity Act, the Criminal Code, the Controlled Drugs and Substances Act, the Corrections and Conditional Release Act, the Youth Criminal Justice Act, the Immigration and Refugee Protection Act and other Acts* (Ottawa: Library of Parliament, 2012).

34   Adam Cotter, Jacob Greenland, and Maisie Karam, *Drug-Related Offences in Canada, 2013*, (Ottawa: Statistics Canada, 2015).

35   Akwasi Owusu-Bempah and Paul Millar, "Research Note: Revisiting the Collection of 'Justice Statistics by Race' in Canada," *Canadian Journal of Law & Society* 25, no. 1 (2010): 97–104.

36   The category "Brown" includes people of South Asian, West Asian, and Arab descent.

37   Jim Rankin, Sandro Contenta, and Andrew Bailey. "Toronto Marijuana Arrests Reveal 'Startling' Racial Divide," *Toronto Star*, 6 July 2017, https://www.thestar.com/news/insight/2017/07/06/toronto-marijuana-arrests-reveal-startling-racial-divide.html.

38   Jim Rankin, "Race Matters: When Good People Are Swept Up with the Bad," *Toronto Star*, 6 February 2010, A1; Jim Rankin, "CARDED: Probing a racial disparity," *Toronto Star*, 6 February 2010, IN1; Jim Rankin et al., "Singled Out: An Investigation into Race and Crime," *Toronto Star*, 19 October 2002, A1; Jim Rankin et al., "Police Target Black Drivers," *Toronto Star*, 20 October 2002, A1.

39   Owusu-Bempah and Wortley, "Race, Crime, and Criminal Justice in Canada."

40   Hayley A. Hamilton et al., "Ethnoracial Differences in Cannabis Use among Native-born and Foreign-born High School Students in Ontario," *Journal of Ethnicity in Substance Abuse* 17, no. 2 (2018): 123–34.

41 Drug Policy Alliance, *From Prohibition to Progress: A Status Report on Marijuana Legalization* (New York: Drug Policy Alliance, 2018), http://www.drugpolicy.org/sites/default/files/dpa_marijuana_legalization_report_feb14_2018_0.pdf.

42 Although recreational cannabis use has been legalized in various jurisdictions, there are still laws regulating the quantity of cannabis that can be possessed or produced and the places where it may be consumed, and stipulating a minimum age for possession, among other things.

43 Drug Policy Alliance, *From Prohibition to Progress.*

44 Colorado Department of Public Safety, *Marijuana Legalization in Colorado: Early Findings, a Report Pursuant to Senate Bill 13-283* (Denver: CDPS, 2016), https://cdpsdocs.state.co.us/ors/docs/reports/2016-SB13-283-Rpt.pdf.

45 Ben Markus, "As Adults Legally Smoke Pot in Colorado, More Minority Kids Arrested for It," *National Public Radio*, 29 June 2016, https://www.npr.org/2016/06/29/483954157/as-adults-legally-smoke-pot-in-colorado-more-minority-kids-arrested-for-it.

46 Drug Policy Alliance, *From Prohibition to Progress.*

47 Ibid.

48 Mick Dumke, "Will Marijuana Decriminalization End the Racial Grass Gap?" *Chicago Reader*, 5 May 2015, https://www.chicagoreader.com/chicago/will-marijuana-decriminalization-end-racial-disparity-in-arrests-prosecution/Content?oid=17599671.

49 Lee Gaines, "Despite Decriminalization, Chicago's Grass Gap Persists," *Chicago Reader*, 19 April 2017, https://www.chicagoreader.com/chicago/marijuana-decriminalization-arrests-ticketing-race-investigation/Content?oid=26258364.

50 Brendan Cheney, "Racial Disparities Persist in New York City Marijuana Arrests," *Politico*, 13 February 2018, https://www.politico.com/states/new-york/city-hall/story/2018/02/13/racial-disparities-continue-in-new-york-city-marijuana-arrests-248896.

51 "House Introduces Marijuana Legalization Bill, Focused on Racial Justice, as Companion to Cory Booker's Senate Bill," *Drug Policy Alliance*, 17 January 2018, http://www.drugpolicy.org/press-release/2018/01/house-introduces-marijuana-legalization-bill-focused-racial-justice-companion.

52 Kanika Samuels, *Examining the Utility of Pre-charge Youth Diversion Programs: A Canadian Context* (Oshawa: University of Ontario Institute of Technology, 2015).

9

What Jurisdiction for Harm Reduction: Cannabis Policy Reform under Canadian Federalism

ALANA KLEIN

As Canada becomes the first country in the Northern Hemisphere to legalize non-medical cannabis nationwide, it seems natural to situate the move within the recent international wave of legalization. Since 2012, recreational cannabis has been legalized in nine US states and in Uruguay. Yet official critique of criminalization has deep roots in Canada, dating back almost fifty years, to the 1972 Le Dain Commission Report. The majority of the commission recommended decriminalization for reasons that still resonate today: Criminalization drew otherwise law-abiding citizens to engage with black marketeers. Low levels of prosecution compounded the injustice for those who did get caught. Exaggerated messages about harm undermined the credibility of drug education. Criminalization fostered disrespect for the law among those who saw it as "perverse and profoundly hostile," given that cannabis is probably not as dangerous as alcohol.[1]

What distinguishes Canada's decriminalization discourse today from that of the 60s and 70s is the dominance of public health and human rights lenses for viewing both the harms of criminalization and its solutions. In its influential Cannabis Policy Framework, for example, the Centre for Addiction and Mental Health treats the disproportionate impact of criminalization on racialized Canadians as discrimination *per se*, and also as a health equity matter, a negative social determinant of health for racialized groups.[2] It was the minister of health at the time, Jane Philpott – rather than, say, the minister of justice – who made the first public legalization announcement on 20 April 2016, at the United Nations General Assembly Special Session on Drugs. Philpott promised that legalization would "protect our youth while enhancing public safety," but also emphasized that a modern approach to drug policy would build on public health–based successes like Insite, Canada's first legally sanctioned safe injection site, and that it would "embrace upstream prevention, compassionate treatment, and harm reduction."[3]

Yet this ostensibly public health– and equity–based project has been hobbled out of the gate by a tenacious ethos of criminalization. For an approach that is said to treat marijuana as primarily a health issue rather than a criminal one, the regime relies heavily on law enforcement, with harsher penalties than the regime it replaces, and often without a clear evidence base in public health or criminological research. The *Cannabis Act* (formerly Bill C-45)[4] serves as a key example of how the dominant discourse of criminalization and stigmatization can overtake more progressive objectives.

Part I of this chapter will dissect the mix of public health, social justice, and traditional criminal law objectives embodied in the *Cannabis Act*. It analyzes the new law and its surrounding discourse through the lens of harm reduction, the primary alternative framework to abstinence-based drug policies that have dominated global drug policy to date. Part II will discuss the role played by Canadian federalism in the persistent domination of criminal enforcement under the new law. Part III will consider how future jurisdictional disputes will channel and reflect government's commitment, and judges' receptiveness, to a shift in Canada's drug policy paradigm from prohibition and enforcement to public health and human rights.

PART ONE – THE CANNABIS ACT:
HARM REDUCTION THROUGH LEGALIZATION OR
REDUCING HARM THROUGH CRIMINALIZATION?

It is tempting to view legalization in Canada as a kind of harm-reduction initiative. The language of reducing harm is all over government discourse surrounding the project. But close attention reveals that government actors avoid using "harm reduction" as a term of art. Minister of Justice Jody Wilson-Raybould says the new law "reflects a public health approach aimed at reducing harm and promoting the health and safety of Canadians."[5] The government's lead on the marijuana file, Bill Blair, parliamentary secretary to the ministers of justice and health, similarly describes it as "...a public health approach directed entirely at reducing both the social and health harms [of marijuana use]."[6] The report of the Task Force on Cannabis Legalization and Regulation, upon which the legislation was based, sought to "identify those system features that will best reduce the risks of health and social harms associated with use."[7]

What is Harm Reduction?

The term "harm reduction" signals a set of practices, a policy approach, and a philosophy that rose to prominence in the 1990s and has since emerged as the primary alternative-policy paradigm to abstinence-based models for addressing addictive or intoxicating substances that dominated the twentieth century.

The moral (or criminal) model construes drug use as morally blameworthy, and endorses prohibitionist policies aimed primarily at supply side reduction – think "war on drugs" and "zero tolerance." The disease model pathologizes addictive behaviours and endorses treatment or prevention services with the goal of abstinence, working on the demand side.

Harm reduction takes a different starting point: the pragmatic recognition that human beings continue to engage in all kinds of behaviour with varying levels of risk. Instead of focusing on use reduction, it seeks to minimize negative individual and social consequences associated with those behaviours. Well-known examples of harm reduction interventions in the drug context include needle exchange, safe consumption sites, and the prescription of opiates to those already living with addiction, in order to avoid the dangers of the illegal market. Advocates have offered sunscreen, bicycle helmets, condoms, and nicotine patches as examples of harm reduction interventions in other areas where people continue to engage in behaviours associated with risk.

Harm reduction is also infused with a set of values that distinguishes it from moral and disease models. These include remaining non-judgmental about the underlying behaviour; elevating evidence and pragmatism over dogmatism and belief; dismissing punitive and authoritarian approaches; and constructing people who use drugs as worthy citizens with full responsibilities and participation rights, and who care about their health and well-being and those of others. Harm reduction's values have been associated with both the ethical duties of care of health professionals to provide compassionate, evidence-based care that honours dignity and promotes and respects informed decision-making,[8] and with human rights to the highest attainable standard of health, to benefit from scientific progress, to be free from arbitrary detention, and to be free from discrimination and degrading treatment.[9]

The Cannabis Act *through the Lens of Harm Reduction*

The *Cannabis Act* reflects an ambivalent relationship to harm reduction. On the one hand, it is rooted in a recognition that prohibition has failed, and seeks to eliminate harms caused by criminalization. Its purposes of "provid[ing] access to a quality-controlled supply of cannabis" recall prescription heroin, a well-supported harm reduction intervention that seeks to avoid risks associated with black market opiates by ensuring access to a licit product with a predictable strength that meets users' needs without exposing them to an increased risk of overdose. The objective of "enhanc[ing] public awareness of the health risks associated with cannabis use" is basic public health policy, but compatible with harm reduction's focus on pragmatism and scientism, and its rejection of stigma, dogma, and demonization of drug use. But in important ways, the new law and the policy supporting it remain within the logic of zero tolerance.

Heavy Reliance on Punitive and Authoritarian Approaches

The Act lifts many current criminal restrictions and abolishes mandatory minimum sentences for cannabis offences, but it continues to rely heavily on criminal sanction, and actually raises maximum penalties in some circumstances. For example, an individual distributing over 30 grams or providing marijuana to a minor now faces imprisonment for up to fourteen years,[10] the same maximum penalty for producing child pornography or aggravated assault of a police officer.[11] Trafficking in amphetamines, LSD, mescaline, or psilocybin (mushrooms), or possession for the purpose of trafficking those substances carries a maximum of only ten years.[12]

Even if the longest sentences will be reserved for the most extreme breaches, raising maximum penalties to fourteen years elevates marijuana offences to the level of the most serious crimes, and creates serious consequences for anyone convicted. For example, 2012 amendments to the Criminal Code removed the possibility of serving a sentence in the community for offences that carry a maximum penalty of fourteen years. Further, raising the penalties will have immigration consequences for permanent residents and foreign nationals. Individuals convicted of these *Cannabis Act* offences will be deemed inadmissible on grounds of serious criminality.[13] This is not an accidental effect of the law. When the Senate tried to amend the bill to specify that cannabis offences do not constitute "serious criminality" for immigration purposes, the government responded that "the criminal penalties and the immigration consequences aim to prevent young people from accessing cannabis and to deter criminal activity."[14]

The contrast with other regulated substances with a high burden of disease is notable. Federal laws on tobacco and alcohol focus on the regulatory goals of taking profits away from the black market through economic penalties. *Tobacco and Vaping Products Act* violations mainly attract fines; imprisonment is contemplated for tobacco manufacturers and advertisers, but generally tops out at two years.[15] Providing tobacco to a young person attracts only a fine.[16] In the case of alcohol, which is governed federally by the *Excise Act*, the highest penalty of five years' incarceration is reserved for fiscal offences.[17]

Provinces will restrict the scope of legalization further, for example, by banning home growing where federal law would allow it. And penalties will be higher than in other comparable contexts: the illegal sale of alcohol in Ontario currently attracts a maximum of one year in jail[18] – as opposed to cannabis's two[19] – and carries a lower fine. Under the new *Smoke-Free Ontario Act*, illegal distribution of tobacco attracts only a fine.[20] Provinces, which enforce both criminal and provincial regulatory law, are also expected to continue to rely heavily on police enforcement. Prohibition and enforcement appear to be so central to the emerging regime that provincial and municipal authorities have secured 75 per cent of cannabis tax revenues[21] to cover the high costs of legalization resulting from the increased burden on policing.[22]

Weak Evidence Base for Punitive Measures

The federal government insists that a "strict regulatory framework"[23] accompanied by harsh penalties is necessary to ensure compliance with its regulatory scheme, and to "keep [cannabis] out of the hands of kids, and the proceeds out of the hands of criminals."[24] Protecting kids is presumably the justification for maintaining criminal prohibition for youth possession of cannabis above five grams, when the same act would be perfectly legal for an adult.

But there is no evidence in criminological or public health literature to support the claim that regulatory effectiveness requires harsh sanction. In fact, the consensus among criminologists is that longer sentences are generally ineffective for deterring behaviour.[25] Measures adopted under zero-tolerance have not reduced cannabis use, especially among Canadian youth, who remain the heaviest users worldwide.[26] And the negative consequences of criminal records, particularly for youth, were the government's main reasons for switching from a criminal to an ostensibly public health–based regulatory framework.[27]

Perpetuation of Stigma and Misinformation

Relying on criminal sanction with harsh penalties despite a shaky evidence base perpetuates stigma, misinformation, and conflicting messages, particularly for youth.[28] Government discourse around legalization has sought to distance itself from the *Reefer Madness*–style moral panic and risk exaggeration that characterized the war on drugs.

Yet the language of keeping cannabis "out of the hands of children" is a constant refrain, reproducing the war-on-drugs–style discourse that consumption among these groups needs to be stopped, rather than made smarter. The Canadian Centre on Substance Abuse found that youth currently have a generally neutral or positive view of the effects of cannabis on development and the brain, a misconception that the Centre traces to inadequate education and conflicting messages linked to prohibition.[29] Researchers have been finding that early-onset cannabis can in fact be harmful to young people's cognitive development and mental health, particularly for those with family histories of such problems. But they have cautioned that it is "unhelpful to slide into a prohibitionist mentality that equates any consumption by youth as harmful."[30] While the *Cannabis Act* leaves space for evidence-based, youth-oriented public health messaging to counter such misunderstandings, maintaining a system that is so much more punitive than it is for other substances commonly used by youth, such as alcohol or tobacco, perpetuates the mistrust and risk distortion that has been an unfortunate consequence of prohibition so far.

Failure to Construct Those Most Affected as Worthy
Citizens with Full Participation Rights

A basic tenet of harm reduction is that those who are most affected know their own needs best. Certainly at the grassroots level, but also within official public health discourse, harm reduction constructs the subject as a worthy citizen whose knowledge deserves respect. But as Anthony Morgan writes, "politicians, the police, political pundits, public policy professionals and professors have overwhelmingly dominated the debate. Sadly, and unsurprisingly, the voices of average citizens from racialized and Indigenous communities have been largely unsolicited, sidelined or silenced."[31] Further, there has been a great deal of discussion about youth and research, but less emphasis on what youths themselves are saying about their own consumption and needs in relation to that consumption.

The strict prohibition on providing cannabis to a minor, which would expose an 18-year-old sharing with a 17-year-old friend to fourteen years in prison, is particularly egregious in the way it ignores how cannabis is used. Despite widespread concerns about imposing serious penalties for "social sharing," a Senate amendment to reduce the penalty for sharing with a minor who is less than two years younger was rejected by the government because it "would be contrary to the stated purpose of the *Cannabis Act* to protect the health of young persons by restricting their access to cannabis."[32]

Exclusion from policymaking may explain why the benefits of legalization are not equally distributed along the lines of race and class. Critics have warned that targeting low-level distributors through criminal sanctions for selling – as opposed to regulatory and economic penalties aimed at the top – will hit people from poor, racialized communities the most.[33] And while the *Cannabis Act* should result in fewer convictions, it does nothing for those who have already been affected by criminalization – disproportionately, "minority communities, Aboriginal communities and those in our most vulnerable neighbourhoods."[34]

PART TWO: FEDERALISM AND THE
PERPETUATION OF CRIMINALIZATION

There are many reasons behind the seemingly paradoxical prominence of criminal law enforcement even under legalization. Legalizing a substance that was once merely tolerated entails some justice system costs, like the development of new impaired driving strategies and technologies, which tend to rely heavily on law enforcement.[35] Lawmakers may also be responding to public discomfort with the pace of change. After nearly 100 years of criminalization in Canada and across the world, cannabis continues to attract a stigma distinct from that of alcohol and tobacco. And legitimate health concerns, particularly related to youth and other vulnerable populations, have prompted tough talk in support of harsh punishment, even if such measures are unlikely to be effective and risk undermining the equity goals of legalization.

Beyond (and in conjunction with) social, historical, political, and technocratic factors, the idiosyncrasies of Canadian federalism also play a role in perpetuating reliance on criminal enforcement–based approaches.

Federal Authority via the Criminal Law Power: Broad but Essentially Punitive and Stigmatizing

There is irony in the fact that Parliament's presumptive source of jurisdictional authority to legalize is the same power it seeks to abdicate – the criminal law. The criminal law power is broad. A valid criminal law need only contain a prohibition, a penalty, and pursue a "criminal purpose" – i.e., be directed at something with an "evil or injurious or undesirable effect on the public."[36] The federal government has used the criminal law power to legislate in a broad range of areas, including food processing, product safety, the environment, tobacco, and assisted reproduction. Outside of the spending power, it may be Parliament's most significant head of jurisdiction to intervene in health matters.

The substantive limit on the criminal law power was strengthened relatively recently in Reference re *Assisted Human Reproduction Act* (AHRA).[37] In that case, a bare majority of Supreme Court judges held that several of the Act's prohibitions related to assisted reproduction (such as performing *in vitro* fertilization or using medical facilities without a federal license) were not directed at any public harm or evil, but rather were directed at ordinary clinical practice and medical research. Essentially, the plurality of judges insisted that there was nothing evil or injurious or undesirable about run-of-the-mill assisted reproduction – in other words, it de-stigmatized it. In so doing, it limited the legitimate place of the criminal law in regulating it.

The upshot is that to claim jurisdictional authority under the criminal law, Parliament must not only frame its law in the form of a prohibition, but it seems it must direct the law at the negative public health or social consequences *of cannabis* – as opposed to criminalization itself. Jean Leclair observes that this constitutional reality was not lost on the legislative drafters of Bill C-45: the overall purpose of the law is to protect public health and public safety, the traditional purposes of a criminal law.[38] Other purposes are to "protect the health of young persons by restricting their access to cannabis"; to "protect young persons and others from inducements to use cannabis"; and to "deter illicit activities in relation to cannabis through appropriate sanctions and enforcement measures."[39] With these purposes, and the harsh penalties central to the overall scheme, the *Cannabis Act* looks far more like a traditional criminal law than any kind of public health framework to promote the safe and healthy use of cannabis.

Provincial Regulatory Authority as Punitive Power

Provinces also have constitutional authority to regulate cannabis punitively. Jurisdiction over "property and civil rights in the province" in section 92(13), and "matters of a merely local or private nature" in section 92(16) of the *Constitution Act, 1867*, allow the provinces to regulate both commercial and public health aspects of legal intoxicants – even to the point of prohibition.[40] Further, section 92(15) provides for "the imposition of punishment by fine, penalty, or imprisonment" as part of a valid provincial regulatory scheme. And though provincial offences can be distinguished from "true crimes" in that they are imposed for public welfare purposes rather than for punishment, consequences can be harsh, including substantial prison time.[41] The proliferation of certain regulatory offences and escalation of penalties has, in recent years, been criticized for its effective and disproportionate criminalization of stigmatized populations,[42] but it continues as an accepted means to enforce otherwise valid provincial regulation.

PART THREE: JURISDICTIONAL CONFLICT AND CRIMINAL/PUBLIC-HEALTH TENSION

Jurisdictional matters may have played a role in keeping criminal sanction a central element of cannabis legalization, but the *Cannabis*

Act nonetheless represents a substantial liberalization of drug policy in the name of public health and pragmatism. While many of the purposes and provisions in the *Cannabis Act* remain consistent with the traditional prohibition-and-punishment model, these are in tension with the liberalizing purposes in section 7 of the Act. These other purposes – "reduc[ing] the burden on the criminal justice system in relation to cannabis" and "provid[ing] access to a quality-controlled supply of cannabis"[43] – are quite novel for a criminal law, and more consistent with the harm reduction paradigm.

These novel policy objectives may be on shaky constitutional ground, however. A jurisdictional dispute is currently brewing in light of Quebec and Manitoba's plans to prohibit personal cultivation altogether.[44] In the zero-tolerance vein, provincial authorities have cited worries that home-grown plants will be diverted to the black market, or left out for kids to sample, or that they will generally increase availability and encourage use, and make policing more difficult.

Federal Paramountcy and Parliament's Source of Jurisdiction

The federal government has claimed that the doctrine of federal paramountcy will render the provinces' plans inoperative if they frustrate the liberalizing purposes of the new law.[45] In a similar dispute in *Rothmans, Benson & Hedges Inc. v. Saskatchewan*, the Supreme Court concluded that a provincial ban on tobacco displays did nothing to frustrate the purposes of a federal tobacco law which permitted such displays.[46] On the contrary, both laws shared the aim of restricting tobacco promotion in the service of public health. With the *Cannabis Act*'s novel objectives of *ensuring access* to cannabis and limiting the burden on the criminal justice system, however, the claim of frustration of purpose appears more viable.

A more substantial obstacle to federal paramountcy is the Court's reasoning in *Rothmans* that Parliament could not have meant to create any positive right to display tobacco products. Provisions enacted pursuant to the criminal law power are "essentially prohibitory," and as such "do not ordinarily create freestanding rights that limit the ability of the provinces to legislate in the area more strictly than Parliament."[47]

The federal government might seize on the word "ordinarily" and argue that although the *Cannabis Act*, as criminal law, is generally prohibitive, its purposes require that Parliament delimit the outside boundaries of prohibition. Yet judges of the Supreme Court have been willing to uphold facilitative provisions under the criminal law power – such as those providing for enforcement, warrants, or even information management – only where they have been in service of, or "ancillary to," other valid prohibitions.[48] Moreover, it is not clear that Parliament has actually created any positive right to have or. exchange cannabis in this law. While certain objectives of the *Cannabis Act* in section 7 are facilitative, the possession, distribution, and promotion provisions themselves are framed in terms of prohibition, mirroring federal criminal tobacco legislation, and consistent with the requirement that criminal laws pursue their goals through prohibition and penalty.

Another possibility, left open in *R v Malmo-Levine*, is to ground federal authority over cannabis in the federal government's power "to make Laws for the Peace, Order, and good Government of Canada" (POGG) in section 91 of the *Constitution Act*, which permits regulation of matters of national concern.[49] Locating federal power here rather than in the criminal law would shift the perceived source of mischief from cannabis alone to the sequelae of the drug war. It would better reflect the government's own position that positive steps – like facilitating access to safe, regulated cannabis that meets users' needs – are needed to ensure the health of Canadians. It would also reflect the importance of addressing the consequences of the war on drugs in a unified way across the country – a recognition that fifty years of war-on-drugs policy has ongoing impacts on a national scale.

The bar for recognizing a matter of "national concern" is understandably high, considering the broad exclusive jurisdiction that it can convey on the federal government.[50] The Supreme Court of Canada has held that a matter of national concern must have "a singleness, distinctiveness and indivisibility that clearly distinguishes it from matters of provincial concern and a scale of impact on provincial jurisdiction that is reconcilable with the fundamental distribution of legislative power under the Constitution."[51] The Court will also "consider what would be the effect on extra-provincial interests of a provincial failure to deal effectively with the control or regulation of the intra-provincial aspects of the matter."[52]

Yet finding a home for marijuana legislation in POGG would not be a complete novelty. A nineteenth-century Privy Council decision ruled that the *Canada Temperance Act* was valid federal legislation because the sale of "intoxicating liquors" was a subject of "general concern to the Dominion, upon which uniformity of legislation is desirable..."[53] In the 1979 case of *R v Hauser*, the Supreme Court found that the *Narcotics Control Act* was valid under POGG.[54] These decisions, however, are hardly constitutional orthodoxy today – Peter Hogg describes the former as "an anomaly" and the latter's reasoning as "tortured" and "unsatisfactory."[55]

More recently, courts have been evasive about whether drug laws might be grounded in POGG, without foreclosing the possibility. In *Malmo-Levine*, finding it was valid criminal law, the Court decided to leave the question as to whether narcotics legislation could be justified under POGG "open for another day."[56] A similar conclusion was reached in relation to federal tobacco legislation in *RJR-MacDonald*.[57]

Locating cannabis regulation in the "national concern" branch of POGG may be a tough sell to courts concerned about federal intrusions into provincial powers, and governments so far have been reluctant to make the argument in court. But as indicated above, the regulation and its surrounding discourse reflect a new understanding of drug policy, of its health and human rights dimensions. Its novel goals of addressing the stigma and misinformation of the drug war through evidence-based policy, and of edging out illegal markets through competition from licit ones, may indeed require some uniformity across the country. The recent opioid crisis, in many ways a consequence of years of wrong-headed abstinence-oriented drug policy, only strengthens the case for treating some aspects of drug regulation as a matter of national concern. If federal legislation were to be located in the POGG power, this could powerfully reflect the message that our drug policy missteps have generated a national-scale crisis that needs to be addressed in ways that ordinary criminal prohibitions never could.

Colourability: Restricting Provinces' Ability to Regulate Punitively

Federal authorities might alternatively claim that Quebec and Manitoba's personal cultivation bans are not really directed at valid provincial objectives like health or market regulation, but are in fact criminal prohibition in disguise, a perpetuation of a war on drugs that only the federal government was ever jurisdictionally entitled to wage, and therefore beyond provincial legislative authority.

This would not be the first time that, in the face of liberalization, provinces attempted to reproduce a defunct criminal law. In *R v Morgentaler* (1993), the Supreme Court concluded that Nova Scotia's law restricting abortions to hospitals was not, as the province had claimed, about ensuring quality medical services. Rather, it was really aimed at prohibiting and punishing clinic abortions as socially undesirable conduct,[58] essentially re-enacting the federal criminal prohibitions that had just been struck down in *Morgentaler* (1988) for violating pregnant women's Charter rights.[59]

Like *Morgentaler* (1993), the home-cultivation ban would reproduce a criminal law, in direct response to federal withdrawal. The validity of the provincial law would come down to whether the provinces can convincingly claim health or local order as a basis for the restriction on home growing. If courts see the ban as primarily a manifestation of stigma or unspecified discomfort with legalization, the law might be viewed as directed at public morals rather than health, and the colourability claim might gain traction. This will in turn depend on judicial receptiveness to claims about inherent health risks and dangers that ostensibly attend home growing.

CONCLUSION

The *Cannabis Act* as it stands can hardly be understood as an example of harm reduction in Canadian drug policy. Canadian federalism – through the presumptive location of the *Cannabis Act* in the criminal law power, and through growing punitive regulatory capacity – has played a role in maintaining the primacy of prohibition, punishment, and stigma even under legalization.

Future jurisdictional disputes may channel and test lawmakers' commitment – and courts' receptiveness – to a new approach grounded in public health and equity. Locating the *Cannabis Act* outside the criminal law power could allow Parliament to more explicitly acknowledge what it means to withdraw from, and repair the damage left by, a war on drugs. Provinces seeking to avoid claims of stepping into criminal jurisdiction may be required to better separate stigma and stereotype from evidence-based policy if they are to maintain their jurisdictional authority. Judges' receptiveness to such claims will test their own attitudes about the harms of cannabis and of the drug war itself. Each of these arbiters of jurisdiction could play a part in moving toward a real paradigm shift in Canadian drug policy.

This article is based on a previous publication: "Paths of least resistance and path dependency: Jurisdiction and the continued criminalization of legalized cannabis in Canada," in *L'Idée Féderale* (Volume 9, No. 1, May 2018). http://ideefederale.ca/documents/Mai_ang_Klein_Cannabis.pdf

The author would like to thank Souhila Baba Ahmed, Dylan Gibbs, Alexandra Klein, and especially Simcha Walfish for their invaluable help preparing this chapter.

NOTES

1   John Kaplan, *Cannabis. A Report of the Commission of Inquiry into the Non-Medical Use of Drugs* (Ottawa: Information Canada, 1972).

2   Centre for Addiction and Mental Health, *Cannabis Policy Framework.* (Toronto: CAMH: 2014).

3   "Plenary Statement for the Honourable Jane Philpott, Minister of Health - UNGASS on the World Drug Problem," Health Canada, 20 April 2016, https://www.canada.ca/en/health-canada/news/2016/04/plenary-statement-for-the-honourable-jane-philpott-minister-of-health-ungass-on-the-world-drug-problem.

4   *An Act respecting Cannabis and to amend the Controlled Drugs and Substances Act, the Criminal Code and other Acts*, S.C. 2018, c. 16.

5   Canada, *House of Commons Debates* (30 May 2017) (Hon Jody Wilson-Raybould), 1235.

6   Canada, *House of Commons Debates* (30 May 2017) (Bill Blair), 1235.

7   Task Force on Cannabis Legalization and Regulation, *A Framework for the Legalization and Regulation of Cannabis in Canada* (Ottawa: Health Canada, 2016), 72.

8   Canadian Nurses Association, *Harm Reduction for Non-Medical Cannabis Use* (Ottawa: CNA, 2017).

9   "How is Harm Reduction a Human Rights Issue?," *Health and Human Rights Resource Guide*, accessed 7 August 2018, https://www.hhrguide.org/2014/03/12/how-is-harm-reduction-a-human-rights-issue.

10 *Cannabis Act*, s. 9(5).

11 *Criminal Code* (R.S.C., 1985, c. C-46), s. 163.1(2), s. 270.02.

12 *Controlled Drugs and Substances Act* (S.C. 1996, c. 19), s. 5(3)(b)(i).

13 *Immigration and Refugee Protection Act* (S.C. 2001, c. 27), s. 36(1).

14 Canada, *House of Commons Notice Paper*, "Motions respecting Senate Amendments to Bills," (13 June 2018).

15 *Tobacco and Vaping Products Act* (S.C. 1997, c. 13), s. 43(1)(b).

16 *Tobacco and Vaping Products Act*, s. 45.

17 *Excise Act*, (R.S.C. 1985, c. E-14), s. 233.

18 *Liquor Licence Act*, (R.S.O. 1990, c. L-19), s. 61(3).

19 *Cannabis Act*, Sched. 1, s. 23(2).

20 *Smoke-Free Ontario Act, 2017*, (S.O. 2017), c. 26, Sched. 3, s. 21.

21 Andy Blatchford, "Feds Agree to Give Provinces 75 per cent of Pot Tax Revenues," *Canadian Press*, 11 December 2017, https://www.ctvnews.ca/politics/feds-agree-to-give-provinces-75-per-cent-of-pot-tax-revenues-1.3716551.

22 Jim Bronskill and Kristy Kirkup, "Legal Marijuana Could See Justice Costs Climb, Not Drop, Alberta Premier Says," *Canadian Press*, 22 November 2017, https://globalnews.ca/news/3875179/notley-legal-pot-marijuana-justice-costs-alberta-police/.

23 Canada, *House of Commons Debates*, (13 June 2016) (Bill Blair), 1250.

24 Canada, *House of Commons Debates*, (13 June 2016) (Hon. Jody Wilson-Raybould), 1425.

25 Daniel S. Nagin, "Deterrence in the Twenty-First Century," *Crime and Justice* 42, no. 1 (2013): 199–263.

26 World Health Organization, *Growing Up Unequal: Gender and Socioeconomic Differences in Young People's Health and Well-being* (Copenhagen: Health Behaviour in School-aged Children Study, 2016), 169.

27 Liberal Party of Canada, "Marijuana," Liberal Party of Canada, accessed 7 August 2018, https://www.liberal.ca/realchange/marijuana.

28 Marsha Rosenbaum, "New Perspectives on Drug Education/Prevention," *Journal of Psychoactive Drugs* 48, no. 1 (2016): 28; Amy J. Porath-Waller et al., *What Canadian Youth Think about Cannabis* (Ottawa: Canadian Centre on Substance Abuse, 2013), 22.

29 Anna McKiernan and Katie Fleming, *Canadian Youth Perceptions on Cannabis* (Ottawa: Canadian Centre on Substance Abuse, 2017).

30 Tara Marie Watson and Patricia G. Erickson, "Cannabis Legalization in Canada: How Might 'Strict' Regulation Impact Youth?," *Drugs: Education, Prevention and Policy* (2018) https://doi.org/10.1080/09687637.2018.1482258.

31 Anthony Morgan, "Where Are Black Canadians in the Cannabis Debate?," *Policy Options*, 24 January 2018, http://policyoptions.irpp.org/magazines/january-2018/where-are-black-canadians-in-the-cannabis-debate/.

32 Canada, *House of Commons Notice Paper*, "Motions Respecting Senate Amendments to Bills," (13 June 2018).

33 Manisha Krishnan, "Why Critics Are Saying Justin Trudeau's Weed Bill Is a Continuation of the War on Drugs," *Vice*, 18 April 2017, https://www.vice.com/en_ca/article/xyjyy4/why-critics-are-saying-justin-trudeaus-weed-bill-is-a-continuation-of-the-war-on-drugs-weedweek2017.

34 Evan Solomon, "A Bad Trip: Legalizing Pot Is about Race," *Maclean's*, 14 April 2017, https://www.macleans.ca/politics/ottawa/a-bad-trip-legalizing-pot-is-about-race/.

35 See *An Act to amend the Criminal Code (offences relating to conveyances) and to make consequential amendments to other Acts*, s.c. 2018, c. 21; For

a critique, see *Submissions to the Senate Committee on Legal and Constitutional Affairs* (Ottawa: The Criminal Lawyers' Association, 2018).

36 Reference re Validity of Section 5 (a) *Dairy Industry Act*, [1949] SCR 1, 1948 CanLII 2 (SCC).

37 Reference re *Assisted Human Reproduction Act*, 2010 SCC 61, [2010] 3 S.C.R. 457.

38 Jean Leclair, "Quelle marge de manœuvre pour les provinces ?," *La Presse*, 29 November 2017, http://plus.lapresse.ca/screens/7ea15b02-f440-4817-ad91-e2c82a19432f__7C___o.html.

39 *Cannabis Act*, s. 7.

40 The Attorney General for Ontario v. The Attorney General for the Dominion of Canada (Canada) [1896] UKPC 20, [1896] A.C. 348.

41 R. v. Wholesale Travel Group Inc., [1991] 3 S.C.R. 154, 1991 CanLII 39 (SCC).

42 Christine Campbell and Paul Eid, *La judiciarisation des personnes itinérantes à Montréal : un profilage social* (Québec: La Commission des droits de la personne et des droits de la jeunesse, 2009).

43 *Cannabis Act*, s. 7.

44 Lauren McNabb, "Manitoba Government to Ban Home-grown Cannabis despite Federal Law," *Global News*, 20 June 2018, https://globalnews.ca/news/4285891/manitoba-government-confident-it-has-right-to-ban-home-grown-cannabis/.

45 *The Standing Senate Committee on Legal and Constitutional Affairs: re Bill C-45, Parts 1, 2, 8, 9 and 14*, 2018 Sen. (Ottawa: 2018), statement of Jody Wilson-Raybould, P.C., M.P., Minister of Justice and Attorney General of Canada. https://sencanada.ca/en/Content/SEN/Committee/421/lcjc/53920-e.

46 *Rothmans, Benson & Hedges Inc. v. Saskatchewan*, [2005] 1 S.C.R. 188, 2005 SCC 13.

47 *Rothmans* at 19.

48 Re *AHRA*.

49 *R. v. Malmo-Levine; R. v. Caine*, [2003] 3 S.C.R. 571, 2003 (SCC) 74.

50 Colleen Flood, William Lahey, and Bryan Thomas, "Federalism and Health Care in Canada: A Troubled Romance?," in *The Oxford Handbook of the Canadian Constitution*, eds. Peter Oliver, Patrick Macklem, and Nathalie Des Rosiers (Oxford University Press, 2017), 469.

51 *R v. Crown Zellerbach Canada Ltd.*, [1988] 1 S.C.R. 401, 1988 CanLII 63 (SCC), 33.

52 *Crown v. Zellerbach*, 33.

53 *Charles Russell v. The Queen*, [1882] UKPC 33, [1882] 7 A.C. 829.

54 *R v. Hauser*, [1979] 1 S.C.R. 984, 1979 CanLII 13 (SCC).

55 Peter W. Hogg, *Constitutional Law of Canada: Student Edition* (Toronto: Carswell, 2016), 17.3(d).

56 *Malmo-Levine*, 72.

57 *RJR-MacDonald Inc. v. Canada* (Attorney General), [1995] 3 SCR 199, 1995 CanLII 64 (SCC).

58 *R v. Morgentaler*, [1993] 3 S.C.R. 463, 1993 CanLII 74 (SCC).

59 *R v. Morgentaler*, [1988] 1 S.C.R. 30, 1988 CanLII 90 (SCC).

PART FOUR

Economics and Taxation

10

Technology, Black Markets, and Retail Marijuana

ANINDYA SEN AND ROSALIE WYONCH

Canada is set to legalize recreational consumption and retail of marijuana on 17 October 2018, after almost a century of prohibition. Despite marijuana being illegal, a large and prolific market for recreational marijuana exists in Canada. For decades, government reports have concluded that the prohibition of cannabis was not sufficient to discourage use and that prohibition has a host of negative consequences that outweigh the possible benefits.[1] The main goals of legalization are the protection of public health, restricting youth access, and limiting the illegal market. To be successful in these objectives, the new legal market will have to successfully compete with the illicit market in Canada. The factors that will determine the success of the legal market are price and convenience.

With respect to prices, the federal and provincial governments have agreed to keep taxes low. Further, the federal government has also committed to keep prices at around $10 per gram. However, large black markets are possible even with quite modest tax regimes.[2] Even absent significant legal–illegal price differentials, a thriving black market will exist if it is more convenient for consumers to access than the legal market, or if it provides products that can't be accessed via legal means. Edible marijuana products and concentrated derivatives that contain large quantities of psychoactive ingredients will be legal to consume, but not to sell, at least at the outset of the legal market.[3] This is particularly relevant given the ease in ordering illegal marijuana online, and the ability of firms to deliver products to consumers through Canada Post.[4]

Most research regarding the marijuana market in Canada has focussed on quantifying the size of the market and estimating appropriate tax levels/prices to facilitate competition. Little attention has been paid to the ease of access and range of products available in the black market and the implications for legalization. This chapter investigates various channels of access to the black market and product availability. Our results indicate that continued prohibition of concentrated or derivative marijuana products would not serve the public interest, as these products are easily accessible through illegal channels. In addition, the small number of brick-and-mortar retail outlets in the legal market in some provinces will be unlikely to match the convenience of the black market.

LEGAL MARIJUANA RETAIL IN CANADA

Most provinces have revealed their plans for retail cannabis access, in terms of private sector/government provision as well as the number of stores (Table 1). Quebec, New Brunswick, Nova Scotia, and Prince Edward Island have followed their existing liquor distribution models and opted for government-owned stores. However, while Quebec, New Brunswick, and Prince Edward Island have chosen to establish stand-alone cannabis stores that are separate from outlets selling alcohol, Nova Scotia has decided to sell cannabis and alcohol together from the same outlets. Alberta and British Columbia have created distribution systems that parallel their liquor retail models, with Alberta going for purely private retail stores and British Columbia choosing a hybrid public/private system. In contrast, despite having mainly government-owned liquor stores, Manitoba, Newfoundland, and Saskatchewan have decided to allow private retail sales with liquor control authorities responsible for regulating private stores. With the election of a new government, Ontario decided against its previous plan of having 30 to 40 government-run stores and instead has opted for a purely private retail distribution system. However, private stores will not be operational until 1 April 2019. Till then, legal recreational marijuana will be available only through online orders.[5]

With respect to the exact number of stores during the first year of legalization, Quebec has decided to operate 20 retail stores. Newfoundland, New Brunswick, Nova Scotia, and Prince Edward Island will have 24, 20, 12, and 4 retail locations, respectively.[6] Saskatchewan and Alberta have decided to open 51 and at least 250

Table 10.1: Legal marijuana sales in Canada.

	Wholesale		Retail		Online Retail	
	Crown	Private	Crown	Private	Number of Stores	Online Retail
Alberta[†]		x*		x	250	x
British Columbia	x		x	x	No cap	x
Manitoba[††]		x		x	No cap	x
New Brunswick	x		x		20	x
Newfoundland	x		x	x	24	x
Northwest Territories	x		x	?	Unknown	x
Nova Scotia	x		x		12	x
Nunavut	x		x	x	Unknown	x
Ontario	x**				40	x
Prince Edward Island	x		x		4	x
Quebec	x		x	x	Not announced	x
Saskatchewan		x		x	51	x
Yukon[†††]	x		x	x***	1	x

* Marijuana wholesale will be similar to alcohol: "The AGLC is the legal importer of record for liquor in Alberta. Manufacturers and suppliers sell liquor products to businesses (licensees) through the AGLC. Licensees then sell liquor products to consumers."

* At the time of writing, Ontario was moving forward with a Crown corporation retail monopoly. There were, however, indications that the government may fully or partially privatize retail in the future.

* Private retail will not be immediate with legalization, but is planned for the future. For more information see: https://senate-gro.ca/news/provinces-territories-preparing-cannabis-legalization/

† https://www.cbc.ca/news/canada/calgary/cannabis-retail-regulations-alberta-1.4538542

† https://www.cbc.ca/news/canada/manitoba/cannabis-retail-stores-manitoba-1.4758488

† https://www.yukon-news.com/news/yukon-cancels-tender-for-government-run-cannabis-store-over-size-and-price/

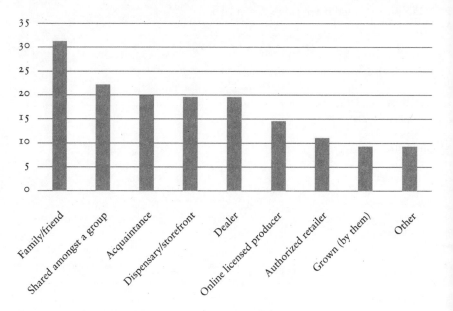

Figure 10.1: Sources of cannabis, % of responses.
Source: National Cannabis Survey (5262), Statistics Canada.

retail outlets, respectively. At the time of writing, British Columbia and Manitoba have not revealed the exact number of stores they are allowing. Finally, all provinces will have online delivery.

Based on these numbers, it is fair to say that Ontario and Quebec are far behind where they should be in terms of allowing consumers to conveniently access marijuana products, especially in relation (on a per capita basis) to Newfoundland, New Brunswick, Saskatchewan, and Alberta. These provinces have shown leadership in terms of their commitment to opening a reasonable number of stores so that consumers may easily access products. If Quebec does not open more stores, it is difficult to see how existing black markets will be stamped out. This is primarily because of the ease with which it is possible to order and obtain a rich variety of products through the internet. The days when it was necessary to locate a street dealer and establish a "safe" relationship are long gone. It is not even necessary to go to an illegal dispensary. It is extremely easy to place orders and have products delivered to residences anonymously through Canada Post.

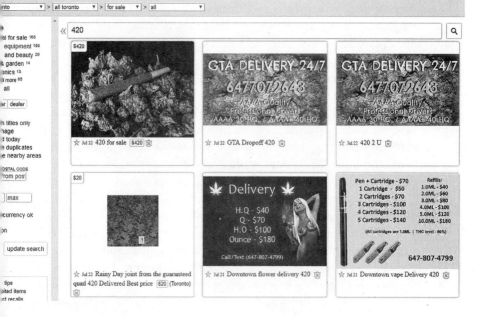

Figure 10.2: Craigslist advertisements for marijuana.
Source: Craigslist.com, Toronto, taken 22 July 2018.

ILLEGAL MARIJUANA RETAIL IN CANADA

The current recreational marijuana market is illegal and mainly supplied through personal acquaintances. Only 14 per cent of cannabis users report accessing their supply through an authorized retailer (see Figure 10.1). After personal connections, dispensaries and storefronts are the most popular way to access marijuana.

Online and physical dispensaries are easily accessible and do not require knowing someone with access to a marijuana supply personally. Some dispensaries do not advertise online, depending instead on word-of-mouth to advertise their business. Advertising online obviously increases the risk of getting caught, as selling marijuana for recreational purposes remains an illegal activity. There are also advertisements for marijuana sales on popular classified ad websites like craigslist.com (see Figure 10.2).

There are also examples of websites that allow prospective consumers to browse different retail storefronts or delivery services and compare products, prices, and customer reviews. A good example is www.weedmaps.com, which can be accessed through the web or its phone app. This technology allows a prospective buyer to locate sellers by neighbourhood and also to choose between storefronts or home delivery. Clicking a specific seller takes the buyer to a separate page (within the website) with different tabs, the most important probably being menu, details, deals, and reviews. The menu tab contains the specific strains offered by the provider, along with corresponding prices for 1/8, 1/4, 1/2, and a full ounce. "Details" contains information on hours of services, store address, and/or text/email address. "Deals" contains information on special promotions, and "Reviews" allows consumers to post ratings on service and product quality. It is also straightforward to search for the best deals for specific strains within a geographic area. And this is but one website. However, it suggests that consumer dissatisfaction with limited legal stores could easily be met through a well-established black market. In addition, the black market supplies more products than will be available through the legal market. Edibles and concentrated marijuana products offer alternate forms of consumption, and the black market has the competitive advantage of being able to supply them.

DISPENSARIES AND DELIVERIES: BLACK MARKET INSIGHTS FROM WEEDMAPS

To investigate the range of products and prices in the black market, we collected data from weedmaps.com in four major cities in Canada: Vancouver, Toronto, Ottawa, and Montreal. In all cities there are over 100 advertised delivery or mail order services. There were 54 dispensary storefronts operating in Toronto and Ottawa alone, more than are planned for the outset of legalization in Ontario (see Table 10.2). Across the country, customer reviews reflect a satisfactory consumer experience, with the average ratings above 4 out of 5 stars for dispensary storefronts. Dispensaries and delivery services also generally provide a large range of products, though there is a lot of variability from outlet to outlet within any city.

To investigate the range of products available and their prices, individual product listings were collected from 20 dispensary storefronts and 8 delivery services advertised on weedmaps.com from 20 to 22 July 2018, yielding 589 observations. The first insight from

Table 10.2: Summary of illicit marijuana retail.

	Storefronts	Rating	# of Reviews	# of Products [min/max]
Toronto	33	4.11	123.8	35.7 [5/151]
Montreal	7	4.17	45	29.6 [8/61]
Ottawa	21	4.29	49.6	61 [12/171]
Vancouver	22	4.65	110.3	93.8 [10/329]
Mail/Delivery	100+*	4.21	24.4	85.9 [1/846]

Data collected from weedmaps.com on 20 July 2018.
*Number of observations used for calculations = 76

the data is that concentrated marijuana products and edibles are widely available. Nineteen of 20 dispensaries and 7 of 8 delivery services listed at least one concentrated marijuana product. Half of dispensaries and 5 of 8 delivery services offered at least one edible marijuana product that won't be available in the legal market.[7] The second insight is that there is substantial variability in price, potency, and product availability in each product category. The most common product listed is dried marijuana flowers ("bud"), but there is substantial variability within this category.[8] Products are listed as "*indica*," "*sativa*," or "*hybrid*," reflecting species of plants in the genus "*Cannabis*." Hybrid indicates a crossbreed between an *indica* and *sativa* "strain." Colloquially, the different strains of cannabis create different psychoactive effects for users: *indica* is associated with physical sedation; *sativa* with invigorating mental effects and minimal physical sensation.[9] Distinct cannabis strains may be biochemically different, but the distinctions commonly applied to the psychoactive effects are not scientifically based:

"There are biochemically distinct strains of Cannabis, but the sativa/indica distinction as commonly applied in the lay literature is total nonsense and an exercise in futility... The degree of interbreeding/hybridization is such that only a biochemical assay tells a potential consumer or scientist what is really in the plant. It is essential that future commerce allow complete and accurate cannabinoid and terpenoid profiles to be available." (Piomelli and Rosso, 2016)

Consumers and sellers of marijuana may hold the belief that different products create different effects, whether they really do or not. Consumers may not actually be getting the strain that is advertised, as there is no way of knowing if the dried bud is actually the strain advertised. When investigating product data, there is more variability in prices by location and purchase amount (many dispensaries offer discounts for larger purchase amounts) than by the of strain (Table 10.3). The price per gram of individual product listing varies significantly and ranges from $6/g to $14/g.

There is also significant variability in the price of different concentrated marijuana products, which vary in potency and quality and may also be associated with a specific strain of marijuana. These products require processing marijuana in different ways, which leads to varying production costs and final consumer prices. Additionally, these products may be associated with a particular brand; for example, oil cartridges likely pair with a specific brand of "vape pen," but hash is more like a commodity product that is consistent regardless of manufacturer.

Edible marijuana products are not included in Table 10.3 due to the complete lack of standardization of potency, servings per package, and products available. For example, the most expensive and potent "gummy" edible in the sample of product listings is $35 and contains ~400 mg of psychoactive ingredients – Tetrahydrocannabinol (THC) and/or Cannabidiol (CBD). The average price of a gummy or a hard candy is only $6.50, with an advertised potency of about 10–20 mg of THC/CBD.

Across all product categories, there are a wide variety of products available in a range of prices. One somewhat surprising aspect of the products advertised on weedmaps.com is the scarcity of repeating products. The most commonly listed marijuana strains are Blue Dream, Death Bubba, Green Crack, and MK Ultra – all with fewer than

Table 10.3: Average prices for various marijuana products, by city ($/g).

		Toronto	Montreal	Vancouver	Ottawa	Delivery
Indica	1 gram	11.05	9.76	10.73	10.46	10.40
	quarter	10.99	8.25	9.62	9.71	9.85
	oz	9.11	7.54	8.66	8.82	8.36
Sativa	1 gram	10.84	9.07	10.86	11.07	10.59
	quarter	10.79	8.11	9.78	10.14	10.26
	oz	9.84	7.71	8.73	9.35	8.89
Hybrid	1 gram	11.41	9.50	10.39	10.23	10.55
	quarter	11.37	8.02	9.25	9.38	9.97
	oz	9.45	7.33	8.45	8.70	8.74
Concentrate	Hash (Afghan, Moroccan, Black)	14.13	18.00	19.67	16.63	17.80
	Oil Cartridge (for vape pen)	60.00	40.00	33.33	53.88	62.50
	Shatter/honey oil	51.67	30.00	56.88	55.00	50.91

Individual product data sourced from weedmaps.com and were collected 20–22 July 2018 (number of observations = 589).

15 listings each. Similarly, there are many listings for unique concentrated or edible products. In the edibles category there are advertisements for THC/CBD capsules, *Rice Crispies* treats, brownies, gummies, sour candies, lollipops, jelly beans, oral sprays, cotton candy, dried apricots, olive/coconut oil, chocolate bars, and even cannabis-infused beverages (tea and lemonade). There is even an advertisement for cannabis-infused dog treats. All told, 59 per cent of the products sampled from weedmaps.com are unique strains or goods.[10]

The lack of repeating products in the edibles and concentrated marijuana categories is somewhat expected. For a dispensary to stock these items, it requires a consistent supplier. The manufacturers of these products are likely small producers, due to the illegality of the activity. Individual producers may choose to pair with a dispensary as their primary retail outlet, resulting in unique product offerings in each dispensary. The lack of repeating strains of marijuana bud is more puzzling, and could be both a strength or a failure in the black market. It could be the case that the different strains don't provide distinct psychoactive effects and the names simply serve to entice consumers. It could be that individual growers create hybrid strains and name them in an attempt to differentiate their products and gain consumers. Our hypothesis is that although consumers hold beliefs about broad strain categories (*sativa*, *indica*, and *hybrid*), individual names do not convey meaningful information. Whether or not their perceptions are accurate, consumers have preferences for a particular strain category.[11] This hypothesis is based on the observation that all dispensaries and online delivery services sampled offer at least one strain in all broad categories.

DISCUSSION AND POLICY IMPLICATIONS

The availability of a wide range of products within each type shows that the black market will readily supply consumers with goods that are unavailable through legal means. In addition, the number of existing retail storefronts and delivery services illustrates the breadth and sophistication of the black market for marijuana in Canada.

In order to minimize the black market, the federal government and Health Canada should immediately develop regulations for edible and concentrated marijuana products. As discussed, these products are already available extensively, which leads to a significant competitive advantage. Edible products are a popular form of cannabis, and consumers may choose to purchase pre-made edibles from the black market instead of using legal cannabis oil to make their own. For example, survey results indicate that 28 per cent of cannabis users consume edibles, 11 per cent consume hashish, 11 per cent use oil cartridges or vape pens, and 8 per cent use solid concentrates (see Figure 10.3). While all these products can currently be purchased through illegal sources, none of them will be available at legal retail locations. Our analysis reveals that the black market in Canada has been diversifying in product offerings and quality ranges. In summary, if the legal market is to be competitive, the federal government should stop prohibiting retail sales of cannabis-derived products.[12]

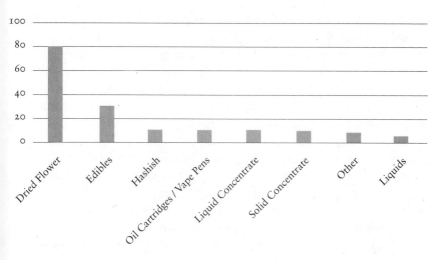

Figure 10.3: Type of products used by cannabis consumers, % of total responses.
Source: National Cannabis Survey (5262), Statistics Canada.

Unfortunately, these are not the only areas in which both federal and provincial governments have offered little guidance. Some of the advertising and product-knowledge regulations surrounding marijuana are unclear. We do know that while products should not be visible to underage individuals, they should be accessible to the general public. While adhering to these rules, New Brunswick and Nova Scotia have made it very clear that convenience and customer satisfaction are extremely important objectives. New Brunswick plans to open "sleek" cannabis stores, while Nova Scotia is also striving towards a consumer-friendly approach by estimating that customers should not have to wait more than fifteen minutes in order to make purchases.[13] In both provinces, customers will be able to browse products on ipads, and there has been some indication that such information will also be made available on the provincial cannabis store websites. This is critical. If sufficient information is unavailable on government websites, consumers will have an incentive to visit black market websites to learn more, which increases the likelihood of illegal purchases, especially if consumers see more interesting products and a greater variety. As noted, these websites also have the functionality of allowing consumers to post reviews and exchange opinions. Therefore, provinces should consider enabling this type of functionality and discussion on their cannabis product websites.

There is a trade-off between giving consumers enough information and restricting that which is misleading or false. Cannabis producers are not allowed to advertise by making any particular therapeutic claims; this protects consumers against information that is either misleading or has not been scientifically validated. Illicit suppliers can make any claims they wish; since they disregard retail and distribution laws, it would be unreasonable to expect them to show restraint with advertising. A functional compromise for the government might be to avoid endorsing any information on cannabis, yet still allow consumers to exchange information with one another.

In a similar vein, illegal dispensaries will also have an advantage over government-mandated stores. Through dispensaries, people are able to see products, perhaps smell them, and inspect their texture, which yields some idea of their quality (or at least perceived quality). This will not be possible in province-run stores, where products will be inaccessible behind frosted glass. In addition, proposed packaging and labelling requirements restrict branding and do not allow the product to be viewed.[14] It is not known how important these features are to consumers in determining cannabis quality. If they are important enough, illegal dispensaries will have a big advantage over province-run stores, and brick-and-mortar retailers will have an advantage over online vendors.[15]

Rather than devoting their resources exclusively to eradicating cannabis black markets, provinces must evaluate these advantages and come up with strategies that offer consumers somewhat comparable experiences through legal purchases. Otherwise, the black market supply will persist.

NOTES

1   Le Dain, *Report of the Canadian Government Commission of Inquiry into the Non-Medical Use of Drugs* (Ottawa: Health Canada, 1972); Nolin, *Report of the Senate Special Committee on Illegal Drugs* (Ottawa: Senate Special Committee on Illegal Drugs, 2002

2   See Anindya Sen and Rosalie Wyonch, *Don't (Over) Tax that Joint, My Friend* (Toronto: C.D. Howe Institute, 2017). Even small increases in taxation can lead to large illegal markets.

3   These products were not included in the *Access to Cannabis for Medical Purposes Regulations*, which governs the medical cannabis market prior to legalization and served as a framework for the new legal recreational market. The federal government will likely develop regulations for derivative, concentrated, and edible marijuana products eventually. They will not be legal for retail purposes at the outset of legalization.

4   For further details please read Colin Perkel, "Pot Black Market Isn't Expected to Disappear even as Marijuana Becomes Legal," *The Canadian Press*, 4 December 2017, https://www.cbc.ca/news/world/pot-cannabis-marijuana-illegal-1.4431419.

5   Ontario Ministry of Finance, "Ontario Announces Cannabis Retail Model," *Government of Ontario*, 13 August 2018, https://news.ontario.ca/mof/en/2018/08/ontario-announces-cannabis-retail-model.html.

6   Jean Lépine, "Ontario's Cannabis-Retail Plan Is a Wreck. But Ford Could Easily Fix It," *Financial Post*, 20 July 2018, https://business.financialpost.com/opinion/ontarios-cannabis-retail-plan-is-a-wreck-but-ford-could-easily-fix-it; Tori Weldon, "Cannabis NB Unveils Sleek, Subdued Look for Pot Shops," *CBC News*, 15 February 2018, https://www.cbc.ca/news/canada/new-brunswick/cannabis-new-brunswick-store-layout-1.4536732; Prince Edward Island Department of Finance, "PEILCC Announces Two Cannabis Retail Outlet Locations," *PEILCC*, 28 February 2018, https://www.princeedwardisland.ca/en/news/peilcc-announces-two-cannabis-retail-outlet-locations.

7   Seven of 8 dispensaries offered edible products, but 2 of these offered only cannabis oils or capsules that have analogous legally accessible products.

8   In our data sample, 397 product listings for bud are associated with 253 distinct strains of marijuana.

9   For more on the "common knowledge" about cannabis strains see "Strains," Lift&Co, https://lift.co/strains?per_page=9&sort=-popularity.

10   We cannot comment about consistency of product availability at each dispensary. It may be the case that a dispensary would offer the same strains/products all the time, but these would not be available elsewhere in the same city. It could also be that an individual dispensary's offerings would be inconsistent over time. Without tracking a particular dispensary over time, it is impossible to know if the uniqueness of product offerings is

intentional market segmentation/differentiation or a failure of the black market to achieve any consistency.

11 It is worth noting that there is very little scientific evidence either in support of or against the hypothesis that biologically distinct species/strains of cannabis create different psychoactive effects. There are multiple psychoactive and bioactive compounds in cannabis, and the interactions and effects of these compounds are just beginning to be understood.

12 The illicit market can offer a wider variety of products, but it may have more difficulty establishing a brand as a signal of consistency or quality, since any brand recognition is inherently associated with openly advertising illegal activity. Legal producers, however, must comply with strict labelling and branding requirements that their illegal counterparts can ignore. It is unclear which market segment will have a better ability to establish brand power with consumers.

13 Please see Paul Palmeter, "Take a Sneak Peek Inside One of Nova Scotia's Legal Pot Stores," CBC News, 18 July 2018, https://www.cbc.ca/news/canada/nova-scotia/nslc-cannabis-legalization-nova-scotia-sneak-peek-1.4751703; Weldon, "Cannabis NB".

14 See Health Canada, *Proposed Approach to the Regulation of Cannabis: Summary of Comments Received During the Public Consultation* (Ottawa: Health Canada, 2018).

15 If legal producers achieve product consistency and some level of brand recognition, consumers may be satisfied with product quality based on that alone. It could be the case that physically inspecting cannabis quality is important to consumers only because of the complete lack of product standardization in the black market. Over time, product consistency and quality could become an advantage to legal producers in the online retail market.

The Legalization of Marijuana and the Remembrance of Things Past[1]

STEPHEN T. EASTON

Canada's choice to legalize marijuana is a bold step. Historically there have been other bold steps, and we need to pay attention to our history. Fundamentally, we will be duplicating the post–World War I experience, during which time Canada instituted and then relaxed alcohol prohibition, while the United States instituted and maintained alcohol prohibition for over a decade. The institutions that we developed during this period provide the directions we could travel and the turns we should avoid in regulating marijuana while the US continues its federal prohibition. Legalization of marijuana consumption is a process, not simply a single event. While we may reduce the footprint of organized crime through legalization, we will also want to minimize the formation of interest groups that will reduce its benefits. Ultimately, as with other prohibited substances that have been legalized, revenue will be a powerful incentive for government to manage the industry. However, too much taxation at the beginning will keep the legal market from reaching its potential.

To see the future more clearly, we begin by looking at Canada's great prohibitions of the past: alcohol, gambling, and increasingly, tobacco. There are, of course, other prohibitions – harder drugs and pornography, to mention two, but regularization of these prohibitions is arguably less imminent in the first case and very difficult in the second. My belief is that increasing government revenue from marijuana will ensure that our regulation of what is currently a vice will become firmly established as a virtue. This perspective should shape our approach to the initial enabling of legalized marijuana. Let us learn from the past and adopt a modern perspective toward what will become the regulatory trajectory of marijuana legalization.

ALCOHOL PROHIBITION IN CANADA

There are two important characteristics of past alcohol regulation that bear on marijuana legalization. Although we had already had experience in producing, regulating, and managing alcohol when we renounced federal prohibition in 1919, the post-regulation period provides some important signals for legalized marijuana. Further, recall that between 1920 and 1933, the United States prohibited alcohol while it was perfectly legal in Canada. This led to a colourful and massively criminal experience in both countries as Canadian rum-runners fed the vast American appetite for illegal booze.

How Did We Get to the Great Prohibition in Canada and the US?

The temperance movement was one of a number of important social movements that arose during the nineteenth century. Prohibition against the vice of alcohol joined restrictions on gambling as one among many important social upheavals. The abolition of slavery and the extension of the franchise to black males, and eventually to women, were among other social restructurings that had their roots in this period of industrialization and market expansion. Socialism, mass immigration, the invention of modern medicine – not to mention the systematic development of academic and industrial chemistry and physics into the early twentieth century – were prominent contemporary developments that bled into the public consciousness. Reduced transportation costs and improved communication technology brought us from the pony express to the telegraph, the telephone, and radio.

The social movements in both the US and Canada produced political action and encouraged national alcohol prohibitions in both countries: in the US from 1919 to 1933 and, in Canada, briefly, from 1918 through 1919. In the latter country, prohibition was more of a response to the need for alcohol for the war effort. In both countries, the anti-alcohol movement was successful in creating legal prohibition, but unsuccessful in retaining it. In Canada a century later, legacies from this period remain. Across the country, state-run liquor stores are ubiquitous. As a testimony to the unique character of our peculiar institutions, Ontario and Quebec are the largest single-source purchasers of alcohol in the world.

The Canadian Experience

In a manner that is quintessentially Canadian, regulation of the *production* of alcohol products is a federal responsibility, while the regulation of distribution and *consumption* of alcohol products is a provincial one. This division of responsibilities helps to explain our early–twentieth century stagger into national prohibition. New Brunswick was the first Canadian province to prohibit consumption of alcohol, in 1851, although it lasted only until 1856. By 1878, Parliament allowed any municipality to hold a plebiscite to prohibit local consumption, and many did. Since it was a federal responsibility, of course production was still permitted. A national referendum in favour of prohibition passed in 1898, but the government decided not to act, since the majority was slim, and the province of Quebec had voted strongly against it. During World War I, the federal government had two cracks at prohibition. The first came in 1916, the second more emphatically in March 1918 under the *War Measures Act*. Federal repeal of prohibition came at the end of 1919, but aside from Quebec, the provinces continued to restrict consumption into the 1920s and in some cases beyond. This was also the period in which liquor control boards were established and most provincial governments began receiving alcohol-related revenue. Table 11.1 identifies the pattern of Canadian alcohol prohibitions. As is apparent from the table, the provinces took their own paths to ending prohibition.

So how did Canadians change production, seeing that consumption was both regulated and illegal in many provinces? Recall that production prohibition ended in 1919 – the federal prohibition. Even while provinces could regulate and curtail the use of alcohol domestically, there was a large and lucrative market for "illegal" liquor in the US. And this is why the analogy of the repeal of prohibition with current marijuana legalization is apt.

The activity of "rum-running" was highly profitable and sometimes highly dangerous. Alcohol from Canada poured into the United States. The two coasts, Montreal, and the Windsor–Detroit border were infinitely porous. Sadly, there is little systematic evidence of the amount of alcohol that moved between Canada and the US, but all accounts suggest that both quantities and values were substantial. Organized crime flourished in the United States during the "roaring

Table 11.1*: Provincial alcohol prohibitions in Canada.

	Year Begun	Year Ended
Alberta	1916	1923
British Columbia	1917	1921
Manitoba	1916	1921
New Brunswick	1853	1856
	1917	1927
Newfoundland	1917	1924
(joined Canada in 1949)		
Northwest Territories	1874	1891
Nova Scotia	1921	1930
Ontario	1916	1927
Prince Edward Island	1901	1948
Quebec	1919	1919
Saskatchewan	1917	1925
Yukon	1918	1920

*There are a host of caveats with the dates in the table as some regulations allowed wine and beer consumption, some restricted locations of consumption, and so forth. References: Stevenson, Chapter VII, and http://www.thecanadianencyclopedia.ca/en/article/prohibition/

twenties," and Canadians were willing and able suppliers of contraband liquor. Gervais provides a wealth of detail about Canadian provisioning of alcohol to the US from Windsor, and others provide details about trafficking elsewhere in Canada.[2]

REVENUE FROM ALCOHOL SALES

Modern revenue from alcohol is substantial. The provinces and the federal government both tax it. Table 11.2 indicates the scale of revenue that accrues to both levels of government.

Table 11.2: Canadian net revenue from alcohol in 2014.

	Provincial Net Liquor Income	Federal Liquor Revenue	Per Capita Provincial	Per Capita Federal
	Millions	Millions	$	$
Alberta	766	218	197	53
British Columbia	935	221	206	48
Manitoba	282	56	225	44
New Brunswick	166	27	220	36
Newfoundland	161	30	305	56
Northwest Territories	25	3	574	69
Nova Scotia	228	42	241	44
Nunavut	1	0	33	9
Ontario	1,817	547	135	40
Prince Edward Island	20	7	136	46
Quebec	1,033	337	128	41
Saskatchewan	244	54	225	48
Yukon	9	3	254	73
Canada	5,687	1,544		
Total Revenue		7,231		

Source: Statistics Canada Cansim: Table 1830025.

To my mind it is most important to prevent what took place after prohibition ended in Canada but remained in the US. Initially, Canada treated alcohol production and export as legal even when it went to the US. By 1927, US complaints and stronger US enforcement reduced the easy flow of alcohol across the frontier. The illegal providers to the US continued successfully to provide legal alcohol in Canada and were given a pass on past behaviour once prohibition ended in the US. Furthermore, rum-runners and gangsters became scions of the new community. Will the Prince of Pot, Marc Emery, be rehabilitated and join respectable society in the same way that Bronfman, Molson, Reifel, and others did?[3] At least one brand touts its past illegal production in advertising.[4] In Canada's history, Seagram's, Molson, and Carling O'Keefe are a few examples of rum-running brand names that are still present in one form or another.

This is one of the serious considerations that make our legalization dicey. Although Canadian companies are producing legal medical marijuana for world markets, I cannot believe that Canadian law enforcement will permit legal export of marijuana to the US if it remains illegal there, at least federally. Will the law be silent? Or will the federal government interdict marijuana shipments to the US, as it was encouraged to do in the late 1920s? How Canadian governments will manage the US federal prohibition and the legalization of marijuana by an increasing number of states will be a delicate dance, considering the current national administration's hostility toward at least some aspects of normal Canadian trade.

Consequently, the production and distribution of marijuana to the US will be remarkably similar to that of alcohol after prohibition ended in Canada and began in the US, albeit with competition from legal US producers. Canadians will have a greater legal supply, some of which may drift south, or those who produce and distribute marijuana illegally today will continue to ply their trade. Leaving aside the potentially profound ramifications of a thickening border for legal trade[5] and mobility, Canadian authorities will be drawn into enforcing a prohibition against exporting to the US, and we will simply be reliving the experience of the 1920s.

GAMBLING

The history of gambling in Canada is an interesting one. Table 11.3 recounts a crude history of the legalization of various aspects of gambling including bingo, horse racing, the "numbers racket" (known today as "the lottery" now that it's legal, casinos, and slot machines. The scale of the revenue gives some insight into the resources provided to organized crime prior to legalization. What has become apparent is that there has been a progressive liberalization of legislation to include more types of gambling and more diverse venues. Interestingly, revenue from gambling is now of the same order of magnitude as the revenue from alcohol.

Table 11.3: Gambling legality in Canada.

1892	All gambling (basically) is made illegal
1900	Bingo and small religious or charitable games are legalized
1910	Horse race betting at the track is legalized
1925	Fair parks are allowed to run games of chance
1969	Provinces are allowed to regulate lotteries and license other forms of gambling
1974	A lottery helps to finance the Montreal Olympics
1985	Provinces gain exclusive control of gambling
1986	First venues for gambling (casinos) open
1989	First private-destination casinos open
since	Slot machines
	Slot machines at racetracks
	Video slot machines and lottery terminals

Source: Derevensky and Meredith Gillespie (2005).

Government Revenue from Gaming

Government revenue from modern gambling is substantial. In 2014–15, BC's net revenue to government was $1.25 billion, while Ontario's was $2.3 billion. Although we continue to hear the obligatory remarks about the social harm created by problem gambling, the expansion of the gaming industry suggests there is little chance that gambling will become less legal. It is a commonplace observation that governments are addicted to revenue, and the data are consistent with this observation. Table 11.4 reports the revenue from gaming in the 2015 fiscal year.

One of the biggest questions facing regulators in the next few years is how the provinces will act to protect their revenue in the

Table 11.4: Net gaming revenue to government, 2015.

	(millions of $)
Alberta	1,528
British Columbia	1,304
Manitoba	335
New Brunswick	153
Newfoundland	146
Nova Scotia	128
Ontario	2,240
Quebec	1,227
Saskatchewan	371
Canada	7,529

Source: Statistics Canada Cansim: Table 3850042.

face of online gambling, since most sites are outside Canada and outside most regulatory enforcement. Since online gambling offers at least equal odds as the domestic regulated industry, the draw will be strong. Although in the future, it is certainly possible that similar pressures from legal marijuana from abroad will continue.

TOBACCO

Tobacco taxation is like prohibition in reverse, moving from legal to illegal. Tobacco's association with cancer and other ailments has gradually tightened the screws on consumption. Although the numbers are a little less certain than official statistics suggest, it seems clear that smoking prevalence has decreased. As you can see in Table 11.5, from 1999 to 2013, the number of smokers fell by nearly 58 per cent.

Table 11.5: Smoking prevalence in Canada (by percentage of the population).

1999	25.2
2000	24.4
2001	21.7
2002	21.4
2003	20.9
2004	19.6
2005	18.7
2006	18.6
2007	19.2
2008	17.9
2009	17.5
2010	16.7
2011	17.5
2012	16.1
2013	14.6

Source: Table 2.1. Tobacco Use in Canada: Patterns and Trends, 2015 Edition. PROPEL Centre for Population Health Impact. www.tobaccoreport.ca accessed 14 March 2017.

Regardless of the decrease in the number of smokers, tobacco revenue has remained robust (see Table 11.6), with each of the provinces benefitting (see Table 11.7).

What is striking when looking at Tables 11.5 and 11.6 is that even though smoking in the population has decreased by 58 per cent over the period, tobacco revenues have increased by 11 per cent in the past 8 years. Governments are clearly increasing their take even as consumption declines.

Table 11.6: Canadian tobacco revenue: 2008–15.

	(measured in millions of 2016 $)
2008	7,438
2009	7,786
2010	8,467
2011	8,128
2012	7,877
2013	8,306
2014	8,353
2015	8,264

Source: Revenue from Cansim: Table 3850042 and population from v466668
CPI – http://www.statcan.gc.ca/tables-tableaux/sum-som/l01/cst01/econ46a-eng.htm.

THE LEGACIES OF ALCOHOL, GAMBLING, AND TOBACCO PROVIDE A TRAJECTORY FOR REGULATION

We have at best a patchwork of legislation governing alcohol consumption. While some alcohol may be available in province-run stores or even some selected private stores, its general distribution as a product like any other is still far away. One hundred years has seen gradual erosion of the prohibition mentality about alcohol, and to a lesser extent, about gambling. In another 100 years Canadians in some provinces will probably be able to buy alcohol at the supermarket or the corner store – as you can today in large US states like California, New York, Illinois, and Texas, to name just a few. Such is the power of tradition – and even more important, the ossification of special interests – that it will take time for Canadian regulation to change. These interests are following today's rules, and any change may imperil their business. While the public may have moved on, changing the rules will harm companies that have simply been doing business under the current regulations and can be ruined

Table 11.7: Provincial and federal tobacco tax revenues, 2015.

	(millions of $)
Alberta	980
British Columbia	734
Manitoba	256
New Brunswick	149
Newfoundland	159
Nova Scotia	217
Ontario	1,226
Quebec	1,080
Saskatchewan	264
Prince Edward Island	33
Federal	3,007
Total Provincial*	5,141
Total Federal and Provincial	8,148

*Includes Northwest Territories, Nunavut, and Yukon (not shown).
Source: Cansim: Table 3850042.

by real legalization. If any store can sell alcohol, provincial liquor stores, wine shops, and the like will also be at risk. It speaks to the strength of the current players that they have been successful at limiting access.

It is not a matter of government revenue over all else, even for governments. There are peculiarly Canadian institutions for which the government clearly forgoes revenue even while inflicting higher prices on the most vulnerable Canadians. We have more than 100 marketing boards for commodities from eggs to pork to maple syrup, but the milk market boards are in some ways the poster child for poor policy. Because of these boards, simple creatures of legislation, the price on the Alberta exchange (for example) of the right to produce milk from one cow is roughly $40,000, which then gets rolled into remarkably higher milk prices than exist in many other countries.[6]

Marijuana is a bit different. In the beginning there are many fewer entirely legal players. Once the first legislation is in place, however, there will quickly be a new set of sellers with a vested interest in the status quo. This "tyranny of the status quo," which has been apparent from liquor to milk, faces the developers of any disruptive technology that may benefit the consumer. Take the experience of trying to bring Uber into the Vancouver market as an example of this kind of intransigence. We need design legislation to prepare transparently for changes in the future so that we are not faced at each step with a debilitating struggle against recently established interests. Consequently, the government (whether federal or provincial) will hopefully plan a trajectory of legalization. This trajectory should allow entrepreneurs to plan for a longer term environment, which will be discussed below.

Of course, if the US were to legalize marijuana, then we had better decide how to manage it all. Tariffs? Quotas? We will surely have entrenched interests here at home. Can a marijuana marketing board be far from mind?

THE REVENUE FROM MARIJUANA

We have several examples of revenue arising from marijuana sales in a semi-legal environment. I call it semi-legal, since the US federal government still regards marijuana as illegal – just try to declare it at the border – while many states have either licensed medical marijuana or legalized it outright under state law.

Let us consider what has happened in Colorado, which has a tax system that discriminates between medical and recreational consumption. The tax rates include a 2.9 per cent sales tax on all marijuana, a 10 per cent retail tax on recreational marijuana, and an excise tax of 15 per cent. Licensing and fees comprise another 6–7 per cent of the total tax burden. Revenue has increased steadily, from $67 million in 2014 to $130 million in 2015, to $247 million in fiscal 2017.[7]

There has been a steady increase in revenue since legalization in 2014. Furthermore, albeit some figures are speculative, total sales of $996 million in 2015 increased to $1.5 billion in 2017, and are forecast to increase by 11 per cent every year through 2020.[8]

How Might this Experience Be Translated into Canadian Dollars?

The 2014 data from Colorado upon legalization suggest total state demand, including visitors, was 130 metric tons (for the population over 21).[9] This estimate is very high relative to my 2004 estimate of the marijuana consumption in Canada (159 metric tons), since the population of Colorado in 2014 was 3.363 million, compared to a population of 30.7 million in Canada in 2000. Reduced to the most simple terms, consumption per capita in Colorado is 22.7 grams per head, while updating Canadian (speculative) consumption to 2014 puts it at 11.7 grams per head. So, leaving aside the ages of consumers, it appears that marijuana consumption in Colorado is significantly higher than what at least one pre-legalization estimate (mine) would suggest.[10]

Washington state has a larger population – 7.06 million (2014) than Colorado, and has a 37 per cent excise tax on marijuana as well as state and local taxes. Leaving aside some exempted transactions, sales in fiscal 2017 were $1.37 billion (US$) and have been rising throughout the year. Taxes collected amounted to (US$) $315 million.[11] Production in Washington state is now substantial: about 22,000 pounds monthly in 2017.[12] Canada has about five times the population of Washington. If Canada had had this tax regime – which is, at least initially, similar to the one being proposed by the federal and some provincial governments – it would suggest total marijuana revenue in the neighbourhood of $1.6 billion, to be split as Canadian politicians negotiate.

CONSUMPTION TODAY AND TOMORROW

Arguments about enhanced levels of consumption and the damage it causes do not impress me. Marijuana is widely consumed today; 12 per cent of all Canadians (over the age of 15) are using and 25.5 per cent of youth between the ages of 15 and 24 have used in the past year.[13] Almost everyone under the age of 60 will have either personal experience with marijuana or know someone who has used it. With 44 per cent of Canadians over the age of 15 already having had experience with marijuana, 5.7 per cent of those between grades 5 and 7 having used, and with so many people able and permitted to produce it in modest quantities, there is simply no way it will not be ubiquitously available to all ages.[14]

There may be additional medical costs. There will be educational costs. These will now have a greater opportunity for success, since the product will be legal. It points toward a more sensible future in which consumption may be treated as an issue of public health rather than a criminal matter, thus paralleling what may be viewed as at least some success with tobacco consumption.

One of the issues right now is the location of marijuana points of sales. The provinces will take different paths consistent with the diversity of sales practices for alcohol. The difficult and substantive issue the federal government faces is how to monitor legal and illegal production. And while the provinces will be concerned with illegal sales and distribution, illegal production must also be a major concern for the federal government. The US is unlikely to legalize marijuana nationally in the near future. Although Canadian rum-runners did well for nearly a decade in the 1920s, legal marijuana production will surely hide illegal production more efficiently than when all production was illegal. And we know how successful that has been; although hardly competing with Mexico, Canadian marijuana historically has moved to the US in substantial quantities.[15]

SAVINGS FROM THE JUSTICE SYSTEM

There are two ways Canadians can benefit from the impact of legalization on the justice system. First, there are and have been many convictions for marijuana-related offences in Canada. In 2016, there were 44,301 arrests for possession, 5,825 for trafficking, 3,014 for production and 1,600 for the import or export of cannabis. These constitute 57 per cent of all 95,417 drug-related incidents and about 3 per cent of all criminal incidents.[16] Consequently, many Canadians will avoid contact with the justice system as a result of simple marijuana offences. Second, if we take the ratio of marijuana-related offences relative to the total number of offences and prorate it over the expenses of the entire justice system, including policing, judiciary, and prisons, we find a modest savings of $660 million. This is not a precise calculation, but it illustrates the order of magnitude of the savings. (Since there will be enforcement costs associated with the new regime, this figure is likely an overestimate.)

THE WAY FORWARD

For the way forward, I want to suggest something completely different. I think we should begin by taxing marijuana only at the rate of the HST, or GST and PST, and possibly local business licenses. That is, initially we should forgo any explicit excise tax on marijuana *per se*. This means an effective rate of between 5 per cent in Alberta, the NWT, and the Yukon, and 15 per cent in Manitoba and the provinces east of Ontario. Although I think that getting provinces to agree on a common tax rate is as likely to be as successful as herding cats, there are several good reasons for doing this.

First, we want to draw as much consumption and production into the legal market as we possibly can. Organized crime has long feasted on the revenues from providing illegal marijuana to an eager market.[17] Since marijuana is the low-hanging fruit for organized crime, we can deny criminals this revenue. To me this is the overarching benefit from legalization. The easy money denied to organized crime is important; insofar as it forces criminals to turn to the next best alternative, the activities they choose will be more expensive for them to exploit and less lucrative.

Second, because they have been so widely violated, the statutes against marijuana legislation have weakened the respect for law and its application. Let us make every effort to draw consumers (and producers) into the legal system, which can act properly as a guardian of standards, transparency, and protection for consumers and producers.

Third, illegal marijuana has given many Canadians criminal records. After legalization, there will be future generations of Canadians, especially youth, who will no longer face interaction with the justice system. Low taxes will encourage the use of the legal market.

Fourth, there is at least a case to be made that the justice system will save money as more people use legal marijuana rather than the alternative.

Fifth, there will be an increase in government revenue from legal marijuana even at modest levels of taxation. How much that revenue will be depends on the details of the legislation, including tax rates, accessibility, and the rules governing distribution, such as advertising. I expect that these rules will change, much as rules have changed with other illegal substances in the past. One feature that has not been explored in the literature is the possibility that marijuana use may have an effect on the markets for tobacco and alcohol (among others). It is an open question whether marijuana use increases or decreases the demand for these products and consequently revenue. Current behaviour while marijuana is illegal may not be a good guide to future consumption patterns. Happily, in a few years we are likely to have real data to guide our analysis.

I am indebted to Dr. Malcolm Easton for comments; errors remain mine.

NOTES

1   This paper is drawn from a larger paper tentatively titled "The Legalization of Marijuana."

2   Gervais, Charles Henry (Marty), *The Rumrunners: A Prohibition Scrapbook (30th anniversary edition)* (Windsor: Biblioasis, 2009); William H. Hagelund, *House of Suds: The History of Beer Brewing in Western Canada* (Surrey: Hancock House, 2003); Gord Steinke, *Mobsters and Rumrunners of Canada* (Edmonton: Folklore Publishing, 2004).

3   Hagelund, *House of Suds*.

4   "Canadian Club advertisement," YouTube, accessed 2 July 2018, https://www.youtube.com/watch?v=r93Oq6VDR_0; "Sleeman advertisement, 2015," YouTube, https://www.youtube.com/watch?v=JnSbL6ZlGiM.

5   Prem Gandhi and Neal Duffy, "Extra Border Security and Its Impact on Canada-United States Trade and Investment: A Focus on the Quebec-Northern New York Corridor," *Journal of Eastern Township Studies* 41 (Fall 2013): 123–42.

6   "Alberta Milk Quota Exchange," Alberta Milk, accessed 2 July 2018, https://secure.albertamilk.com/secure/abm/quotainfo/quotaprices.aspx.

7   "Marijuana Tax Data," Colorado Department of Revenue, accessed 2 July 2018, https://www.colorado.gov/pacific/revenue/colorado-marijuana-tax-dat

8   Miles K. Light, *The Economic Impact of Marijuana Legalization in Colorado* (Denver: Marijuana Policy Group, 2016), 22.

9   Miles K. Light, *Market Size and Demand for Marijuana in Colorado* (Denver: Colorado Department of Revenue, 2014), 32.

10 Stephen T. Easton, "Marijuana Growth in British Columbia," *Public Policy Sources* 74 (June 2004): 40.

11 "Sales and Tax Grouped by Fiscal Year," Washington State Liquor and Cannabis Board, accessed 2 July 2018, https://data.lcb.wa.gov/Sales/Sales-and-Tax-Grouped-by-Fiscal-Year-Chart-/g9n8-n3mg.

12 "Dashboard Usable Production by Month Chart," Washington State Liquor and Cannabis Board, accessed 2 July 2018, https://data.lcb.wa.gov/Production/Dashboard-Usable-Production-by-Month-Chart/6fks-6k8d

13 Canadian Centre for Substance Use and Addiction, *Canadian Drug Summary: Cannabis* (Ottawa: CCSA, 2018), http://www.ccdus.ca/Resource%20Library/CCSA-Canadian-Drug-Summary-Cannabis-2018-en.pdf.

14 Canadian Centre for Substance Use and Addiction, *Canadian Drug Summary: Cannabis*.

15 Easton, "Marijuana Growth in British Columbia"; "Canada-United States Border Drug Threat Assessment, October 2004," Public Safety Canada, last modified 2 December 2015, https://www.publicsafety.gc.ca/cnt/rsrcs/pblctns/archive-us-cnd-brdr-drg-2004/index-en.aspx#a06.

16 "Incident-based crime statistics, by detailed violations," Statistics Canada, Table: 35-10-0177-01, https://www150.statcan.gc.ca/t1/tbl1/en/tv.action?pid=3510017701.

17 Easton, "Marijuana Growth in British Columbia," 40.

12

Cannabis Legalization: Lessons from Alcohol, Tobacco, and Pharmaceutical Industries

MICHAEL DEVILLAER

All living Canadians were born after the creation of our alcohol, tobacco, and pharmaceutical industries. The legalization of cannabis, representing the emergence of a new legal recreational drug industry, is an unprecedented event in their lives. The end of cannabis prohibition has been welcomed by human rights and justice advocates and celebrated by users of the drug who have experienced, or lived in fear of, the personal consequences of prohibition. Legalization has also been embraced by those who see an opportunity for financial benefit from a new commercial drug industry serving both therapeutic and recreational use.

However, many Canadians are apprehensive. A 2016 Nanos poll showed that 57 per cent have at least minor concerns or questions, or are unsure.[1] Some have major concerns. Clinicians are troubled about the impact on the welfare of their patients, particularly those with drug-related problems and/or mental health challenges. Concerns include the conduct of the cannabis industry itself. In an Environics Communications survey of Canadians' level of trust for twenty business sectors to "do what is right for Canada, Canadians, and our society," the cannabis industry was ranked dead last, behind even recently controversial sectors such as energy and resources, banks, and the pharmaceutical sector.[2]

In the face of these concerns, the government has insisted that Canadians should not worry because, in contrast to the illegal trade in cannabis, a new legal trade will be strictly regulated like our alcohol, tobacco, and pharmaceutical industries.

This chapter will explore the question of whether Canadians should worry about the commercial legalization of cannabis. To responsibly address this question, it must be broken down into three more manageable ones:

1   How well have existing drug industries prevented harm from the use of their products?
2   How might the legalization of a formerly illegal drug impact its use and misuse?
3   How well has government regulation balanced the pursuit of revenue with the protection of public health?

HOW WELL HAVE EXISTING DRUG INDUSTRIES PREVENTED HARM FROM THE USE OF THEIR PRODUCTS?

The alcohol industry is a legal, government-regulated, commercial drug industry. Alcohol misuse in Canada is a public health crisis. In 2014, alcohol was responsible for 87,911 hospitalizations, 35,777 individuals absent from the workplace, and 14,827 premature deaths associated with 244,144 years of lost life. The total economic cost was $14.6 billion.[3]

The tobacco industry is a legal, government-regulated, commercial drug industry. Tobacco use in Canada is a public health crisis. In 2014, tobacco was responsible for 145,801 hospitalizations, 39,727 individuals absent from the workplace, and 47,562 premature deaths associated with 326,870 years of lost life. The cost to Canada's economy was $12 billion.[4]

It should be emphasized that, for both alcohol and tobacco, these are annual figures, the magnitude of which has been occurring for decades. The annual levels of harm actually increased between 2007 and 2014.[5]

The pharmaceutical industry is another legal, government-regulated, commercial drug industry. Federal Health Minister Ginette Petitpas-Taylor is the third consecutive Canadian minister of health to declare opioid overdose deaths a public health crisis in this country.[6]

Public Health Agency of Canada has released counts of opioid-related deaths at 2,861 for 2016 and 3,987 for 2017. Both figures are considered incomplete.[7] The opioid crisis is not restricted to Canada, having reached epidemic proportions in the US and parts of Europe as well. Nor is the problem restricted to opioids. The US Center for Disease Control has declared the misuse of prescribed medications in general as "an epidemic" in that country.[8]

In summary, we have three legal, government-regulated, commercial drug industries and we have three public health crises. Clearly, legal drug industries are no panacea against harm to the public's health in epidemic proportions.

HOW MIGHT THE LEGALIZATION OF A FORMERLY ILLEGAL DRUG IMPACT ITS USE AND MISUSE?

We can gain some insight into likely trajectories for a new legal drug industry from our other, longer-lived, legal drug industries. The key determinants of the overall impact of legalization of cannabis will be the individual impacts of several factors:

- granting people legal permission to use the drug
- increased product promotion (e.g., advertising, marketing, event sponsorships, celebrity endorsements)
- increased ease of access
- the relationship between the prevalence of use and the prevalence of associated harm

Impact of Legal Permission

Many Canadians have not waited for permission from their government to use cannabis. Nonetheless, a 2015 Forum Poll suggests that, after legalization, new users will number approximately 900,000.[9] The Office of the Parliamentary Budget Officer provided a more conservative projection of 600,000 new users.[10] Given some margin for error, we can probably expect somewhere between half a million and a million new users following legalization.

Impact of Product Promotion

A near-decade of research has shown that more promotion of alcohol is associated with more consumption.[11] This is true for use by children and youth as well.[12] The same relationship has also been shown to hold for tobacco.[13] There is no reason to believe that this relationship will not be found for cannabis, another conclusion reached by the Office of the Parliamentary Budget Officer.[14] In a meeting in February 2017, the federal government's Cannabis Secretariat confirmed for this author that a desire to advertise was the major issue raised by lobbyists representing the cannabis industry.[15] This is not surprising, given the potential of advertising to be a key factor in market expansion.

Thus, all sources indicate that we should expect various forms of product promotion to increase aggregate cannabis use among the Canadian population.

Impact of Ease of Access

A decade of research has shown that easier access to a drug is associated with more use of that drug in the population. This is true for alcohol[16] and for tobacco.[17] The same relationship is apparent with increased access to opioid medications. Again, there is no reason to expect that cannabis will be different. Legal cannabis retail outlets will have several advantages over illegal ones. Legal outlets will operate with no fear of a police raid. They will be local and visible at fixed locations and with regulated hours of operation. They will also provide an assured supply. In sum, a legal, safer, more reliable and convenient supply relative to illegal sources should provide easier access to cannabis and increase aggregate use.

Increases in aggregate use following legalization also seem likely upon consideration of use by the following sub-populations under the facilitative forces described above.

- current cannabis users will continue to use
- some current users will use more often
- some former users will resume use
- some lifetime abstainers will try it and some of these will continue to use it

Thus, all sources and lines of reasoning suggest that aggregate use of cannabis will increase upon commercial legalization.

Impact of the Prevalence of Use on the Prevalence of Related Problems

About one in ten (10.5 per cent) cannabis users experience serious problems related to their use,[18] meaning that approximately nine out of ten do not. Accordingly, some people might be inclined to ask why there should be concern about increases in use. However, research on the most comparable recreational drug, alcohol, consistently demonstrates that increases in prevalence of population use is correlated with increases in the prevalence of related problems in the population[19] (it is also apparent that increases in use of tobacco and opioids would also lead to increases in their respective expressions of illness and/or death). There is no reason to believe that the same dynamic will not prevail for cannabis. As the number of users increases, the number of people represented by 10.5 per cent will also increase. This translates into a variety of increased challenges at both individual and societal levels. We could expect harm to more individual users, to their significant others, to co-workers, and to total strangers who perhaps have the misfortune of being in the path of a cannabis-impaired driver. We could also expect more demand for treatment, longer waiting lists, and delayed treatment. In sum, the prevalence of harm to individuals and to society in general would be expected to increase.

The exact impact of cannabis legalization on public health problems in Canada remains uncertain. However, drawing upon the information available from our other legal, regulated, commercial drug industries, the most likely scenario can be expressed as follows:

legal permission + increased promotion + easier access =
increased aggregate use = increased aggregate harms

It is also reasonable to expect that as harms increase, so too will adverse economic impacts.

HOW WELL HAS GOVERNMENT REGULATION BALANCED THE PURSUIT OF REVENUE WITH THE PROTECTION OF PUBLIC HEALTH?

The Alcohol Industry

Reports of the alcohol industry and its regulation by government spanning two decades (1980 to 2000) have documented industry and regulatory indifference to public health and the rule of law.[20] The authors describe smuggling operations involving hundreds of legal drinking establishments in Canada, industry-launched disinformation campaigns to sway public opinion and policy, aggressive lobbying, use of charitable donations to leverage permissive policy by threatening to withdraw those donations, and bribery of elected officials with campaign contributions.

Within the realm of regulatory permissiveness and failure, the authors report a trend of increased commercialization and increased liberalization of restrictions on alcohol, fewer advertising restrictions, industry self-regulation of advertising practices, and the continued absence of health warnings on alcohol product packaging. This general trend towards liberalization has occurred despite well-communicated evidence linking increased consumption to increased problems.

The early years of this millennium have seen new causes for concern emerge. One of the principal promises of a regulated trade relative to an illegal one is product quality and safety at retail. However, recent events challenge this promise. In 2011, the Ontario government's alcohol retail monopoly, the Liquor Control Board of Ontario (LCBO), was found to have unknowingly sold at least 221 bottles of low-quality, counterfeit wine from the shelves of its outlets. Upon investigation by the York Region police department, several individuals were arrested and charged with fraud.[21] An interesting facet of this case is that the fraud was not detected through government regulation, but rather by sophisticated consumers.

Consumers, rather than regulators, have also been instrumental in detecting production failures in legitimately produced alcohol products. In 2017, the LCBO recalled bottles of Bombay Sapphire London Dry Gin and Georgian Bay Vodka which, when returned by customers, were found to contain 77 per cent and 80 per cent alcohol by volume, respectively, as opposed to the intended 40 per cent as labelled.[22]

The promise of propriety of a legal trade is also called into question when licensed companies and/or their executives collude with criminal elements. Such was the case when, in 2015, a Montreal winery sold over two million bottles of its wine on the contraband market, avoiding the payment of at least $14 million in provincial taxes in the process. The former CEO of an Ontario winery was among the twelve individuals arrested on charges of fraud, conspiracy to commit fraud, and recycling the proceeds of crime.[23]

An important indicator of regulatory due diligence is the extent to which government adopts evidence-based policies that reduce harm. Such policies include:

- charging higher taxes on alcohol products
- decreasing maximum blood-alcohol level allowed while driving from .08 to .05
- setting the legal blood-alcohol level to zero for new young drivers
- increasing the minimum drinking age
- providing Safer Bars training for staff and managers
- delivery by health care professionals of brief interventions for early-stage alcohol problems.[24]

An analysis of the extent to which these proven policies and other promising practices have been adopted by Canadian provinces found that no province performed well. Ontario scored the highest at 56 per cent, while the national average was 47 per cent.[25]

Another study[26] assessed the impact of adopting better alcohol policies in Canada, specifically, what would be the impact on the amount of alcohol-related harm and its cost? The study found that each year in Canada, there would be 800 fewer preventable deaths, with a reduction of 26,000 years of lost life. There would also be 88,000 fewer acute-care days spent in hospital. The economic benefit to the Canadian economy would be $1 billion. The authors emphasize that these reductions in harm and cost would be realized on an annual basis. They also emphasize that because of the way the estimates were calculated, they should be considered conservative. In other words, the return on investment is likely to be even greater than reported.

These compelling findings were submitted to government, along with additional warnings against increased liberalization of alcohol policy[27] and a call for a renewed, comprehensive, public health–based alcohol policy.[28] Undaunted by the data, neither industry nor governments in Canada have made policy changes to reduce harm. The Ontario government has implemented even higher-risk practices – introducing beer and expanding wine retail in grocery stores.[29] This move is inconsistent with advice from the expert organizations that government funds to obtain guidance on such matters. In contrast, the alcohol industry continues to have a significant impact on shaping government policy in Canada.[30]

Governments in Canada are not alone in their apparent indifference to evidence-based alcohol policy. The same failure has been documented in the US.[31] Nor is there cause for complacency elsewhere. The conduct of the alcohol industry in developing countries has been shown to cause and worsen poverty. The industry exploits poor and illiterate populations with deceptive advertising, and bribes governments for favourable regulation at the expense of human welfare.[32]

The Tobacco Industry

The last half-century has witnessed an epic battle among the tobacco industry, public health authorities, government regulators, and the courts in both Canada[33] and the US.[34] Over the course of this battle, the task of bringing the tobacco juggernaut in line with both the rule of law and aspirations of public health often seemed hopeless.

However, the turn of the century has brought increased cause for optimism. In the 2006 landmark case of the *United States of America vs. Philip Morris USA, Inc.*, Justice Gladys Kessler reviewed hundreds of depositions and thousands of exhibits before submitting her 1,742-page judgement. A couple of passages convey the essence of Kessler's judgement:

> "Defendants have marketed and sold their lethal products with zeal, with deception, with a single-minded focus on their financial success, and without regard for the human tragedy or social costs that success exacted."

> "Over the course of more than 50 years, Defendants lied, misrepresented and deceived the American public, including smokers and the young people they avidly sought as 'replacement' smokers, about the devastating health effects of smoking and environmental tobacco smoke."[35]

The direct relationship between US and Canadian tobacco companies meant that the crimes described by Kessler also occurred in Canada at the same time. In the early 1990s, Canada's three legal tobacco companies were involved in tobacco smuggling, from which government lost billions in unpaid taxes. Along with his verdict of guilt for fraud, conspiracy to commit fraud, possession of the proceeds of crime, deceit, fraudulent misrepresentation, and spoliation, Justice E.F. Ormston described the case as *"...the largest offense of its nature in Canadian history."*[36]

Undaunted by this judgement, the industry continued to engage in smuggling activity. In 2008 and 2010 cases, tobacco companies pled guilty, but no individuals were convicted. The eventual settlements recovered very little of the taxes that were lost. Furthermore, the payment schedules of ten to fifteen years meant that the companies could pass on these costs to their customers with modest price increases. One is challenged to discern an incentive for the industry to modify its conduct.[37] Recent reports confirm that the tobacco industry continues to engage in global smuggling operations and to interfere with attempts to contain this illegal activity.[38]

Most Canadian provinces and territories have launched healthcare cost-recovery actions against Canadian cigarette manufacturers and their foreign parent companies. At the time of writing, only New Brunswick had set a trial date (4 November 2019).[39] Public health advocates worry that in the end we will see additional small, out-of-court settlements and more lost opportunities to reform this industry.[40] The industry does not seem concerned. It continues its opposition to plain packaging,[41] bans on flavourings,[42] increased taxation,[43] and improved safety of e-cigarettes.[44] And governments continue to abide by the interests of this industry. One of the first acts of a newly elected Ontario government, in June 2018, was to block recently passed legislation designed to provide further protections against the effects of tobacco smoke and vapour. The halt came two days before the legislation was to come into force.[45] The struggle to protect the Canadian public from the tobacco industry is far from over.

Globally, like the alcohol industry, the tobacco industry is increasing its efforts in undeveloped countries. In response to this industry's continued opposition to and sabotage of international public health efforts, in 2008 the World Health Organization came to this stark conclusion:

"The tobacco industry is not and cannot be a partner in effective tobacco control."[46]

The Pharmaceutical Industry

In 1996, Purdue Pharma introduced their opioid product OxyContin through an aggressive, misleading marketing campaign to prescribers that led large numbers of pain sufferers to become dependent on the medication.[47] A wave of opioid-related deaths ensued. Eventually, in response to considerable pressure, Health Canada eliminated access to oxycodone-based medications, which prompted a fentanyl replacement. Not only did this fail to curtail legal prescriptions of opioid medications; it also emboldened a contraband market.[48] The crisis spiraled out of control.

A warning about the problem came as early as 2004 from the government of Newfoundland and Labrador's *Oxycontin Task Force Final Report*, which recommended:

"...that Health Canada ensure that pharmaceutical manufacturers use appropriate marketing strategies that include information on the dangers of drug abuse and diversion."[49]

The position of Purdue Canada during much of the crisis was articulated by its president, Mr. John H. Stewart:

"The answer to abuse of prescription medications is greater education and substance-abuse treatment. The answer to diversion is tough law enforcement, not restrictions on patients and physicians who treat them."[50]

This perspective may have been partly responsible for the lack of attention to industry misconduct by government in Canada, where there have been multiple calls for industry reform and improved regulation.[51] In 2015, federal Health Minister Rona Ambrose noted that Health Canada's guidelines allowed it to consider only a medicine's effectiveness for its intended purpose (e.g., painkiller), and not its potential for public health or safety implications.[52] This statement would seem to reflect the systemic low priority in federal regulation of protecting the safety of Canadians.

In 2016, Health Canada released its *Action on Opioid Misuse*.[53] While it contained some promising provisions, important interventions were conspicuous by their absence. There are no recommendations for improving the regulation of industry practices related to introducing a new drug to market. Nor is there any provision for holding a company accountable for deceptive practices in bringing a new product to market.

In 2017, federal Health Minister Jane Philpott and Ontario Health Minister Eric Hoskins were reportedly having "some conversations" about legal action against Purdue to recover health care costs.[54] Both ministers have since left their portfolio posts with no legal action in sight.

In 2018, Health Canada has continued to come under criticism for placing the fiscal interests of the pharmaceutical industry ahead of protecting public health.[55]

Regulatory reactions to the pharmaceutical industry in the US, particularly in relationship to the opioid crisis, have been more punitive. Purdue executives were found guilty of making false claims and fraudulently marketing a drug for an unapproved use. The company was fined $634 million (US).[56] No individuals were punished. The executives deflected responsibility to lower-level employees, whom they claim made "*misstatements*."

Following the retirement of its CEO in 2007, Purdue USA filled the position with (previously mentioned) Mr. John Stewart from Purdue Canada. By 2012, Mr. Stewart was being chastised by the US Senate Committee on Finance for the continued economic harm his company was causing the US health insurance industry, and for a lack of cooperation in responding to government requests for information. Shortly thereafter, Mr. Stewart left Purdue and returned to Canada (where he was granted a licence by Health Canada to produce cannabis medications).[57]

Apart from the protection of a country's citizens, there is another reason why companies like Purdue should be held accountable for their actions. Without meaningful consequences, they are likely to become emboldened in their conduct. Under the campaign banner "*We're Only Just Getting Started*," Purdue is now taking OxyContin to undeveloped countries in Latin America, Asia, the Middle East, and Africa. They are using the same deceptive marketing strategy, but this time accompanied by promotional videos that include actors of diverse ethnicities. The campaign also vows to combat "*opiophobia*."[58]

These are worrisome developments. The advanced and well-resourced health care systems in North America were unprepared for, and continue to struggle to contain, the opioid crisis. Undeveloped countries have much less capacity to prevent an epidemic and respond to one. The outcomes could be horrific. These countries will also possess less capacity to hold Purdue accountable.

Despite the enormous amount of premeditated harm perpetrated by Purdue thus far, no one from the company has gone to prison. However, Walter James McCormick, a British Columbia street dealer, did. In January of 2017, he was convicted of trafficking in fentanyl and sentenced to fourteen years. Presiding Justice Bonnie

Craig admonished McCormick for contributing to the suffering and potential death of others, but may have shown some insight into the bigger picture when she added,

> "McCormick did not create the problem with opioid addiction in the community. He is just one of the players in a far more complicated problem."[59]

McCormick is not alone in his treatment by the judicial system. Fentanyl street dealers in Alberta and Ontario have faced manslaughter charges. [60]

The opioid crisis is not the only example of pharma misconduct. An examination of journals, court cases, and government/health/ justice agency investigations documented illegal, unethical conduct at no fewer than sixty-four companies in no fewer than thirty-one countries, spanning all populated continents.[61] The review details a dizzying list of malfeasance on the part of this industry, including:

- manipulation of research practices and findings
- intimidation and suppression of uncooperative researchers
- using overly aggressive, misleading, and illegal advertising/marketing practices
- tampering with court proceedings and legislative processes; bribery
- testing new drugs in countries with weak regulations, harming vulnerable populations
- causing deaths of children in illegal trials; pressuring parents into uninformed consent
- non-payment of court-ordered settlements to parents whose children died
- selling drugs to publicly funded medicare programs at inflated prices
- receiving tax breaks from donations of expiring drugs that were useless or harmful to the recipients
- committing workplace safety, environmental, and animal rights violations

The review also exposes regulatory permissiveness on the part of governments, including the following examples:

- high-risk, highly profitable drugs were allowed onto the market
- industry whistleblowers were not protected and were sometimes prosecuted by the state
- regulators were complicit with industry in commission of crimes

This analysis would not be complete without some additional comments on how drug industry transgressions are rarely met with meaningful consequences. We have already noted that even with guilty verdicts, executives rarely bear any personal consequences for their actions. A report by the advocacy group Public Citizen examined pharmaceutical industry cases between 1991 and 2012. During this time, US pharmaceutical companies settled at least 239 cases for a total of $30.2 billion.[62] Given the widespread recidivism by this industry, it is apparent that individual settlements, even in the hundreds of millions of dollars, are insufficient as deterrents. Perhaps this is in part because fines and settlements tend to punish company shareholders more than those who make the decisions.

In summary, alcohol, tobacco, and pharmaceutical industries are legal, government-regulated, commercial drug industries. These industries have uniformly failed to balance their pursuit of revenue with the protection of public health. Sometimes they engage in illegal behaviour to maximize revenue – often with dire consequences for public health. Government regulation has not been effective in discouraging such conduct.

In bringing its cannabis legalization campaign to Canadians, our government has promised that the cannabis industry, like other legal drug industries, will be strictly regulated. *Strict regulation* has become the clarion call of many governments, public health authorities, drug-policy academics, and other advocates for the introduction of this new drug industry. However, the evidence is that our regulation of existing drug industries is not merely less than perfect – it is substantially less than adequate. Strict regulation would appear to be the unicorn of drug policy. It is a lovely concept, but it simply does not exist – not in Canada and not elsewhere. The World Health Organization has recognized this bleak reality in the following statement:

"Market power readily translates into political power. Few governments prioritize health over big business."[63]

EPILOGUE: THE CANNABIS INDUSTRY

The cannabis industry is an emerging legal, government-regulated, commercial drug industry. Already, there are indications that the conduct of this industry and its permissive and otherwise inadequate regulation by government are on a trajectory like that of other drug industries.

Since the legalization of cannabis for therapeutic purposes in 2001, we have seen repeated intentional violations related to advertising and product safety, as well as collaboration with criminal elements. Health Canada has repeatedly failed to hold the industry accountable for these violations. Furthermore, the process of legalization for recreational purposes was tainted with conflicts of interest, and ultimately favoured the maximization of industry revenue over the protection of public health. Recommendations from public health advocates for greater constraints on commercialization, including adoption of a public health governance model for the industry, were assigned little weight or were dismissed by government.[64] A more detailed treatment of the many failings of the process is available elsewhere.[65]

The Canadian government's legalization campaign, including the legislation (Bill C-45), also continues to criminalize minor cannabis infractions by issuing harsh penalties, including prison terms of up to fourteen years. There has been no record expungement for those who carry criminal records for past minor cannabis transgressions. Long-time advocates of reform, less mesmerized by the spectacle of a glamorous, lucrative new industry, are justified in asking what has happened to the compassion and sense of justice that fueled the drive for reform over the course of the issue's history. These humanitarian concerns appear to have been strategically marginalized.

No one knows for certain how commercial cannabis legalization will play out in Canada. This will be an experiment, and not the controlled kind. The legacy of duplicitous conduct by existing drug industries and the attendant harm should evoke concern regarding the introduction of yet another for-profit drug industry. The potential for the commercial legalization of cannabis to serve as an accelerator for an eventual fourth drug crisis should not be dismissed.

The position of the Canadian government continues to be that Canadians should not worry, given that the cannabis industry will be strictly regulated like other drug industries. The prudent public health perspective suggests that, in the absence of significant improvement in drug industry regulation, Canadians may have a great deal to worry about.

NOTES

1 Jesse Tahirali, "Seven in 10 Canadians Support Marijuana Legalization: Nanos Poll," CTV News, 30 June 2016, https://www. ctvnews.ca/canada/7-in-10-canadians-support-marijuana-legalization-nanos-poll-1.2968953.

2 Susan Krashinsky Robertson, "Marijuana Industry Faces Challenge in Gaining Canadians' Trust, Survey Finds," The Globe and Mail, 15 June 2017, https://www.theglobeandmail.com/report-on-business/industry-news/marketing/marijuana-industry-faces-challenge-in-gaining-canadians-trust-survey-finds/article34466751/.

3 Canadian Substance Use Costs and Harms, Scientific Working Group, Canadian Substance Use Costs and Harms (2007–2014) (Ottawa: Canadian Centre on Substance Use and Addiction, 2018), 1–4.

4 Scientific Working Group, Costs and Harms, 1–4.

5 Scientific Working Group, Costs and Harms, 2.

6 Paul Wells, "Canada's New Health Minister Faces the Opioid Crisis," Maclean's, 12 September 2017, https://www.macleans.ca/politics/ottawa/canadas-new-health-minister-faces-the-opioid-crisis/.

7 Government of Canada, National Report: Apparent Opioid-related Deaths in Canada (Ottawa: Public Health Agency of Canada, 2018), section 1.0.

8 "Opioid Overdose: Understanding the Epidemic," Center for Disease Control and Prevention, accessed 26 July 2018, https://www.cdc.gov/drugoverdose/epidemic/index.html.

9 Patrick Cain, "Canada Will See 900,000 New Pot Smokers under Legalization, Poll Implies." Global News, 12 October 2016, https://globalnews.ca/news/2995390/canada-will-see-900000-new-pot-smokers-under-legalization-poll-implies/.

10 Office of the Parliamentary Budget Officer, Legalized Cannabis: Fiscal Considerations (Ottawa: Government of Canada, 2016), 9–17.

11 Thomas F. Babor, "Alcohol: No Ordinary Commodity – A Summary of the Second Edition," Addiction 105, no. 5 (May 2010): 769–79;

Canadian Public Health Association, *Too High a Cost: A Public Health Approach to Alcohol Policy in Canada* (Ottawa: CPHA, 2011), 6; Rosalie L. Pacula et al., "Developing Public Health Regulations for Marijuana: Lessons Learned from Alcohol and Tobacco," *American Journal of Public Health* 104, no. 6 (April 2014): 1021–28; Public Health Agency of Canada, *The Chief Public Health Officer's Report on the State of Public Health in Canada 2015: Alcohol Consumption in Canada* (Ottawa: PHAC, 2016), 3–4 and 38.

12 Carly M. Heung, Benjamin Rempel, and Marvin Krank. "Strengthening the Canadian Alcohol Advertising Regulatory System," *Canadian Journal of Public Health* 103, no. 4 (2012): 263–6.

13 Babor, "Ordinary Commodity," 769–79; Tobacco Control Legal Consortium, *Cause and Effect: Tobacco Marketing Increases Youth Tobacco Use: Findings from the 2012 Surgeon General's Report* (St. Paul: TCLC, 2012), 17–20; Pacula et al., "Developing Public Health," 1021–28.

14 Budget Officer, *Legalized,* 43.

15 Meeting with Federal Tobacco Control Program and Cannabis Secretariat at Main Stats Building, 150 Tunney's Pasture Driveway. Ottawa, 16 February 2017.

16 Jürgen Rehm et al., *Avoidable Cost of Alcohol Abuse in Canada 2002* (Toronto: Centre for Addiction and Mental Health, 2008), 29–31; Canadian Public, *Too High,* 6–9; Pacula et al., "Developing Public Health," 1021–28.

17 Ontario Tobacco Research Unit, *Prohibition of Tobacco Sales in Specific Places: Monitoring Update* (Toronto: OTRU, 2011); Christine Navarro and Robert Schwartz, *Evidence to Support Tobacco Endgame Policy Measures* (Toronto: Ontario Tobacco Research Unit, 2014), 3–4.

18 Benedikt Fischer et al., "Crude Estimates of Cannabis-attributable Mortality and Morbidity in Canada – Implications for Public Health–focused Intervention Priorities," *Journal of Public Health (Oxf)* 38, no. 1 (2016): 183–8.

19 Rehm et al., *Avoidable Cost,* 40; Babor, "Ordinary Commodity," 769–79; Canadian Public, *Too High,* 4; Norman Giesbrecht et al., *Strategies to Reduce Alcohol-related Harms and Costs in Canada: A Comparison of Provincial Policies* (Toronto: Centre for Addiction and Mental Health, 2013), 12.

20 Norman Giesbrecht, Andrée Demers, and Gina Stoduto, "Alcohol Smuggling in the 1990s: Policy Opportunism and Interventions," in *Sober Reflections: Commerce, Public Health, and the Evolution of Alcohol*

Policy in Canada, 1980–2000, eds. Norman Giesbrecht et al. (Montreal & Kingston: McGill-Queens University Press, 2006).

21   Josh Rubin, "Fake Wine Discovered at LCBO Prompts Police Probe," *Toronto Star*, 18 March 2011, https://www.thestar.com/business/2011/03/18/fake_wine_discovered_at_lcbo_prompts_police_probe.html.

22   The Canadian Press, "LCBO Recalled Bottles of Bombay Sapphire London Dry Gin and Georgian Bay Vodka," CBC *News*, 3 May 2017, https://www.cbc.ca/news/canada/toronto/lcbo-gin-recall-bombay-gin-1.4096746.

23   Graeme Hamilton, "Illegal Tipple," *National Post*, 12 December 2015.

24   Babor, "Ordinary Commodity," 769–79.

25   Giesbrecht et al., *Strategies,* 49.

26   Jürgen Rehm et al., "Avoidable Cost of Alcohol Abuse in Canada," *European Addiction Research* 17, no. 2 (2011): 729.

27   Norman Giesbrecht, *Selling Alcohol in Grocery Stores: Hidden Risks and Alternative Options* (Toronto: CAMH, 2015).

28   Centre for Addiction and Mental Health, *Why Ontario Needs a Provincial Alcohol Strategy* (Toronto: CAMH, 2015).

29   Giesbrecht, *Selling Alcohol.*

30   James Wilt, "Alcohol Industry Officials Lobbied Yukon to Halt Warning-Label Study, Emails Show," *The Globe and Mail*, 22 May 2018, https://www.theglobeandmail.com/canada/article-alcohol-industry-officials-lobbied-yukon-to-halt-warning-label-study/.

31   Ziming Xuan et al., "The Alcohol Policy Environment and Policy Subgroups as Predictors of Binge Drinking Measures among US Adults," *American Journal of Public Health* 105, no. 4 (2014): 816–22.

32   Aneel Karnani, "Impact of Alcohol on Poverty and the Need for Appropriate Policy," in *Alcohol: Science, Policy, and Public Health*, eds. Pete Boyle et al. (Oxford: Oxford University Press, 2013).

33   Rob Cunningham, *Smoke and Mirrors: The Canadian Tobacco War* (Ottawa: International Development Research Centre, 1996).

34   Richard Kluger, *Ashes to Ashes* (New York: Vintage Books, 1997).

35   *United States of America vs. Philip Morris USA, Inc., Amended Final Opinion* (Civil Action No. 99-2496 GK). United States District Court for the District of Columbia, 2006: 4 and 1500.

36   Garfield Mahood, *What Were They Smoking? The Smuggling Settlements with Big Tobacco* (Toronto: The Non-smokers Rights Association, 2013), 1–5 and 22–3.

37   Mahood, *Smoking*, 1–5 and 22–3.

38   Anna B. Gilmore and Andrew Rowell, "The Tobacco Industry's Latest Scam: How Big Tobacco Is Still Facilitating Tobacco Smuggling, while

Also Attempting to Control a Global System Designed to Prevent It," *Tobacco Control Blog*, last modified 19 June 2018, https://blogs.bmj.com/ tc/2018/06/19/the-tobacco-industrys-latest-scam-how-big-tobacco-is-still-facilitating-tobacco-smuggling-while-also-attempting-to-control-a-global-system-designed-to-prevent-it/.

39 André Picard, "The Long, Long Fight against Big Tobacco," *The Globe and Mail*, 16 July 2018, https://www.theglobeandmail.com/canada/ article-theres-a-big-legal-battle-between-the-provinces-and-the-tobacco/.

40 Mahood, *Smoking*, 6–21.

41 Jenny L. Hatchard et al., "A Critical Evaluation of the Volume, Relevance and Quality of Evidence Submitted by the Tobacco Industry to Oppose Standardised Packaging of Tobacco Products," *British Medical Journal Open* 4, no. 2 (2014): 3757.

42 Jennifer Brown et al., "Tobacco Industry Response to Menthol Cigarette Bans in Alberta and Nova Scotia, Canada," *Tobacco Control* 26, no. e1 (July 2016): 71–4.

43 Bo Zhang and Robert Schwartz, *What Effect Does Tobacco Taxation Have on Contraband? Debunking the Taxation-Contraband Tobacco Myth* (Toronto: Ontario Tobacco Research Unit, 2015).

44 Elisha G. Brownson et al., "Explosion Injuries from E-cigarettes," *New England Journal of Medicine* 375 (October 2016): 1400–02; Nicholas Kusnetz, *How Big Tobacco Lobbies to Safeguard E-cigarettes* (Washington DC: The Center for Public Integrity, 2016).

45 Robert Benzie, "Doug Ford Halts Introduction of Additional Anti-vaping Rules," *Toronto Star*, 4 July 2018, https://www.thestar.com/news/queen-spark/2018/07/04/doug-ford-halts-introduction-of-additional-anti-vaping-rules-for-more-study.html.

46 World Health Organization, *Tobacco Industry Interference with Tobacco Control* (Geneva: WHO, 2008), 22.

47 Art Van Zee, "The Promotion and Marketing of OxyContin: Commercial Triumph, Public Health Tragedy," *American Journal of Public Health* 99, no. 2 (2009): 221–7.

48 Benedikt Fischer, "Fentanyl: Canada's Homemade Drug Crisis," *The Globe and Mail*, 14 April 2016, https://www.theglobeandmail.com/ opinion/fentanyl-canadas-homemade-drug-crisis/article29626211/.

49 Government of Newfoundland and Labrador, *OxyContin Task Force Final Report* (St. John's: Government of Newfoundland and Labrador departments of Health and Community Services, Justice, and Education, 2004), 55.

50 G. Robertson, "OxyContin Creator Expands into Canadian Pot Industry," *The Globe and Mail*, 3 December 2016.

51 Newfoundland, *OxyContin*, 55; J. Lexchin and J. Kohler, "The Danger of Imperfect Regulation: OxyContin Use in the United States and Canada," *International Journal of Risk and Safety* 23 (2011): 233–40; Centre for Addiction and Mental Health. *Prescription Opioid Policy Framework*. (Toronto: Centre for Addiction and Mental Health, 2016), 9–11.

52 John Ivison, "Ottawa Moves to Rein in Oxycontin," *National Post*, 15 May 2015.

53 Health Canada, *Health Canada's Action on Opioid Misuse* (Ottawa: Health Canada, 2016).

54 Karen Howlett, "Ottawa Urged to Prosecute Purdue Pharma over Marketing of OxyContin," *The Globe and Mail*, 19 July 2017, https://www.theglobeandmail.com/news/national/ottawa-urged-to-prosecute-purdue-pharma-over-marketing-of-oxycontin/article35729663/.

55 Joel Lexchin, "Health Canada Might Make Your Prescription Drugs Less Safe," *Maclean's,* 10 January 2018, https://www.macleans.ca/society/health/health-canada-might-make-your-prescription-drugs-less-safe/; Kelly Crowe, "Judge Orders Health Canada to Disclose Industry Documents. Meanwhile, Almost All Other Requests under the Same Law Have Been Denied," CBC *News: Second Opinion*, 14 July 2018.

56 CBC News, "Court Fines OxyContin Maker $634M US," CBC *News*, 10 May 2007, https://www.cbc.ca/news/technology/court-fines-oxycontin-maker-634m-us-1.636582.

57 Robertson, "OxyContin Creator."

58 Harriet Ryan, Lisa Girion, and Scott Glover, "OxyContin Goes Global — 'We're Only Just Getting Started,'" *Los Angeles Times,* 18 December 2016, http://www.latimes.com/projects/la-me-oxycontin-part3/.

59 Justin McElroy, "B.C. Fentanyl Dealer Sentenced to 14 Years in Prison," CBC *News,* 30 January 2017, https://www.cbc.ca/news/canada/british-columbia/fentanyl-dealer-mccormick-1.3959167.

60 The Canadian Press, "Manslaughter Charges against Alleged Fentanyl Dealers Mount across Canada," CBC *News,* 9 October 2017, https://www.cbc.ca/news/canada/toronto/fentanyl-manslaughter-dealers-overdose-death-1.4346539.

61 Graham Dukes, John Braithwaite, and J.P. Moloney, *Pharmaceuticals, Corporate Crime and Public Health* (Cheltenham and Northampton: Edward Elgar Publishing, 2014).

62 Sammy Almashat and Sidney Wolfe, *Pharmaceutical Industry Criminal and Civil Penalties: An Update* (Washington, DC: Public Citizen, 2012), 9–10.

63 Margaret Chan, "Opening Address at the 8th Global Conference on Health Promotion, Helsinki, Finland," World Health Organization, 10 June 2013, http://www.who.int/dg/speeches/2013/health_promotion_20130610/en/ .

64 Michael DeVillaer, *Cannabis Law Reform in Canada: Pretense and Perils* (Hamilton: McMaster University, Peter Boris Centre for Addictions Research, 2017), 79–90; Maude Chapados et al., *Legalization of Nonmedical Cannabis: A Public Health Approach to Regulation* (Québec: Institut National de Santé Publique du Québec, 2016), 37–43.

65 DeVillaer, *Pretense and Perils*, 57–78.

PART FIVE

The International Context

13

Cannabis Legalization Is the Inconvenient Test of Canada's Commitment to the Rule of International Law and a Rules-Based World Order

ROOJIN HABIBI AND STEVEN J. HOFFMAN

The international law of treaties may not necessarily be the first thing that comes to mind when we think about the legalization of cannabis. And yet drug control is the focus of one of the oldest and most widely ratified international treaty regimes in place today. Three United Nations (UN) treaties, implemented in succession over the past fifty years, collectively aim to address drug use.[1] They also require over 180 countries, including Canada, to prohibit the use of cannabis for non-medical and non-scientific purposes.

Canada's *Cannabis Act*, which received royal assent on 21 June 2018, was originally referred to the Senate Standing Committee on Foreign Affairs and International Trade as Bill C-45 on 15 February 2018. The Standing Committee was tasked with studying the bill's subject matter insofar as it relates to Canada's international obligations. All witness testimonies before the Standing Committee, including the testimony of the Honourable Chrystia Freeland, minister of foreign affairs, concurred that the legalization of cannabis, without any further action to formally re-adjust Canada's international legal obligations, will violate international law.[2]

Since the Liberal Party of Canada ran and won on a campaign that included a pledge to "legalize, regulate, and restrict access to cannabis,"[3] debates on Parliament Hill have shed little light on how the Canadian government plans to reconcile specific international obligations under the treaties with national drug policy priorities. Officials from Global Affairs Canada advised the Standing Committee that, as of March 2018, Canada had no intentions of taking any treaty actions, though it planned to "monitor and observe the legal and political reactions from the international community."[4]

By forging ahead to meet electoral promises, Canada has also become the first G7 country to legalize cannabis for recreational use. This means it will have to contend with criticism from international authorities such as the International Narcotics Control Board (INCB) and other Parties to these treaties, who will inevitably ask whether Canada is committed to the rule of international law and the rules-based international order in which we live today.

If the Canadian government intends to restore "constructive Canadian leadership" in the world,[5] it must view the *Cannabis Act* as the inconvenient test where it can prove its commitment to the rule of international law, and as its opportunity to pursue a bold and pioneering role in the international drug control agenda. This means that it must modify – rather than shirk from – its international legal obligations.[6] And the sooner, the better.

WHAT IS THE INTERNATIONAL DRUG CONTROL REGIME?

Three UN drug control treaties form today's international drug control regime: (1) the 1961 *Single Convention on Narcotic Drugs* (referred to as the *Single Convention*; (2) the 1971 *Convention on Psychotropic Substances* (*Psychotropics Convention*)[7] and (3) the 1988 *Convention Against Illicit Traffic in Narcotic Drugs and Psychotropic Substances* (also known as the *Trafficking Convention*).[8]

The *Single Convention* was adopted in 1961 to streamline several previous international agreements on drugs and set the normative tone and rules prohibiting the production, use, and trade of narcotic drugs in the world. By the 1970s, a dramatic increase in drug use prompted countries, at the insistence of the United States (US), to convene again and conclude two significant agreements. The first was the 1972 *Protocol Amending the Single Convention on Narcotic Drugs*, which modified the *Single Convention* to strengthen efforts to reduce the supply and demand of drugs.[9] The amending protocol also reinforced the public health view of drug dependence as a medical condition that should be treated through various ways, including education and rehabilitation.

The *Psychotropics Convention* was the second agreement concluded, a reaction to the high uptake of synthetic drugs such as amphetamines and benzodiazepines appearing during that decade. Since these substances were not previously covered by the *Single Convention*, the *Psychotropics Convention* reiterated with minor variations the prohibitive rules of the former convention, applying them specifically to psychotropic drugs.

In 1988, countries convened again to adopt a convention addressing the concerning rise in drug trafficking, especially among organized criminal groups. The *Trafficking Convention* provided for comprehensive measures, such as extradition and confiscation of assets, to tackle the illicit production, trafficking, and demand for drugs.

At their core, these treaties aim to curtail drug use by requiring Parties to prohibit the possession, cultivation, production, importation, sale, and distribution of drugs for non-medical and non-scientific purposes. While the terms "narcotic drug" and "psychotropic substance" are not explicitly defined in the treaties, restricted or prohibited substances are listed in four schedules within the *Single Convention* and the *Psychotropics Convention*, respectively. Cannabis extracts, including cannabis, hashish, and cannabis oil, are doubly listed in Schedules I and IV of the *Single Convention*.[10] Synthetic forms of tetrahydrocannabinol – the principal active agent in cannabis – are covered by Schedule II of the *Psychotropics Convention*.

WHAT DOES THE INTERNATIONAL DRUG CONTROL REGIME SAY ABOUT CANNABIS?

Cannabis legalization will violate several provisions of the three international drug control treaties. Under the *Single Convention*, Parties have a general obligation to:

> "...take such legislative and administrative measures as may be necessary... to limit exclusively to medical and scientific purposes the production, manufacture, export, import, distribution of, trade in, use, and possession of drugs."[11]

While the term "medical and scientific use" is not defined anywhere in the treaties, it is reasonable to conclude that the recreational possession and consumption of cannabis would not qualify as a legitimate exception to the general prohibition. Taken on its own, however, the general obligation also does not require for Parties to *criminalize* the enumerated activities.

Further in the *Single Convention*, Article 33 states that Parties "must not permit the possession of drugs except under legal authority."[12] Article 36(1)(a) states that the possession and production of narcotic drugs must be "punishable offences" subject to the constitutional limitations of the Party.[13] An analogous provision is also found in the *Psychotropics Convention*.[14] These provisions bring into clearer focus the requirement to impose sanctions for activities prohibited by the treaties. Up to this point, the treaties say nothing about possession of drugs for personal consumption.

It is within the *Trafficking Convention* that Parties have a requirement to explicitly prohibit personal consumption. Article 3(2) states that treaty parties must "establish as criminal offences under [their] domestic law, when committed intentionally ... the possession, purchase, or cultivation of narcotic drugs or psychotropic substances for *personal consumption* contrary to the provisions of the 1961 Convention ... or the 1971 Convention."[15]

The collection of these provisions leads to the conclusion that, for over 180 states that have ratified the international drug control treaties, there must be some form of prohibition on the possession of cannabis for personal use.

INHERENT FLEXIBILITIES WITHIN THE TREATIES

Treaty drafters and diplomats alike know that every treaty must contain some built-in flexibilities to allow for Parties to implement, within certain parameters, the regime that suits their own state. Applying this principle to the international drug control regime, we find that punishment leading to incarceration and/or a criminal record for engaging in prohibited activities is not required. The treaties call on Parties to implement sanctions for the possession, use, and sale of drugs, but they leave it open to interpretation exactly what kind of punishment there must be. Portugal, for instance, prohibits drug use but diverts offenders towards mandatory education classes, treatment sessions, and administrative fines.[16]

The treaties also require that states have, in law, state punishment, but they do not require countries to enforce those legal provisions. In the Netherlands – famous for its "coffee shops" – cannabis is prohibited by law, but police are not expected to enforce this prohibition against people possessing small quantities.[17]

Finally, the treaties also allow room for constitutional override through "safeguard clauses" appearing throughout the treaties. As a result, Parties are afforded a degree of latitude in crafting legal and policy responses to drug control that are suited to their national legal context. After failing to convince Parties to amend the *Single Convention* to allow for the chewing of coca leaf, Bolivia withdrew from the convention and amended its constitution to include protections for the use, production, commercialization, and industrialization of coca leaf (Article 384 of the 2009 Constitution). In 2013, Bolivia re-acceded to the *Single Convention* with a reservation that the chewing of coca leaf, now a constitutional right, be permitted for its people.

The 1969 *Vienna Convention on the Law of Treaties* (*Vienna Convention*), which has been ratified by Canada, guides Parties to interpret their treaty obligations in "good faith," according to the "ordinary meaning" given to terms in the treaty context, and considering the "object and purpose" of the treaty.[18] While experts recognize that the drug control treaties are saturated with textual ambiguity,[19] consensus dictates that the *de jure* legalization of a regulated market for the sale of cannabis for personal consumption falls definitively outside of the ambit of the treaties.

In June 2018, as Parliament celebrated the adoption of Bill C-45 as Canadian law, the INCB expressed "great concern," and cautioned that "the legalization of the use of cannabis for non-medical purposes ... undermines the international legal drug control framework and respect for the rules-based international order."[20] The INCB is responsible for monitoring and enforcing compliance with the treaties.

WHAT ABOUT URUGUAY AND THE UNITED STATES?

In addition to Canada, two countries already have regulated markets for cannabis today. Both are contravening the treaties, but their logics for doing so are very different. Importantly, these logics are unique to the politico-legal context within these countries, and inapplicable to Canada.

At the time of writing, ten US states and the District of Columbia have legalized cannabis personal use. The US has defended itself by invoking a unique feature of its criminal law system that gives US states criminal law powers independent from the federal government.[21] This reasoning overlooks the common understanding that, even in federalist countries, the onus is on the federal government to ensure that its constituents abide by their international legal obligations. In any event, this logic cannot be leveraged in the Canadian context, since criminal law falls squarely within federal jurisdiction in Canada.

In 2017, motivated by a concern for public health, security, and human rights, Uruguay also legalized and began regulating the sale of cannabis for personal use. At international drug policy forums, Uruguay consistently cited the overriding importance of human rights principles over drug control obligations, specifying that cannabis legalization had become a national priority after the country led a "critical and realistic reflection on the negative impacts on human rights brought about by ... drug policies agreed at the international level in the last 50 years."[22] While the strength of this argument can also be debated on the basis of certain well-recognized principles of law,[23] the Supreme Court of Canada previously found that banning the simple possession of cannabis via Canada's *Criminal Code* does not breach the rights and freedoms enshrined in Sections 7 and 15 of the *Canadian Charter of Rights and Freedoms*.[24] As a result, it would be difficult for Canada to similarly mount a human rights argument for treaty non-compliance.

OPTIONS AVAILABLE TO CANADA

The international drug control regime need not be an obstacle to a sensible drug policy agenda. While no solution is perfect, there are several clear and defined avenues in international law allowing countries to modify their legal obligations in any treaty regime.

First, it must be recognized that consensus on the international drug control regime, once exhibited through the high rate of accession to the treaties, has fractured considerably since the final treaty was negotiated in 1988. When the most recent global meeting on drug control took place in 2016 – at the 30th Special Session of the UN General Assembly on the World Drug Problem – Parties continued to avoid discussing the adequacy of the treaties, especially as they relate to the legal status of cannabis possession and use.[25] Yet these discussions have already begun to take place at national and sub-national levels in Uruguay, and in several US states.

While most contemporary treaties now contain built-in provisions for periodic treaty review, older international agreements like the drug control treaties lack such future-proofing mechanisms. As a G7 country, Canada has the reputation and political leverage to make the case for treaty reform that would benefit all Parties to the treaties. A treaty-reform initiative might involve requesting to change certain provisions of the treaties, or it might attempt a wholesale overhaul of the current system. With an unprecedented number of like-minded Parties interested in the cause, there has never been a more appropriate time to trigger reform on the status of cannabis and other drugs in the UN drug control treaties.

Some have also suggested using creative lawyering to find a possible legal workaround. For instance, the treaties limit the use of cannabis consumption to medical or scientific purposes.[26] Canada could leverage this workaround, claiming that cannabis legalization was necessary to conduct a big natural experiment on the inter-generational effects of legal cannabis. But this workaround is a stretch, and certainly the *Cannabis Act* has not been presented to the Canadian public or the international community as a longitudinal public health experiment to date.

Others have proposed the possibility of using a little-known mechanism of international treaty law known as an *inter se* agreement.[27] This term, a Latin phrase for "among or between themselves," describes an approach where a Party may modify the legal effects of certain provisions between itself and another likeminded Party or Parties to a treaty, if these changes are in line with the object and purpose of the treaty and do not detract from the full enjoyment of the provision for the non-agreeing Parties.

If Canada were to initiate an *inter se* agreement, it could expect the collaboration of several Parties, including Uruguay, the Netherlands, and Jamaica. This is likely not a fruitful avenue to explore, especially as proponents of this mechanism even concede it would be "uncharted legal territory," with a paucity of practical examples to draw upon from any area of international treaty law.[28]

It is also worth remembering that joining international treaties is an exercise of a country's sovereignty, and withdrawing from them is an equally legitimate and legal exercise of that sovereignty. The *Vienna Convention* allows Parties to cite a historical "error" or a "fundamental change of circumstances" when depositing a notification to withdraw from a treaty.[29] And countries including Canada have withdrawn from treaties in the past for reasons that are far less convincing.

For instance, in 2013, Canada withdrew from the widely ratified *UN Convention to Combat Desertification*. At the time, former foreign affairs minister John Baird explained via the news media that Canada had a disinterest "in continuing to support bureaucracies and talkfests."[30] Canada also controversially withdrew from the *UN Framework Convention on Climate Change*'s Kyoto Protocol in 2011.[31]

What makes treaty withdrawal understandable in this instance is that, as nearly everyone familiar with the international drug control regime would agree, these treaties are outdated and reflective of another era; they describe drug addiction as an "evil" rather than as a medical challenge faced by individuals in conditions of vulnerability.

The consequences of withdrawal from the three UN drug control treaties are not negligible. Ultimately, these are the instruments through which we obtain narcotics for medicines and coordinate law enforcement efforts tackling drug trafficking. But alternative arrangements for access to narcotics and coordination of law enforcement can be made in ways that do not require international law.

If Canada did really want to be part of these treaties, the country could always withdraw from them and then rejoin, with reservations to the treaty provisions that are incompatible with cannabis legalization. That means that we would be rejoining with a condition that the treaties do not apply to cannabis. The approach offers the advantage of having a precedent in Bolivia's saga to earn the international community's acceptance of its indigenous coca leaf–chewing practices.

But the challenge here is that withdrawal cannot take effect immediately. The time from notice deposition to treaty withdrawal varies according to the treaty and the time of year in which notice is given. If Canada's Cabinet had given the UN Secretary General notice of its intent to withdraw from the *Single Convention* or *Psychotropics Convention* in October 2018, the withdrawal would take effect only in January 2020.[32] A notice of withdrawal from the *Trafficking Convention* would always require one year from the time of notice deposition.[33] Compliance with the treaties is better than temporary non-compliance. Temporary non-compliance, followed by appropriate measures to restore compliance through modifying legal obligations, is much preferred over continued flagrant violation of international law – even if those international laws are outdated, just about drugs, and relate to a not-so-harmful substance that was consumed by many (12.3 per cent) Canadians in the past year.[34]

WHY DOES ALL THIS MATTER?

For some, the weight of international law lends itself to interpretation and perspective. When international law stands in the way of a national or an activist agenda, it is said to be abstract and to lack teeth. When it offers support for the chosen policies of a given group, it is deemed to be just and unquestionably "the law."

In testimonies to the Canadian Senate's Standing Committee on Foreign Affairs and International Trade, officials from Global Affairs Canada submitted that "strict compliance with every technical aspect of the conventions" was not a priority for the government, effectively characterizing contravention of the international treaties as a minor issue.[35] This was not the approach that was later taken by Minister Freeland, who stated before Committee members that "the issue of the conventions is an important one, and [the government] need[s] to be clear about it."[36] Her position was supported by other witnesses and the Standing Committee's final report itself.[37]

When accepting the 2009 Nobel Peace Prize, former US president Barack Obama astutely stated that no state can "insist that others follow the rules of the road if we refuse to follow them ourselves. For when we don't, our actions appear arbitrary and undercut the legitimacy of future interventions, no matter how justified." Put differently, states cannot pick and choose which international treaties to follow without encouraging others to do the same.

Already, Canada has been singled out by the Russian Federation, whose ministry of foreign affairs stated soon after the *Cannabis Act* became law that it "expect[s] Canada's partners in the G7 to respond to its 'high-handedness' because [the G7] has repeatedly declared its adherence to the domination of international law between states."[38]

The international drug control regime is old, slow to change, and desperately in need of evolution. Whatever our opinions on the legality of cannabis use may be, we cannot ignore the fact that a country's ability to influence international dialogue depends on its perceived credibility and its respect for a rules-based international order. International law is an imperfect system, but it is our best shot at solving the complex global problems – climate change, conflict, human rights, migration, and trade – that we are facing today.

When asked how Canada intends to reconcile its views on the importance of a rules-based world order with the *Cannabis Act*'s violation of international treaties, Minister Freeland reasoned that while the Canadian government would be in contravention of the treaties, the country would continue to be "very much committed to preserving the health and safety of Canadians, and ... very committed to working in close partnership with its international partners."[39] Such transparency about non-compliance is a good start; now Canada must take appropriate measures to restore compliance, either through modifying its own legal obligations or by using its political clout to advocate for treaty reform that would benefit all Parties. Doing nothing to address Canada's current non-compliance with the three UN drug control treaties would lead to a national cognitive dissonance brought on by respecting some treaties while ignoring others – and all of the international consequences that would follow from such hypocrisy

NOTES

1   *Single Convention on Narcotic Drugs, 1961, as Amended by the Protocol Amending the Single Convention on Narcotic Drugs, 1961, 8 August 1975, 976* UNTS 105, 23 UKTS 1 (entered into force 8 August 1975) [*Single Convention*].

2   Standing Senate Committee on Foreign Affairs and International Trade (AEFA), *Report of the Senate Standing Committee on Foreign Affairs and International Trade: The Subject Matter of Bill C-45 – An Act Respecting Cannabis and to Amend the Controlled Drugs and Substances Act, the Criminal Code and Other Acts, Insofar as It Relates to Canada's International Obligations* (Ottawa: Canada Senate, 2018), https://sencanada.ca/content/sen/committee/421/AEFA/reports/AEFA_BILLC-45_Report_Final_e.pdf.

3   David Johnson, "Making Real Change Happen," Speech from the Throne to open the first session of the forty-second Parliament of Canada, delivered in Ottawa, Government of Canada, 4 December 2015, https://www.canada.ca/en/privy-council/campaigns/speech-throne/making-real-change-happen.html.

4 AEFA, *Report of the Senate Standing Committee on Foreign Affairs and International Trade,* 11.

5 Justin Trudeau, "Minister of Foreign Affairs Mandate Letter," Prime Minister of Canada, 1 February 2017, https://pm.gc.ca/eng/minister-foreign-affairs-mandate-letter.

6 Roojin Habibi and Steven J. Hoffman, "Legalizing Cannabis Violates the UN Drug-Control Treaties, but Progressive Countries Like Canada Have Options," *Ottawa Law Review,* Working Paper No. 1 (13 March 2018), https://papers.ssrn.com/sol3/papers.cfm?abstract_id=3136881; Steven J. Hoffman and Roojin Habibi, "International Legal Barriers to Canada's Marijuana Plans," *Canadian Medical Association Journal* 188, no. 10 (2016).

7 *Convention on Psychotropic Substances,* 1971, 21 February 1971, 1019 UNTS 175, 10 ILM 261 (entered into force 16 August 1976) [*Psychotropics Convention*].

8 *United Nations Convention Against Illicit Traffic in Narcotic Drugs and Psychotropic Substances,* 1988, 20 December 1988, 1582 UNTS 95, 28 ILM 493 (entered into force 11 November 1990) [*Trafficking Convention*].

9 *Protocol Amending the Single Convention on Narcotic Drugs, 1961,* 25 March 1972, 976 UNTS 3, Can TS 1976 No 48 (entered into force 8 August 1975) [1972 *Protocol*].

10 A review of cannabis extracts was initiated by the World Health Organization's Expert Committee on Drug Dependence (ECDD) in June 2018.

11 *Single Convention,* Article 4(c).

12 *Single Convention,* Article 33.

13 *Single Convention,* Article 36(1)(a).

14 *Psychotropics Convention,* Article 22.

15 *Trafficking Convention,* Article 3(2).

16 Serviço de Intervenção nos Comportamentos Aditivos e nas Dependências, "A Public Health Approach as a Base for Drugs Policy: the Portuguese Case" by João Goulão (Presentation delivered at UNGASS 2016 on World Drug Problem Side Event, 20 April 2016), http://www.unodc.org/documents/ungass2016//CND_Preparations/Reconvened58/PT_Special_Event9December_Ministry_of_Health.pdf.

17 Justus Uitermark, "The Origins and Future of the Dutch Approach towards Drugs," *Journal of Drug Issues* 34, no. 3 (2004): 511.

18 *Vienna Convention on the Law of Treaties,* 23 May 1969, 1155 UNTS 331, 8 ILM 679, art 31(1) (entered into force 27 January 1980), art 31(1) [*Vienna Convention*].

19 Neil Boister, *Penal Aspects of the UN Drug Control Conventions* (The Hague: Kluwer Law International, 2001), 22.

20 International Narcotics Control Board, "International Narcotics Control Board Expresses Deep Concern about the Legalization of Cannabis for Non-Medical Use in Canada," Press Release, INCB, 21 June 2018, https://www.incb.org/incb/en/news/press-releases/2018/incb-expresses-deep-concern-about-the-legalization-of-cannabis-for-non-medical-use-in-canada.html.

21 Jonathan Rauch, "Marijuana Legalization Poses a Dilemma for International Drug Treaties," Brookings Institute, 16 October 2014, https://www.brookings.edu/blog/fixgov/2014/10/16/marijuana-legalization-poses-a-dilemma-for-international-drug-treaties/.

22 Junta Nacional de Drogas [National Drug Board], Impact of the World Drug Problem in the Exercise of Human Rights: Uruguayan Contribution to the Implementation of the Resolution, "Contribution of the Human Rights Council to the Special Session of the UN General Assembly on the World Drug Problem of 2016, report submitted to the Office of the High Commissioner on Human Rights of the United Nations (Montevideo, Uruguay: Junta Nacional de Drogas, 2015) at 3.

23 For instance, it is a well-recognized principle of law that specific requirements (*lex specialis*) generally trump broad requirements (*lex generalis*) – meaning, in this case, that the specific requirements of the UN drug control treaties related to cannabis should trump the general human rights norms that are not specific to drugs or cannabis.

24 *R. v. Malmo-Levine; R.v. Caine* [2003] 3 S.C.R. 571 at para 168, 185.

25 Jamie Bridge, *The United Nations General Assembly Special Session (UNGASS) on the World Drug Problem: Report of Proceedings* (London: International Drug Policy Consortium, 2016), 2.

26 Megan Fultz et al., "Reconciling Canada's Legalization of Non-Medical Cannabis with the UN Drug Control Treaties," in *Global Health Law Clinic Publication Series*, ed. Steven J. Hoffman (Ottawa: Global Strategy Lab, 2017).

27 Martin Jelsma et al., *Balancing Treaty Stability and Change: Inter Se Modification of the UN Drug Control Conventions to Facilitate Cannabis Regulation* (Swansea: Global Drug Policy Observatory, Transnational Institute and Washington Office on Latin America, 2018).

28 Transnational Institute, *Cannabis Regulation and the UN Drug Treaties: Strategies for Reform* (Amsterdam: Transnational Institute, 2016), 11.

29 *Vienna Convention*, art 48.

30 Wayne Kondro, "Canada Pulls Out of UN Treaty to Combat Desertification," *Science*, 29 March 2013, http://www.sciencemag.org/news/2013/03/canada-pulls-out-un-treaty-combat-desertification.

31 Canada's Notification to Withdraw from the Kyoto Protocol to the *United Nations Framework Convention on Climate Change*, UN Doc C.N.796.2011.TREATIES-1 (Depositary Notification) (15 December 2011).

32 *Single Convention*, art 46(2); *Psychotropics Convention*, art 29(2).

33 *Trafficking Convention*, art 30(2).

34 "Canadian Tobacco, Alcohol and Drugs (CTADS): 2015 Summary," Health Canada, last modified 27 June 2017, https://www.canada.ca/en/health-canada/services/canadian-tobacco-alcohol-drugs-survey/2015-summary.html.

35 "Proceedings of the Standing Senate Committee on Foreign Affairs and International Trade," Standing Senate Committee on Foreign Affairs and International Trade, 21 March 2018, https://sencanada.ca/en/Content/SEN/Committee/421/aefa/41ev-53882-e.

36 "Evidence," Standing Senate Committee on Foreign Affairs and International Trade, 1 May 2018, https://sencanada.ca/en/Content/Sen/Committee/421/AEFA/54008-e.

37 AEFA, *Report of the Senate Standing Committee on Foreign Affairs and International Trade*, 22.

38 Adam Frisk, "Russia Rips Canada's 'High-Handedness' in Legalization of Recreational Marijuana," *Global News*, 28 June 2018, https://globalnews.ca/news/4302624/russia-canada-recreational-marijuana/.

39 "Evidence," Standing Senate Committee on Foreign Affairs and International Trade.

14

The Portuguese Experience with Decriminalization

JOÃO CASTEL-BRANCO GOULÃO

(Editor's Note: This is a transcript of a talk on cannabis legalization given at McGill University on 29 May 2018. It has been edited for length and clarity.)

Good afternoon everyone, thank you for your kind introduction. I have learned a lot throughout this conference. It is good that you made it clear that I am not presenting testimony on the legalization of anything, because this is not the case in Portugal. We simply *decriminalized* the use of every drug. It happened seventeen years ago, and we are happy with the results. My role here, in presenting during this important moment of the conference, is to share our experience with you and to explain why it happened, what were the historical conditions, and where we stand nowadays. I will start by saying that the complicated name of my service, Addictive Behaviours and Dependencies, comes from the fact that we are now a service under the ministry of health, and we currently deal not only with illicit drugs but also with alcohol, prescribed medicines, new psychoactive substances, gambling, screen dependency, etc. That is why we dropped the drug issue from the name.

As you can imagine, there is a lot of popular interest and curiosity about the so-called "Portuguese model." We are visited every week at least by one delegation from various countries or invited to speak to different audiences globally. Even then my English is not as good as I would like, but as it is better than your Portuguese, I will keep going.

HISTORICAL BACKGROUND

I think it is important to understand that we lived for a long time under a dictatorship. You would do well to remember the name António Salazar.[1] We spent fifty years under his dictatorship, during which we had no problems with drugs. Of course, there were some accounts of people using drugs. Health professionals, for instance, that could prescribe opioids and the like.[2] But it was not a massive phenomenon. We were a tightly controlled society beholden to a ruthless police force and severe censorship. It was practically impossible for us to travel abroad or to host people visiting us, and as such we were kept isolated. At the same time, in the last years of this authoritarian regime, we were dealing with a colonial war in our nation's colonies (Angola, Mozambique, and so on).[3] A substantial proportion of our young male population was sent to that war. Down there, similar to the situation of the American armed forces in Vietnam, drug use was tolerated and even incentivized. In our colonies, whisky was cheaper than water and cannabis was readily available. It could be used without any form of control by officials. Suddenly, on 25 April 1974, we had our Carnation Revolution;[4] an explosion of freedom. Shortly after, we also had the return of soldiers and settlers from the colonies. Suddenly, almost a million people with habits of using drugs and bringing in tons of cannabis came back to the Portuguese mainland. I was twenty at the time, so I remember the curiosity the young population had for these drugs. This was because we had heard distant echoes of events that happened during our dictatorship, such as the hippie movement or the student movement in France, but that had not directly touched us. We were really longing to interact with those new things that came with freedom. And suddenly, cannabis was there, available to everybody for free because the soldiers and settlers brought it and distributed it, so everybody began experimenting. At the time, we knew nothing about drugs, we had no information at all about drugs. Shortly after, certain criminal organizations came into our territory, bringing with them all the other drugs and making them available. Suddenly we had access to everything; we could obtain cocaine, heroin, LSD – everything. People were not aware of the differences between the several drugs. It was easy to shift from one to the other because there was no oversight, and the State had other priorities than informing the people about drugs. As such, there was an explosion of experimentation, not only of cannabis but of every drug. This situation, shortly after, caused a real epidemic, devastating our youth. The following AIDS epidemic complicated things, and we started to have a really devastating situation on our hands, with deaths due to HIV infection. We also observed significant overdose deaths and the development of increasing criminality (petty crimes; no violent criminality related to drugs, but rather, acquisitive crimes for people to sustain their habits).

Drug use in Portugal has always been under the European average, but the gap between the total number of drug users and the problematic ones was very narrow. In other societies you typically had a much lower level of problematic users compared to total users. It was as if most individuals experimenting with drugs then became problematic users. To address this, we started to develop some responses. The previous framework we had established, as in most parts of the world, was based on criminalization. Nevertheless, we started to develop responses in the health system through a network of centres meant to treat those affected and deal with the situation. It is curious to recall that these first prevention- and treatment-focused centres were installed under the ministry of justice. Even if the aim of these centres was to deal with drug abuse as a health issue, the basis for its organization was the ministry of justice. It took some years until it moved under the umbrella of the ministry of health.

Continuing on, in the 70s, the first of these three centres for treatment were inaugurated in the main cities (Lisbon, Porto, and Coimbra), and for almost a decade no other initiatives took place. This was a time when private responses popped up everywhere, most of them religion-oriented. Some of them were very good and are still present, but many were quite problematic, even in terms of human rights respect. We started to develop more responses in '87; the first big centre under the ministry of Health was created (Centro das Taipas in Lisbon). And starting then we began to develop a network of centres guided by the Centro das Taipas model. Taipas was a very powerful centre, a kind of comprehensive hospital addressing all the problems of the drug user population, with inpatient clinic, outpatient responses, day centre, emergency room, and much more. We then started to develop a network of smaller centres inspired by that model. I am a general practitioner who works with families and, in the late '80s, I worked in the Algarve (the south of Portugal). I had no training at all to deal with addiction problems. But I started to be sought out for help by my families experiencing problems related to it. The only tool I had at the time was simply being available and trying to help. In time, the leaders of the Centro das Taipas located me there, they invited me to training, which I attended for six months, and then I went back to the Algarve to open a new centre. What happened to me happened to other colleagues around the country, which is how we started to develop a network inspired by Taipas, as mentioned before. At this time, the government was paying more and more attention to those problems because it became the main priority of the Portuguese people. In some nationwide polls of the time, people were asked "What are your main concerns about the future of your children?" People tended to respond spontaneously, "Drugs and drug addiction." As such, it became a high priority for the government. But the problem remained that we, the professionals, still felt the lack of a clear guidance to deal with the phenomenon.

DEVELOPING A RESPONSE

In '97, I became responsible for the aforementioned network of treatment. In '98, António Guterres (who is now the secretary general of the UN) was our prime minister, and he recruited a group of experts on drug abuse from several areas. I was included in that group. He invited us to publish a report on the situation and to propose a strategy to address the problem. And we did so. Concerning preventative measures, we proposed new ways to address drug abuse prevention. Concerning the use of methadone, we were not able to reach a consensus, despite being faced with important heroin abuse problems. As for harm-reduction initiatives, we were already developing responses such as needle exchange, street teams, shelters, etc.

For the reintegration of drug users, we presented a comprehensive strategy proposal. Prior to this, we had all had the opportunity to visit other countries (as countries visit us nowadays), such as the Netherlands and Switzerland, to observe what they were doing. Taking all this information, we then proposed new ways to address drug problems, based on the idea that we were dealing with a health and social problem rather than a criminal one. Accordingly, we proposed the decriminalization of use and possession for use for every drug. Our proposal was to change only one article of the previous law, the one which deals with possession for use and use of every drug. Of course, we discussed prior if we were going to propose the decriminalization solely for cannabis or for other drugs. And what we determined really matters is the relation that the subject establishes with the substance and not the substance itself, so why have different approaches for different drugs? With that in mind, the proposal was targeted to all drugs.

One of the main concerns during the process, and the only boundary that António Guterres enforced at the time, was that you may propose anything you want, but you must fit within the spirit of the treaties of the United Nations. So we had advice from the top jurists of Portugal, who told us, "If you keep administrative sanctions, you can remove the criminal ones, you are still in line with the treaties." Therefore, this was the middle ground that we proposed. We then proposed a complete strategy package to go along with this new framework.

DETAILING THE STRATEGY

One of the principles on which the strategy is based is the principle of humanism: assuming that a problematic drug user/addict is someone who has a disease, and that disease has the same dignity as any other disease, such as diabetes or someone suffering from hypertension. Decriminalizing contributed a lot to lower the stigma associated with drug use and to provide the opportunity for an inclusive set of policies. It's been much easier since this process was accomplished, but it's not a silver bullet. The most important effect of decriminalization is to make all policies/actions much more coherent with the idea that we are dealing with a health and social condition rather than a criminal one. I am sure that if we just decriminalized and did nothing else (i.e., if we did not provide treatment to the ones who are in need of it, if we did not develop a drug-abuse prevention set of policies, if we did not develop a network of services concerning harm reduction, and also, if we did not develop policies aimed at positive discrimination towards the employment of drug addicts under treatment (such as tax benefits for companies that accept these individuals), then we would not have achieved the level of success we've experienced. Pragmatism is another important component principle of our strategy: you must take all the successful experiences found elsewhere and adapt them to your local reality. We have now a broader strategy in place from 2013 to 2020, targeting drug use and other addictive behaviours as a balanced approach.

Before I forget to mention this important fact, since we decriminalized drug use the efficiency of the police forces that deal with drug traffic increased a lot. Mainly because instead of spending their time and energy targeting the victims ("small fish") and finding grams or kilos at street level, they can now address the "sharks" and improve the cooperation with international police and customs forces and intelligence. This means seizing tons of drugs in open sea or containers instead of seizing those grams or kilos, so they are the happiest people in the world nowadays. Also, increases in quantities of seizures has resulted in more success at lowering the availability of illicit substances in the market.

THE ISSUE OF LIMITS

We have a national coordination of our policies, which in my view is quite an important aspect of our model. The politician responsible for drug policies in Portugal is the minister of health. In my institute, I work as the national drug-policy coordinator, on behalf of the minister of health. I work with the personal representatives of eleven ministries as part of an inter-ministerial commission, and we evaluate results, we produce legislation, and we present our work to the ministers to adopt them and make them work in line with our political and legal framework.

As mentioned before, the proposal that we had made was the decriminalization of use and possession for use. Possession for use is outlined using pre-established threshold quantities for each drug, calculated based on average personal use over ten days. Those amounts are likely currently outdated, an issue that will have to be addressed, but for practical purposes they are nevertheless very important. The lack of a quantified possession limit can act as a tool for abusive discretionary actions, as will be exemplified later. In Portugal, if someone is arrested by the police in possession of illicit substances, they are brought to the police station and the substances are apprehended. In the presence of an objective quantity limit, if they have more than the established amount, they are sent to be processed through the criminal justice system. If they have less, they are sent to a dissuasion commission under the ministry of health that has to evaluate what kind of medical needs that citizens may require. Even if the commissions have the power to apply administrative penalties, such as social work or prohibiting someone from going to certain places or seeing some people, the main goal remains to assess what kind of healthcare-related needs that citizen has. Is he or she in need of treatment? This is mainly enabled by facilitating access: "Have you ever thought about treating yourself?"; "Oh yes, but it's so complicated"; "Oh, what about tomorrow? I have an appointment for you tomorrow with Doctor X at Centre X." Eighty per cent of them accept. Even if those who present themselves in front of the commission are not problematic users (most of them are just occasional or recreational users), the goal of the commission remains to assess if there is any problematic aspect in their life that could benefit from any type of intervention. For example: "Okay, I only smoke a joint on weekends with friends. But my parents are divorcing, or my father just lost his job, or myself, I am imbalanced with my gender choices." If the commission can refer this person to adequate services, it likely means we are interrupting a harmful life choice precociously before it becomes more problematic. And that is the aim of the dissuasion commissions, as we call them. As mentioned before, having clearly established quantifiable possession quantity limits allows us to avoid abuse of discretionary power. In countries such as Spain, for instance, there was never any criminalization, so they never had to decriminalize. But they never established clear possession amounts that would not be subjected to criminal sanction. As such, in practice, someone is taken to the police station. He is a good-looking guy, middle class, blue eyes. The response will be, "Okay, go in peace, you are just a user." But if you are Black or Romani, for example, you will likely be charged as a trafficker. Having an objective threshold is therefore important to avoid that kind of discretion. In addition, the police feel much more comfortable because they do not need to exercise discretionary judgements on the spot.

Humanism, pragmatism, participation, prevention, and reinforcing commitment: these are the objectives of the dissuasion commission system. It only works if you have a network of services to which you can refer those who are caught with drugs. To quickly address the sanctions that may be applied to users by the dissuasion commissions, they allow the members of the commission to address situations with a tailor-made approach for the person involved. It is possible to apply a monetary fee, but only for non-addicted individuals (drug-dependent individuals cannot be imposed a monetary fine).

INTERNATIONAL REACTION

The strategy was approved by the executive government in 1999, but the issue of decriminalization had to be discussed in our parliament. This only took place in 2000, and the resulting statutory changes came into force in 2001. Shortly after, we had the first visit of the International Narcotics Control Board (INCB). They were very critical, but never took concrete action to oppose our policies. In fact, concerning the enforcement of international treaties, I never saw any practical effect of decriminalization that would be in violation. But the reports coming from international bodies were nevertheless very critical. In 2009, we started to obtain and present our first results. Both Glenn Greenwald and Caitlin Hughes visited us for the first time, and they each wrote articles detailing the Portuguese policy. That got people talking about the Portuguese model. Then in 2009, the United Nations Office on Drugs and Crime (UNODC) report, for the first time, starts to be more apprehensive of our policies: "Even if they decriminalized, the Portuguese decriminalization of drugs falls within the convention's parameters." Then fifteen years later, at the United Nations General Assembly Special Session (UNGASS) 2016 in New York, the president of the INCB participated in a side event concerning the Portuguese model, and he showed this: "Portuguese approach is a model of best practices." So fifteen years later, we think we achieved recognition for our success. And what we are happy to do nowadays is to offer our solidarity to countries such as Canada and Uruguay. Because we were victims of the same international pushback, we feel the greatest responsibility we now have is to help countries to approach drug-abuse issues in a more humanistic manner.

Nowadays we are quite comfortable with our model. Don't expect Portugal to push it further (as sometimes people ask me, "Why doesn't Portugal push forward for legalization?"). There is a broad consensus, and our society has deemed it satisfactory to leave our policies be. When our decriminalization model was approved by parliament, there was a fracture between the left-wing parties and the right-wing parties, even if many common citizens were very much in favour. They were in favour because, as I explained, we had an explosion of consumption that happened across all social groups. It was not something that happened only among lower-class people. It happened among the middle class, the upper class, everybody. It was impossible to find a Portuguese family that had no problems relating to drug abuse. The overall feeling of the population was one of acceptance towards decriminalization. I can imagine a middle-class parent of the time discussing with a priest, "Oh, my boy is not a criminal, he is someone in need of help." But at the political level it seemed a little more complicated, there was talk of, "Oh, Portugal will become a paradise for drug addicts from all over the world, we will have planes coming to Lisbon every day with people to use drugs," or "Our children will start using drugs with the milk bottle." Nowadays, seventeen years later, we can say for a fact that none of this happened.

DATA

Concerning interventions of the dissuasion commissions from 2001 until 2016, we had a total of ~124,000 processes with ~110,000 different offenders. Fifty-seven thousand were evaluated as non-problematic users, but even then, ~16,000 of those non-problematic users were assessed with having a problem that could benefit from some intervention and accepted to be referred for it. For the ~12,000 problematic drug users (people in need of treatment for their addiction), ~10,000 accepted to be referred to treatment centres. This is a supplementary gateway from which an individual can enter the treatment system for drug abuse (people can also admit themselves freely or be referred by a doctor, a teacher, and even their family). It should be noted that we have quite a solid healthcare network; everything is almost free and with practically no waitlists. In 2016, we had ~27,000 people in treatment for drug use–related problems, plus ~13,000 in treatment for alcohol problems. Just to note, in 2011–12, we had more re-admissions than new patients. Those were the years of a social crisis, when we had many longtime heroin users relapse, so they came to access the services en masse. Concerning HIV infections among drug users, this affected a huge proportion of drug users in the '90s, and then it started to drop. Nowadays, if we consider three groups (heterosexuals, homosexuals/bisexuals, and injecting drug users), injecting drug users are the group with the lowest rate of new infections in Portugal. As for overdose deaths, in the mid-'90s we had around one overdose death a day, about 360 a year. In 2016, we had twenty-seven overdose deaths throughout the country during one year.

NEW CHALLENGES

We are not yet confronted with big numbers related to new psychoactive substances. But as we look to other European countries, we see the rising importance of new psychoactive substances. We are therefore trying to prepare to deal with what we perceive as an oncoming issue. The same with fentanyl, for instance. It's not yet very present in Europe, namely in my country, but we try to prepare ourselves to deal with it by seeing the experiences arising from North America. Another big problem we face nowadays is the aging of the ancient heroin users. We had first contact with them when they were twenty or thirty years old. Nowadays they are fifty, sixty, seventy years old, while also mentally and physically very sick. This poses a lot of new problems. Additionally, even if they are provided for in our legislation, we had previously decided not to open safe injecting rooms in the last decade because injection drug use rates were dropping so fast that we felt it would send the wrong message to society.[5] But currently we have decided (two weeks ago) to open some safe injecting rooms in Lisbon.

CONCLUSION

Since our decriminalization policy has been in place, we've seen some small increases in illicit drug use among adults. But more important are the results pertaining to a reduction in illicit drug use among adolescents, reduced burden of drug offenders in the criminal justice system, reduction in the prevalence of injection drug use, reduction of opiate-related deaths and infectious diseases, reduced stigmatization of drug users, increase in amounts of drugs seized by authorities, and reduction of the public resource burden caused by drugs. The primary concern of Portuguese society in the '90s, drugs and drug addiction, now ranks in thirteenth or fourteenth place in surveys. It is not a solved problem in our society, but we are quite comfortable with those results. There is a coherent articulation among all Portuguese policy and actions based around the idea that the drug user is a person with health and social needs instead of a criminal or delinquent. And, just to end, nowhere do international drug conventions require that personal use be criminalized. This is just food for thought, but I think it is an important fact to pass on to other countries.

QUESTIONS

Q: Could you provide us with a little more detail about the dynamics around the political decision to take this bold step? Was there a particular event? Was there a particular person? How did the political forces coalesce around this policy?

A: I was part of a group of experts that were nominated by the government to build the strategy. We had judges (from the Supreme Court), doctors, psychiatrists, psychologists; we were nine people. The leader of the group was the only one who had nothing to do with drugs, he was a scientist very much used to leading working teams. We had all the resources that we needed to visit other places, to contact politicians, professionals, and all that. Then we just wrote our proposals and they were presented to the government, who just adopted it. But the particular issue of decriminalization, which was just a component of the proposed strategy, was the one which created the most friction at the political level because it had to be discussed at the parliament. During that period, from the approval of the strategy by the executive until the parliamentary debates, we (the proponents) organized a huge number of public discussions. And what I can testify to was a substantial support coming from common citizens to the idea. At the political level, the right-wing parties were opposing decriminalization: "Oh, this is going to be a disaster!" But well, they lost. Nowadays, they support it. Shortly after decriminalization, we had changes in government, but no one tried to reverse the process. Nowadays there is a stagnant consensus; nobody proposes to regress, but also nobody is willing to take any kind of step forward. We are comfortable, no one wants to open a Pandora's box.

Q: You mentioned the issue of novel psychoactive substances being an emerging problem. When you use a threshold table to determine decriminalization quantities, how are you addressing thresholds with novel psychoactive substances or new and emerging substances? Or are police *de facto* issuing arrests for those substances?

A: Those new psychoactive substances, since they are not under the schedule, those are not controlled yet and are not included in those tables. Solely if they are included in those tables can we establish a limit, and the people in possession of those substances are submitted to the same procedures as the others. For the new ones that are not controlled, there is no administrative procedure to be done, and they are subject to criminal sanction.

Q: Portugal is not a wealthy country, and in order to provide the kinds of services you're talking about, you've obviously had to draw on more than just a handful of specialists. So how have you coordinated the different groups involved in the process? How have you managed to get the different elements of Portuguese society to work together and coordinated them for the common goal?

A: Well, Portugal is in fact a country of limited resources. But I restate that this was a top priority at the time, so there was a lot of investment in it. It is not the case nowadays; we are doing what we can with limited resources. Especially during the financial crisis, we dealt with severe cuts that had repercussions on mostly the research and knowledge of the phenomenon. But we could almost keep wholly intact all responses in terms of treatment and harm reduction. I must tell you, for instance, that one important source of resources for harm-reduction policies comes from the profits of the state lotteries. This is allocated to us and is the source of an important part of our budget. And with that, my service, at its maximum, was able to reach numbers of approximately 1,600 professionals working in the network at the state level, plus some NGOs funded by the state working on it as well. I think that the Portuguese state made a very brave effort to deal with the catastrophic situation that we were facing, and from this we can now take the opportunity to show our results. Nowadays, this system is included in the general healthcare service, which is a universal service that serves the entire population almost for free. This is one of the greatest achievements of our democracy since the revolution.

Q: I must admit I'm a little bit saddened to hear Australia and Portugal take such a conservative view of marijuana, considering that this is about marijuana policy and that we're discussing "heavy duty" drugs like LSD or heroin, grouping them all together and calling cannabis a drug in the same category as LSD or heroin. As opposed to countries like Uruguay. The question being, what will Canada do and, obviously, industry? Clearly, cannabis has been proven to have medical applications, and there are more and more medical patients being treated with it. We talk about taking the stigma out of cannabis, but we're still grouping it in with drugs that are going to be stigmatized. Why are countries that are decriminalized still talking about cannabis as a class-1 narcotic?

A: I believe in the therapeutic potential of cannabis, but that is a different set of issues. Talking about therapeutic cannabis for me is different from talking about recreational use. There is also potential therapeutic use of opiates, which is very important in dealing with certain medical conditions, and yet I do not advocate for recreational use of opioids. I think it was a wise measure to decriminalize all drugs. When the moment comes to legalize drugs and to empower the citizen with the capacity of choosing, of making informed choices, I think we must have the same kind of policy: "All drugs, they are available, and you decide if you want." That is my position.

Q: Anybody, I wanted to know what they think Canada's position will be on cannabis. Is it going to be considered in the legal or health department?

A: I respect the decisions taken by different countries, and you can count on our support for those decisions, okay?

NOTES

1 Leading figure of an authoritarian regime known as the Estado Novo, which held control of Portugal from 1926 to 1974.
2 An example of one of the rare sources of drugs during the Estado Novo regime.
3 Series of uprisings in Portuguese colonies, resulting in a war that lasted from 1961 to 1974.
4 Military coup d'état that ended the authoritarian Estado Novo regime and was the first step in the country's rebirth into a constitutional democracy.
5 From a political perspective, it would have previously been untenable to obtain broad support for safe-injection sites if usage rates were going down.

Acknowledgments

The editors wish to acknowledge the contribution of the staffs of the Institute for Health and Social Policy and of the McGill Institute for the Study of Canada. In particular, we wish to thank Kanita Ahmed, Daniel Caron, Anaik Fortin, Gabriella Kranz, Jacqueline Rosenhek, Ema Shirom-Chao, and Eloisa Xel Ha Ochoa. Publication of this volume was made possible by the financial support of the Institute for Social Policy of McGill University, and by a research grant from the Canadian Institutes for Health Research on "Harm Reduction: Public Health Reasoning in Law and Public Policy in Relation to Morally Controversial Behaviour."

Contributors

MALCOLM G. BIRD is Associate Professor, Political Science, University of Winnipeg.

JEAN-FRANÇOIS CRÉPAULT is Senior Policy Analyst, Centre for Addiction and Mental Health; and PhD candidate, Dalla Lana School of Public Health, University of Toronto.

MICHAEL DEVILLAER is Assistant Professor, Dept of Psychiatry & Behavioural Neurosciences; Faculty Associate, Peter Boris Centre for Addictions Research; and Faculty Associate, Centre for Medicinal Cannabis Research, McMaster University & St Joseph's Healthcare Hamilton.

STEPHEN T. EASTON is Professor of Economics, Simon Fraser University.

BRANDON M. FINLAY is a PhD Candidate, Department of Sociology, Indiana University Bloomington.

JOÃO CASTEL-BRANCO GOULÃO, General Directorate for Intervention on Addictive Behaviours and Dependencies (SICAD), Portugal.

ROOJIN HABIBI is Research Fellow, Global Strategy Lab, York University.

STEVEN J. HOFFMAN is Director of the Global Strategy Lab and Professor of Global Health, Law, and Political Science, York University.

ALANA KLEIN is Associate Professor, Faculty of Law, McGill University.

ALEX LUSCOMBE is a PhD Candidate, Centre for Criminology and Sociolegal Studies, University of Toronto.

CHRIS MACDONALD is Associate Professor, Ted Rogers School of Management and Director of the Ted Rogers Leadership Centre, Ryerson University.

AKWASI OWUSU-BEMPAH is Assistant Professor, Department of Sociology, University of Toronto.

ANDREW POTTER is Associate Professor, the McGill Institute for the Study of Canada.

ANINDYA SEN is Professor of Economics and Director of the Master of Public Service, University of Waterloo.

JACOB STILMAN is a criminal defence practitioner in Toronto.

DANIEL WEINSTOCK is James McGill Professor of Law and Director of the McGill Institute for Health and Social Policy.

JARED J. WESLEY is Associate Professor, Political Science, University of Alberta.

ROSALIE WYONCH is a policy analyst with the C.D. Howe Institute.